SO, YOU WANT TO BE A LAWYER, EH?

2ND EDITION

SO, YOU WANT TO BE A LAWYER, EH?

Law School in Canada

2nd Edition

Adam Letourneau, BSc, BA, LLB

Part of the
Writing on Stone Press
Canadian Career Series

Writing on Stone Press
PO Box 259, Raymond, AB T0K 2S0
(403) 752-4800
www.writingonstone.ca

Published by:
Writing on Stone Press Inc.
P.O. Box 259
Raymond, Alberta, Canada T0K 2S0
(403) 752-4800
Fax: (403) 752-4815
Email: info@writingonstone.ca
Web: http://www.writingonstone.ca

LIBRARY AND ARCHIVES CANADA
CATALOGUING IN PUBLICATION

Letourneau, Adam, 1974-
So, You Want to be a Lawyer, Eh? : Law School in Canada / Adam Letourneau. -- 2nd ed.

(Writing on Stone Canadian Career Series)
ISBN 978-0-9738092-8-2

1. Law schools--Canada. 2. Law--Study and teaching--
Canada. 3. Law students--Canada. I. Title. II. Series.

KE330.Z82L48 2007   340.071'171   C2007-906138-9
KF297.Z9L48 2007

For my children, Zoë, Soleil, Zane, and Samuel.

May you reach every big goal you set.

TABLE OF CONTENTS

INTRODUCTION

Law is king of all.
— Henry Alford

WHY THIS BOOK NEEDED TO BE WRITTEN OR WHY I WROTE THIS BOOK

SO, you want to be a lawyer, eh? In 2001, I began the formal journey towards becoming a lawyer. I was as green as they come. I had made the decision that I wanted to take a shot at law school and was wondering "now what?" I was lost. I started my research using the Internet and calling various law schools across Canada. After a gruelling double attempt at the LSAT, and after a lot of sifting through and seeking out information from anybody and everybody that I knew connected to law, I was finally able to complete my applications to law school. Then after months of eager anticipation, I gained acceptance into the fold. Although this was a difficult and confusing procedure, it was only a taste of what law school had to offer in terms of challenges, obstacles and sessions of hair pulling.

As I approached the end of the law school journey and embarked upon the practical field of law, I often wished that I had obtained a sufficient guide to succeeding in law school. I read several American "guidebooks" on the subject, both before and during law school, and although they offered some introductory information about what law school was all about, I was really in need of a guidebook that contained information specifically applicable to the Canadian law student. I never did find that guidebook, so I decided to write it myself.

It is my hope that the contents of this book will help you in your decision to enter the field of law, help you gain entrance into law school, and in particular, help you succeed in law school and beyond.

WHAT QUALIFIES THE AUTHOR TO WRITE THIS BOOK?

From the very moment I made that decision to apply for law school, my life has been non-stop information gathering. I do not mind admitting that I have become a compulsive law-related information junkie. I have pored over law school rankings, law firm rankings, law firm Web sites, articling pamphlets, etc. I have also been incredibly interested in what law graduates are doing with their education; reading whatever articles I can find related to law-graduate career choices.

So, with all of this information swimming around in my head, it seemed natural to make it available to others following the same path. A real-life chance to help others presented itself—one of the aspirations of all future lawyers, and I jumped on it. I am excited about my career in law, am thankful for the opportunity, and am satisfied in the choices that I have made so far. I made those choices only after thoroughly scanning the horizon, which was really a lot of work! I received many interviews for articling positions and received a good number of offers from some very prestigious firms. I hold a wide range of experience in law from academics to extracurricular activity, to summer jobs to articling, even starting my own law firm (Letourneau Law, Barristers & Solicitors—http://www.lelaw.ca) and succeeding as a lawyer. The things I have learned and experienced, the things that cannot be found in other law resource books (I've looked)—I share with you now in this book. It will answer the questions I was asking when I first decided on law school, and will provide valuable information on how to get that elusive and cherished first job in law. I sincerely hope that you will eagerly accept the information contained in this book and that it will help you in your mission to succeed in your journey through law school and beyond. I hope that it saves you time and that you will share this knowledge with your colleagues.

Comprehensive Canadian Law Students' Guide

This is the second of hopefully many editions of this guidebook. As a result, it is a work in progress. I plan to update the information contained in the pages of this book biyearly, resulting in the most comprehensive guidebook for the Canadian law student available. The first edition proved to be very popular and well received, with many five star reviews on Amazon.com, Amazon.ca and Chapters.ca. It is with this encouragement that we released this second edition as quickly as possible.

In this book, you will find personal anecdotes, both from the author and from colleagues of the author. This second edition contains many more useful comments from colleagues. In addition, you will find the most in-depth and up-to-date research and information about law schools in Canada, the application process, law school study habits, summer jobs, the articling process, and more.

No guidebook can cover everything. The law and legal education are big topics. Further, it is not always easy to understand the subtle differences between Canadian law schools. If you have any information to add, or think that I should be including information particular to a certain law school or region, please let me know and I will include that information in the next edition of this book. I will also make sure that such information is accessible in the meantime on the Web site http://www.CanadianLawSchool.ca.

Please email your comments, suggestions, or criticisms to adam@CanadianLawSchool.ca and I will get back to you as soon as possible.

You will also find other useful information at http://www.CanadianLawSchool.ca, including law links, links to online CANS/ outlines (condensed annotated notes—basically, a summary of what you have learned in the term—more about these later), prospective and current law student surveys on important questions facing these groups, and more. Also, feel free to visit my blog, *Law Eh?* (http://canadalawstudent. blogspot.com), where I provide many informal comments about law school, the law, and being a lawyer.

THE ULTIMATE CANADIAN LAW SCHOOL SOURCE

If you find any information contained within this book to be inaccurate, outdated, or misguiding, please contact me immediately at adam@CanadianLawSchool.ca. By doing so, you will ensure that your colleagues will have the information they need to succeed. All updates you provide, along with updates researched by the author, will be added to subsequent editions of this guidebook and to http://www.CanadianLawSchool.ca.

OPINION COUNTS

To augment the material in this book, I have asked a number of classmates, current law students, and colleagues to answer a number of key questions about their law school application, law school experience, and about landing a job. I include answers to these questions throughout as **Obiter Dictum**, a Latin term literally meaning, "said by the way". This is usually a remark or observation made by a judge that is included in the body of the court's opinion, but does not form a necessary part of the court's decision. I chose students or graduates of law school who I thought were examples of success. This second edition includes a number of additional comments from various individuals. I have also included a section written by a colleague who is much more knowledgeable and experienced on the specific topic of applying for court clerkships.

Acknowledgments

First, I would like to thank my wife, Carmen, for her emotional and intellectual support through law school, articling and opening my law firm, and for editing this book. If it were legal to have her added to my LLB parchment, I would arrange to have it done in a heartbeat. She deserves the degree as much as I do. I would also like to thank my test readers, Shawn and Maiko Davis, along with the contributors to *Obiter Dictum* that are interspersed throughout this book. Your support is greatly appreciated. Lastly, thank you to Mr. Mike Gunther, a law student at the University of Alberta Faculty of Law, for his diligent research and suggestions for this second edition.

CHAPTER 1: WHAT DOES THE ROAD LOOK LIKE?

*Law school taught me one thing: how to take two situations
that are exactly the same and show how they are different.*
— Hart Pomerantz

REASONS FOR APPLYING TO LAW SCHOOL

EVERY law student or lawyer to whom I have posed
the question, "What made you decide on law school?"
has provided a different answer. There are literally thousands of reasons for embarking on this new career. I have heard of
people who wrote the LSAT on a dare, who have done it because
they love lawyer movies and TV shows, or who found inspiration
from a court case they read about in the newspaper. I have heard
people say they felt they had no choice—that nothing else looked
appealing. I often hear people say (some sheepishly and some un-
abashed) that the money attracted them. Others have indicated that
they like the idea of power, prestige, and wearing a pinstripe suit on
Bay Street. I have heard many times that they wanted to help others.
There is no right reason or wrong reason, but there must be a compelling personal reason.

For me, law was a real career change. Before applying to law
school, I was Vice President of Operations for an electronic publish-

ing house that specialized in electronic travel and outdoor activity guidebooks to be uploaded on a Personal Digital Assistant or PDA (i.e., Palm, Pocket PC). The idea being to bring all your cumbersome guidebooks in your pocket-sized PDA while backpacking, cycling, or traveling. It was a fantastic job, always putting me on the cutting edge of Internet and computer technology. However, I was ready for new challenges, and the Internet and technology fields had already dropped from their incredible peak in popularity and economic sky-rocketing. My body was suffering from being in front of a computer for hours at a time—I had repetitive strain in my wrists, back, and legs. So after raising tons of money and making huge progress, our company looked like it was about to fizzle out. It was the perfect time to jump on an opportunity that I had been considering for some time. I read an article that suggested that the best time to embark on further education was during a downtime in the economy. I did not need much more incentive. I signed up for the LSAT exam, and found myself suffering along with a couple of hundred other students in a large auditorium. My desire to succeed was evidenced by my terror—a feeling that lasted until I was finally accepted into law school.

Obiter Dictum

For me, going to law school was more accident than plan. As I was finishing my first degree, I was not sure what I wanted to do, but I knew I wanted a change. Studying law seemed like it would be both an intellectual challenge and something with a direct practical application, so I decided to try it.

— *Robin Penker, Law Graduate 2005, Risk Manager and Legal Counsel, Maple Trade Finance*

I thought that no matter what I chose to do in the future, a law degree would provide a great foundation. One can do so many things with a legal background—e.g., teach, open up a business, work as in-house counsel for a company, etc.

— *Kim Yee, Law Graduate, 2006, Associate, Brownlee LLP*

I was always interested in law. I really enjoyed writing and argumentation. I thought law would be a good degree to have regardless of what I ended up doing.

— *Mike Kariya, Law Graduate, 2005*

Law school has always been a lifelong dream. I was inspired by the thought of advocating for others in addition to participating in large business transactions.

— *Rob Nelson, Law Graduate 2005, Associate in Dubai, United Arab Emirates*

I wanted to go to law school for a number of years before starting my post-secondary education....I chose to apply to law school mainly because I felt unsatisfied with my current education and couldn't see myself working in the field that I was studying.

— *Jamie Johnson, Law Graduate, 2005, Associate at a major Canadian municipality*

I had always wanted to go to law school. It was probably in grade nine that I decided I wanted to go to law school because of my interest in social studies and politics. In fact, in grade nine I had to write a paper about my career goals and describe some goals and steps to get there. So at that point, I researched and learned a lot about how to apply and what I needed to go to law school. After my first degree in Arts, I decided to work for a while. After working for about eight months (and after applying to law schools in western Canada), I was offered an opportunity of a lifetime—to work on Parliament Hill in Ottawa (a dream job for a Poli Sci grad). I then moved to Ottawa and after a year...of working there and an issue of job security, I decided to look back to my original goal of attending law school and so reapplied to some schools and considered some deferrals I had at other schools.

— *Lorne Randa, Law Graduate, 2005, Associate, Brownlee LLP*

I had completed a three-year contract job. I wanted to embark upon a career. Truthfully, I somewhat romanticized the profession of law and did not know nearly as much as I should have about what lawyers do before applying to law school.

— *Shawn Davis, LLB/MBA Graduate, 2005, Associate, Shearman & Sterling LLP, Abu Dhabi, United Arab Emirates*

Finances, Pay, and Underemployment

As you read this book, you will find that the subject of law is not all roses. One of the most popular reasons for entering law is because of the potential for high personal income. It *is* possible to make good money as a lawyer. It *is* true that lawyers are at the upper end in terms of annual income and bonuses in Canada and the US. And these are not necessarily terrible reasons to enter into law. Although annual salaries are very high for some lawyers, if you were to break down the hourly income for many lawyers compared to others, you might be surprised. This is especially true for junior and mid-level lawyers who are striving for that pot of gold called partnership. I will address the daily life of a lawyer in a later chapter.

Status

Contrary to many jokes and popular belief, one of the most prevalent reasons for becoming a lawyer is that the professional designation of being a lawyer brings with it prestige, and in some cases, power. If this is important to you, law is probably a good choice. Lawyers are trusted members of the community that often carry the appearance of prestige and power. However, note that prestige and power can be dangerous in large quantities.

GRUELLING, VERY COMPETITIVE, BUT REWARDING

Pursue your passion and live your dream.
— Katherine Logan

Law school is hard. There are a few super-human individuals who will argue that they slid through law school unscathed. Nevertheless, for most mere mortals, law school is just plain hard. It is time-intensive, extremely competitive, and the material is often new and challenging. It is my hope that this guidebook will help.

You may have heard stories about law students putting in twelve to fourteen hour days, and often more. You may have heard about students who have hidden library books before exam time, or about students who have deliberately tried to throw off fellow students before exam time. While these things do happen, for many, the overall experience is very rewarding, filled with camaraderie and teamwork. The feelings of self-worth that come with grasping a legal concept, nailing a law exam, or winning a moot competition are incalculable and make all of the hours spent studying and preparing well worth the effort.

Obiter Dictum

What makes a good lawyer?

Big Firm: Time management, ability to consistently bill hours at a tepid pace, ability to meet competing expectations thrown at you from multiple directions, having a spouse/significant other who is eternally understanding.

Small Firm (fewer than ten lawyers): All the same as big firm but billable hours usually not as earth shatteringly important.
— *Shawn Davis, LLB/MBA Graduate, 2005, Associate, Shearman &*
Sterling LLP, Abu Dhabi, United Arab Emirates

Prior to attending law school, I had to deal with many lawyers on a daily basis. The best ones were very practical, tenacious, and equally good at seeing the big picture and finding the details. They would listen to the client, provide the services asked for, and not get bogged down in superfluous issues. They were tenacious and able to find the answers and communicate effectively in a timely manner.
— *Carissa Browing, Class of 2008*

What makes a good lawyer? This is a tough question, because this really depends on the type of law one wishes to practice. In some areas, people skills are essential; in others, being aggressive and outgoing is key; and in others, being passive and calm is needed. Overall however, any good lawyer requires the ability to think analytically, listen well, and be able to pull out relevant information. A good lawyer is also one with strong research skills (which law schools also teach) and the ability to communicate well, whether it be in oral or written form.

— *Lorne Randa, Law Graduate, 2005, Associate, Brownlee LLP*

CHALLENGING JOB MARKET

Current lawyers and personal research tell that there was a time when most law students could obtain a law article position. Today, there are far fewer articling positions available relative to the numbers of graduates, with available positions dwindling over the last decade. It is now common to have 30–40 percent of second year law students exit the articling summer without articles lined up. Frightening as this may be, like the LSAT and the law school admission process, the articling application process is another opportunity to weed out those students who are not up to the standard required of a very demanding career.

With that thought, however, I believe that there will always be a need for lawyers. There will always be legal work. If you work hard and have a sincere desire to be a lawyer, you will succeed and will find a job in the field. If you follow the strategies outlined in this guidebook, you may even love your end position.

2nd Edition Update: Almost all of my classmates eventually obtained an article and most have continued on towards their legal career. Only a very few were unsuccessful in achieving their goals, and it is likely there were good reasons for this, such as a lack of focus in law school or a general attitude that was not conducive to working.

DO I WANT TO TRAVEL THAT ROAD?

Like all important decisions, it is important to take stock and to analyze the pros and cons before embarking upon a new path. Law school is not for everyone. It is a huge commitment in terms of time and money, along with emotional energy. I would encourage you to really think about the decision and write down all of the pros and cons for you personally. Talk to as many people as you can about your decision. Talk to any significant partners, friends, or parents about the decision. For me, it was useful to envision what it would be like to be a lawyer. What emotions were attached to that vision? Could I imagine myself dressed up in a suit? In court? Defending a murderer? Making a big deal in a large corporation? Dealing with prisoners? Caught in the middle of a fighting couple in a divorce? Could I imagine myself preparing for a case or a settlement?

Note: Writing these things down may be important to lift you up later when you feel discouraged or overwhelmed.

Obiter Dictum

Talk to current law school students, articling students, junior associates, and don't always believe the propaganda on the websites of the large firms. Also consider other careers and whether the skyrocketing law tuition costs will be reasonable vis-à-vis the credentials you obtain.
— *Shawn Davis, LLB/MBA Graduate, 2005, Associate, Shearman & Sterling LLP, Abu Dhabi, United Arab Emirates*

Make sure that you have done your research into the legal profession. Know what you're getting into. Law school is too much hard work to do for three years and then decide that the profession is not what you thought it would be
— *Mike Kariya, Law Graduate, 2005*

Many people are not fit for law school; you really, really need to understand the dedication necessary to succeed in law school. You need to have a lot of humility (there is no room for arrogance) and you need to understand that you may be disappointed. Law school is not for the faint of heart—getting into law school and being in law school are two different things. You need to crave it, fixate on it, and have a passion for it or you won't succeed.
— *Gayle Hiscocks, Law Graduate, 2005, Associate, North & Company LLP*

To be a successful lawyer (or law student), there is a threshold of intelligence needed. This intelligence is not the "engineering" sort of intelligence, but rather an intuition and ability to make mental links that others might not be able to forge. I know many intelligent people who would make terrible lawyers. I also see colleagues in my program who are in law because they know that a hefty payday awaits. If you are not truly interested in the law, a legal career is probably not for you. Law school is a lifestyle: I have learned just as much about the law from reading newspaper articles about the law, reading *Lexpert* and *Canadian Lawyer* magazines, and spending random time on Wikipedia reading about historical cases. Sadly enough, I do this for fun. Not everyone needs to be as much of a nerd as me, but you definitely should have an interest in the law that extends beyond the classroom.

— *Michael Gunther, Class of 2008*

Be very sure that law school is something that you really want; otherwise, it could prove to be an arduous process.
— *Rob Nelson, Law Graduate 2005, Associate in Dubai, United Arab Emirates*

STATISTICS—HOW MANY LAWYERS ARE THERE?

The Federation of Law Societies of Canada puts out statistics on Canadian Lawyers each year. The last available set of statistics is from 2005. You can get full access to all statistics at http://www.flsc.ca/en/lawsocieties/statisticslinks.asp.

As of 2005, there were around 56,000 practicing, insured member lawyers in Canada. There were actually over 94,000 lawyers in Canada including practicing members exempt from insurance, non-resident practicing members, and non-practicing members.

If you look carefully at these statistics, you will find a few interesting things. The first item of note is the relatively high number of sole practitioners in most provinces. The second thing is the decreasing number of lawyers as you progress through years as a member of the bar. Evidently, there are not so many runners at mile twenty as there were at the starting line.

You will find some other very interesting information provided for each province and territory such as: how many law firms (of various sizes) there are, admission rates to articles and calls to the bar, average practicing fees, insurance coverage, complaint rates, and full contact information for law societies in each province.

HOW MANY APPLY? HOW MANY ARE ACCEPTED?

You will see details in Appendix B on the number of applications and the number of spots available at each law school in Canada. There is a large discrepancy across the country. Many prospective law students are curious about where they may have the best chance of gaining acceptance. The number of spots and the number of admissions are not clearly indicative of your chance for success. It is important to consider other information, such as the average GPA and average LSAT for incoming students. It is also useful to find out what percentage of in-province and out-of-province applications each law school accepts on a percentage basis for any schools in which you may be interested. This information is not included in this book, but should be readily available from the admissions office at the respective school where you apply.

Another consideration for prospective law students is to realize that the numbers in the Appendix B spreadsheet can be misleading. There is a lot of crossover between applications at the various schools. There are also a relatively large number of acceptance letters sent out each year, with many students declining offers from particular schools. The truth is, most prospective students apply to multiple schools. Those at the top of the heap will gain acceptance at more than one school. However, they can only attend one school, and so must turn down one or more offers. This forces the schools to move down their list until they have all of their positions filled.

Apply to more than one law school. Apply to as many as possible within your guidelines for location, school prestige, school offerings, and tuition. It is surprising to hear how many students are accepted to more than one school. On the other hand, I am aware of students who only applied to one law school. I would advise against this, as the odds will not favour you. Personally, I applied to four law schools and was accepted to three.

All prospective students should put their all into every application that they submit. Those students who believe they may be closer to the middle of the pack should put even more into their applications. Make sure that there is nothing that would cause an admissions officer to put your application into the reject pile. **No spelling errors, nothing missing, all signatures included, and a smashing personal letter will all give you an advantage over those less careful. Each law school is going to fill every available spot. Take every advantage that you can to ensure your success.**

LSAT AND GPA STATS

Law schools are looking for the best. Most admissions offices believe that the LSAT is a good indicator of future potential as a law student, and ultimately as a lawyer. Different law schools give the LSAT score more or less weight compared with the GPA. See the chart in Appendix B to see the LSAT/GPA ratios of different law schools. When you write your LSAT, you will be given a raw score as well as a percentile score. For those of you who are unfamiliar with percentile scores, they basically work like this: If you are in the 75th percentile that means that you scored equal to or higher than 75% of those who have written the LSAT. That includes many people! (Note—this includes other jurisdictions, such as the US). It is important that you know what the average LSAT score is for each school you apply to, whether in raw score or percentile form. Also, become aware of what the minimum LSAT score was last year, and any other information that you can get from the admissions officer about what the matrix of LSAT and GPA scores for the previous entering class was. This matrix will provide you with a more accurate scope of what calibre of students the school is letting in and where you might fit into such a matrix. It will differ from school to school.

Most schools will look at your last two years of undergraduate work for your considered GPA. There are some subtle nuances between each school, and you should become very familiar with these to give yourself the most advantage in the application process.

WHAT IS LAW SCHOOL LIKE ANYWAY?

This is a very good question to ask if you are considering becoming a lawyer. Law school has a very different atmosphere from most other undergraduate and graduate programs out there. It has an extremely high workload, and is peculiarly competitive. This book is a great place to start to get a feel for what law school is really like. I explore some of the social aspects, some of the type of work, and many of the challenges that you will face in law school. You will find that throughout this book, I try to be as honest as possible about what law school is really like. I try not to take the all-too-common pessimistic viewpoint, but rather try to look at the process of becoming a lawyer in a positive manner.

Law school is not for everybody. Nevertheless, if after reading this book, and after consulting with a number of people already involved in the legal community, you decide that it is for you, you may find yourself immersed in the most challenging, most rewarding experience of your life.

Retrospectively, I think law school was an excellent experience. Now that I have been away for a couple of years, I look back with great fondness. The stresses were high, but they were manageable. I met such great friends, and proved to myself what I was really capable of.

CHAPTER 2: HOW DO I PASS THE LSAT?

For many persons, law appears to be black magic—an obscure domain that can be fathomed only by the professional initiated into the mysteries.
— Susan C. Ross

THERE are many books and articles devoted entirely to this subject. This chapter will give you an overview of the important information and point you to places where you can go to learn more.

The Law School Admission Test (LSAT) "is a half-day standardized test required for admission to all ABA-approved law schools, most Canadian law schools, and many non-ABA-approved law schools. It provides a standard measure of acquired reading and verbal reasoning skills that law schools can use as one of several factors in assessing applicants. The test is administered four times a year at hundreds of locations around the world."[1]

According to LSAC:

The test consists of five 35-minute sections of multiple-choice questions. Four of the five sections contribute to the test taker's score. These sections include one reading comprehension section, one analytical reasoning section, and two logical reasoning sections. The un-scored section,

---

[1] http://www.lsac.org/LSAC.asp?url=lsac/about-the-lsat.asp.

commonly referred to as the variable section, typically is used administratively to test new questions or to equate new test forms. The placement of this section in the LSAT will vary. The score scale for the LSAT is 120 to 180. A 35-minute writing sample is administered at the end of the test. The writing sample is not scored by LSAC, but copies are sent to all law schools to which you apply.

The LSAT is designed to measure skills that are considered essential for success in law school: the reading and comprehension of complex texts with accuracy and insight; the organization and management of information and the ability to draw reasonable inferences from it; the ability to think critically; and the analysis and evaluation of the reasoning and arguments of others.[2]

According to informal surveys, most people write the LSAT more than once. Some say that rewriting will not significantly improve your score. In my case however, my second try resulted in a marked improvement. After my first poor showing, I then took a personal inventory of how I had prepared the first time and came up with a methodology that I was sure would work for me. I have heard this same strategy has worked for others who have had to write the LSAT more than once. I found strategies that allowed me to more fully comprehend the games section of the LSAT, which brought my scores up considerably on the practice exams, to which I dedicated myself the second time around.

On my second attempt, I received a score that was well within the acceptable range for law schools in Canada. I was terrified that the first score would ruin my chances to gain acceptance, but I was accepted to three out of the four law schools to which I applied.

---

[2] *Ibid.*

Obiter Dictum

I completed three practice exams under strict time constraints. I used an alarm clock and allowed myself one minute less than normally allowed on each section.
— *Shawn Davis, LLB/MBA Graduate, 2005, Associate, Shearman & Sterling LLP, Abu Dhabi, United Arab Emirates*

I took the Renert tutorial course and practiced in my third year of undergrad twice per week for three months.
— *Gayle Hiscocks, Law Graduate, 2005, Associate, North & Company LLP*

I took the Kaplan LSAT class, and spent about one hour each day studying for the month and a half prior to the test.
— *Michael Gunther, Class of 2008*

To prepare for the LSAT, I purchased a study guidebook with CD ROM and obtained as many old LSAT exams as I could. From there I relied on the guidebook to practice strategies for answering questions and then practiced writing as many exams as I could in exam-like situations (i.e., timed sessions). I did this about two to three months before writing the actual exam.
— *Lorne Randa, Law Graduate, 2005, Associate, Brownlee LLP*

I bought a few LSAT prep books from Chapters and spent three months going through study guides and doing timed tests. Learn some of the techniques to improve your time on logic questions but work hard on getting your time down and calming your nerves. It's stressful and almost impossible to finish the sections. Fill in and move on. Breathe. Fill in and move on. Breathe.
— *Carissa Browing, Class of 2008*

To prepare for the LSAT I went online to the LSAC website and ordered a number of different practice LSATs from previous years. I spent the Saturdays for the last month before the LSAT timing myself and taking the practice tests. Other than the practice test, I only went through the LSAC website and read different hints and suggestions that were available.
— *Jaime Johnson, Law Graduate, 2005, Associate, major Canadian municipality*

I took an LSAT prep course and completed lots of practice exams.
— *Rob Nelson, Law Graduate 2005, Associate in Dubai, United Arab Emirates*

Law School Admission Council (LSAC): http://www.lsac.org/.

PREP COURSES

Many prospective law students feel more confident going into the LSAT having taken a preparatory course. Kaplan and The Princeton Review are probably the most well known. In Canada, Oxford Seminars offers courses throughout the country. Numerous private companies in each city or university in Canada offer courses as well. It is a good idea to visit your local law school to look at the bulletin boards where you will be sure to find advertisements for numerous LSAT prep courses. You can also find advertisements on other bulletin boards in undergraduate university buildings. It is helpful to ask around—ask classmates or friends that you know who have written the LSAT or taken a prep course to see what they think about the various prep courses offered in your area.

Oxford Seminars
LSAT Test Preparation Courses, Including Free Practice Prep Tests, Canada-wide http://www.oxfordseminars.com/Pages/LSAT/lsat_about.htm

Powerscore
http://www.powerscore.com/

Kaplan
http://www.kaplan.com

The Princeton Review
http://www.princetonreview.com/law/testprep/testprep.asp?TPRPAGE=5&TYPE=LSAT

The LSAT Center
http://www.lsat-center.com/

LSAC Prep Tests
https://os.lsac.org/Release/Shop/Shop_Books.aspx?po=Y#prep

BOOKS

There are a number of books out there that are reasonable in cost and useful, but only if you are very self-motivated. All of these can be found and purchased from http://www.CanadianLawSchool.ca.

Kaplan LSAT 2008, Premier Program (w/ CD-ROM)
by Education Center Kaplan Can$28.98
http://www.amazon.ca/exec/obidos/ASIN/1419551353/canadala
wstud-20/701-3675836-3447539

Kaplan LSAT 180, 2007-2008
by Kaplan Can$19.53
http://www.amazon.ca/exec/obidos/ASIN/1419550977/canadala
wstud-20/701-3675836-3447539

Kaplan GMAT/GRE/LSAT 2004 Deluxe Edition
by Topics Entertainment. Can$49.99
http://www.amazon.ca/exec/obidos/ASIN/B00008QOE1/canadal
awstud-20/701-3675836-3447539

Master the LSAT with Disk
by Jeff Kolby, Scott Thornburg Can$25.19
http://www.amazon.ca/exec/obidos/ASIN/1889057118/canadala
wstud-20/701-3675836-3447539

LSAT Logic Games Bible
by David M. Killoran Can$40.97
http://www.amazon.ca/exec/obidos/ASIN/097212960X/canadala
wstud-20/701-3675836-3447539. One of the best selling books on
Amazon.com

Cracking the LSAT, w/ DVD 2007 Edition
by Princeton Review Can$28.97
http://www.amazon.ca/exec/obidos/ASIN/0375765557/canadala
wstud-20/701-3675836-3447539

Cracking the LSAT, 2007 Edition
by Princeton Review Can$15.34
http://www.amazon.ca/exec/obidos/ASIN/0375765549/canadala
wstud-20/701-3675836-3447539

Official LSAT Next 10 Actual PrepTests (August 2007)
by Law Services Editorial Can$23.28
http://www.amazon.ca/exec/obidos/ASIN/0979305055/canadala
wstud-20/701-3675836-3447539

Actual, Official LSAT PrepTests (August 2007)
by Law Services Editorial Can$18.92
http://www.amazon.ca/exec/obidos/ASIN/0979305047/canadala
wstud-20/701-3675836-3447539

10 More Actual Official LSAT PrepTests (July 2007)
by Law School Admission Council Can$18.92
http://www.amazon.ca/exec/obidos/ASIN/0979305039/canadala
wstud-20/701-3675836-3447539

Ultimate Verbal and Vocabulary Builder for the SAT, ACT, GRE, GMAT, and LSAT
by Lighthouse Review Inc Can$10.96
http://www.amazon.ca/exec/obidos/ASIN/0967759412/canadala
wstud-20/701-3675836-3447539

The LSAT Advantage with Professor Dave 2004–2005
by David Scalise Can$16.13
http://www.amazon.ca/exec/obidos/ASIN/0970175612/canadala
wstud-20/701-3675836-3447539

LSAT for Dummies
by Amy Hackney Blackwell Can$12.00
http://www.amazon.ca/exec/obidos/ASIN/076457194X/canadala
wstud-20/701-3675836-3447539

CD-ROMS

I found a couple of excellent CD-ROMs at my local bookstore that guided me through the various sections of the LSAT. I found these to be very useful, as they were interactive, inexpensive, and included a few prep tests. However, be aware that completing a test on a computer is not the same as writing an actual prep test on paper. You should be sure to try at least one (preferably more) prep test in paper format, as you would in the LSAT exam.

Cambridge Educational Services
http://www.cambridgeed.com/ooshop/controller.php?v=prddet&p id=185

STRATEGIES

There are many LSAT prep courses, books, and CD-ROMs that may help you gain an edge over other LSAT test writers. However, everybody will find the best success through gaining a strategy of his or her own. This comes through practice, pondering, and practicing again. Learn from your mistakes. Come up with shortcuts and strategies that work for you. Increase your mental endurance through more regular, prolonged study sessions and repeated mock LSAT test writing situations.

Some people suggest that the score you receive on your first attempt at the LSAT is an accurate reflection of your potential and your abilities. I think that it is possible to increase your score, but you may need to work very hard and approach the LSAT in a new way in order to see a significant change in your score.

Other than that, I cannot really provide any strategies. You may find more helpful information in the books and CD-ROMs mentioned in this book.

TRY, TRY AGAIN!

Just don't give up trying to do what you really want to do.
— Ella Fitzgerald

As I mentioned, I wrote the LSAT twice. This is common. It is an overwhelming experience the first time round, and many people are unprepared, especially in terms of the mental and physical strain and the endurance required. Alternatively, perhaps nerves got in the way. Do not be too embarrassed if you find that you need to write it more than once. If you have decided that law is your dream, do not let this obstacle get in your way. Do not give up that easily. **Under normal circumstances, you can take the LSAT up to three times in any two-year period.** This applies even if you cancel your score or if it is not reported otherwise. You may hear from different authorities that LSAT scores do not differ greatly under normal circumstances from one test to another. You can find more detailed information on this at http://cachewww.lsac.org/pdfs/2004-2005/registration-book-ca-2004b.pdf (LSAT Registration & Information, Canadian Law School). This document includes a great matrix of differences between multiple test attempts. Do not be thrown off by this information. It is a matrix of averages. Not everyone will fall within his or her averages. If you feel that you might do better if better prepared, both mentally and physically, it is definitely worth trying the LSAT more than once.

DO NOT Share Your Score With Anybody!

What you think of yourself is much more
important than what others think of you.
— Seneca

As with your GPA, your LSAT score should be a private matter. Some students like to boast about their LSAT score. However, the LSAT is not always indicative of your real potential in law school or as a lawyer. There are so many other factors that come into play, such as ability to handle stress, social ability, study habits, whether some or numerous areas of law catch your fancy, your relationships with other law students and law professors, and so on.

Sharing your LSAT score is not necessary. It does not help anybody. It can make people feel bad about themselves, or cause them to categorize you. Unless someone shares their score with you in a non-hostile, non-threatening manner, and in an atmosphere that you are comfortable with, I would suggest that you tuck your score sheet in a locked file cabinet and forget about it. Nobody important should ever ask that question of you again, although I have heard stories of recruiters asking for your score.

IMPORTANT DATES AND INFORMATION

It is very important that you are aware of the deadlines associated with the LSAT test dates and your law school application deadlines. As indicated on the LSAC Web site (http://www.lsac.org), "Many law schools require that the LSAT be taken by December for admission the following fall. However, taking the test earlier—in June or October—is often advised." As of publication of this edition, the upcoming test dates are scheduled for Saturday, December 1, 2007, and Saturday, February 2, 2008.

Please note that there is an associated registration fee of Can$123 for taking the LSAT. Also, please note that test takers must report to the test centres for the September, December, and February administrations of the LSAT no later than 8:30 a.m. The reporting time for the June LSAT is 12:30 p.m.

LSAC provides the following information about receiving your LSAT scores:

- LSAT takers who have LSAC online accounts will automatically receive their LSAT scores by e-mail approximately three weeks after taking the test. This is the quickest way to obtain your LSAT score, and there is no additional charge.

- Test takers can obtain test scores via TelScore, for a fee of $10 (credit card only), approximately three weeks after taking the test. TelScore: 215.968.1200; available at all times except 6:00 a.m. to 8:00 a.m. (EST) Sundays.

- LSAC will send score reports by mail approximately four weeks after each test. Test takers who have LSAC online accounts will pay a one-time fee of $25 to obtain hard-copy mailings of account information that is available online.[3]

Please note that you can cancel an LSAT test score. Why would you do this? Perhaps you panic during the test or get sick. Perhaps you just have a gut feeling and you don't feel confident about your performance. If you must cancel your score, LSAC "must **receive** a signed fax or overnight letter with your request within six calendar days of the test. You can also cancel your score at the test centre if you are absolutely certain you want to cancel your score."[4] Do not cancel your score unnecessarily. If you simply lack faith in yourself without legitimate cause, take a chance and wait for the score, especially if you are taking the test for the first or second time. You may just surprise yourself!

---

[3] http://www.lsac.org/LSAC.asp?url=/lsac/faqs-and-support-lsat.asp#1.
[4] *ibid.*

CHAPTER 3: THE APPLICATION PROCESS

Law school has been described as a place for the accumulation
of learning. First-year students bring some in;
third-year students take none away. Hence it accumulates.
— Unknown

WHICH SCHOOL?

THERE are quite a few law schools in Canada, and it can be difficult to choose which one is the best one for you. Assuming you have choices, you may want to consider some factors such as the cost of living, moving yourself or your family, the types of classes, the size of faculty, and especially where you would like to work after law school. Unlike US students, Canadian students tend to stay in their home jurisdiction more often than not.

Law schools also tend to accept applicants within their own province more readily, usually due to the fact that the highest percentage of applications received are from their own province. Loyalty also plays a role, and there is a hope that the majority of the law students will stay within the province where they attend school. However, law schools are very accepting of applications from anywhere in the country, as well as international applicants.

There is some differentiation between law schools in the west and law schools in the east. It may seem obvious, for example, that Ontario law schools are better primed to prepare students for Bay Street firms than schools in Alberta or Saskatchewan. In turn, the University of Calgary and University of Alberta have more classes directed towards an energy-boosted economy driven by oil and gas. These are just single factors of many, and should not sway you one way or the other too readily. After reading this book, you may carry out further research into various law schools, the cities where they are located, and the types of firms and establishments within those cities. However, as you will see below, ranking various law schools is difficult and rather unscientific.

For some people, school rankings are the highest consideration because they want the best chance possible at a great job and a successful career.

Rankings—Do They Mean Anything?

Canadian Lawyer puts out a list of law schools in Canada each year, ordered by rank, which can be found at http://www.canadianlawyermag.com. I have provided the rankings for the past few years for your convenience below.

2000 Results
1. University of Calgary
2. University of Toronto
3. University of Victoria
4. University of Moncton
5. University of New Brunswick
6. University of Western Ontario
7. McGill University
8. University of Alberta
9. University of Windsor
10. University of Montreal
11. Dalhousie University
12. University of Manitoba
13. Osgoode Hall, York University
14. Queen's University
15. University of Saskatchewan
16. University of British Columbia
17. University of Ottawa

2001 Results
1. University of Victoria
2. University of Alberta
3. University of Calgary
4. University of New Brunswick
5. University of Windsor
6. Queen's University

7. Dalhousie University
8. University of Toronto
9. University of Saskatchewan
10. University of British Columbia
11. University of Western Ontario
12. McGill University
13. University of Manitoba
14. University of Ottawa
15. Osgoode Hall, York University

2002 Results
1. University of Victoria
2. University of Calgary
3. University of Alberta
4. University of Windsor
5. University of New Brunswick
6. Dalhousie University
7. Queen's University
8. University of Toronto
9. University of British Columbia
10. University of Western Ontario
11. McGill University
12. University of Ottawa
13. Osgoode Hall, York University

2003 Results
1. University of Victoria
2. University of Alberta
3. University of Toronto
4. University of New Brunswick
5. University of Western Ontario
6. Queen's University

7. University of Windsor
8. University of Moncton
9. McGill University
10. University of Ottawa
11. University of Manitoba
12. Osgoode Hall, York University
13. Dalhousie University
14. University of Montreal
15. University of British Columbia

2004 Results
1. University of Calgary
2. Osgoode Hall, York University
3. University of Toronto
4. University of Victoria
5. McGill University
6. Dalhousie University
7. University of New Brunswick
8. University of Windsor
9. University of Western Ontario
10. University of Saskatchewan
11. University of Alberta
12. Queen's University
13. University of British Columbia
14. University of Ottawa
15. University of Manitoba

2005 Results
1. University of Victoria
2. University of Toronto
3. University of New Brunswick
4. Osgoode Hall, York University

5. University of Western Ontario
6. University of Alberta
7. University of Saskatchewan
8. Queen's University
9. University of Ottawa
10. University of Manitoba
11. University of Windsor
12. Dalhousie University
13. University of British Columbia

Insufficient responses from:
University of Quebec at Montreal
McGill University
University of Sherbrooke
University of Laval
University of Calgary
University of Moncton

2006 Results
1. Osgoode Hall, York University
2. University of Toronto
3. University of Victoria
4. University of Calgary
5. University of Windsor
6. McGill University
7. Dalhousie University
8. University of New Brunswick
9. University of Western Ontario

10. University of Alberta
11. Queen's University
12. University of Saskatchewan
13. University of Ottawa
14. University of Manitoba
15. University of British Columbia

Insufficient Responses from:
University of Quebec at Montreal
University of Lava
University of Sherbrooke
University of Moncton

2007 Results
1. University of Toronto
2. University of New Brunswick
3. McGill University
4. University of Victoria
5. Osgoode Hall, York University
6. Queen's University
7. University of Western Ontario
8. University of Windsor
9. Dalhousie University
10. University of Manitoba
11. University of Ottawa
12. University of Calgary
13. University of Saskatchewan
(What—no University of Alberta!!!)

As you can see from the above lists, the rankings change from year to year. The rankings published by Canadian Lawyer Magazine are not without bias. If you understand how they are ranked, you can better understand how to interpret the lists. First, the rankings are based on the input of graduating or recently graduated students. The magazine asks many questions about what the students thought of their particular school. It is in the student's best interest to score her school as high as possible (a degree from a #1 ranked school looks better on that job application than a degree from a #13 ranked school). Additionally, unless the students have been to more than one law school they really do not have anything with which to compare their experience. Most law students have only attended a single law school. Of course, one's own school is usually thought of as the best school.

A quick analysis on the rankings over the past five years shows that many of the schools jump from one end of the scale to the other. For example; Osgoode Hall, York University, was at the bottom of the scale at #15 (last) in 2001, #13 (last) in 2002, then #13 (fourth from last) in 2003. Then, in 2004, it miraculously leaps to the #2 spot and the front runner (#1) in 2006!!! This example alone should give you a good idea of how much credence you should give to these rankings. Unless Osgoode received millions in funding, got an entirely new faculty and a brand new building; it is hard to legitimately justify an increase in rank this big.

However, some things might be worth considering. For example, Victoria, Calgary, Toronto, and Alberta are consistently at the top end, while British Columbia, Manitoba, and Ottawa seem to be consistently near the bottom end. Again, digest this analysis with a grain of salt.

I mentioned in the first edition that it would be more useful to have ranking as done by Maclean's Magazine[5] for the universities, which used to be published each year. Many years ago, Maclean's did a ranking of the law schools, but for some reason they have not published one out for a long time. "To conduct the survey, Maclean's distributed a seven-page questionnaire to the country's sixteen law schools and mailed a second questionnaire to 3,997 law school graduates who had been called to the bar in the past three years. In all 1,227—more than thirty percent—responded and their opinions kept UVic at or near the top of several categories."[6] Such a ranking would take into account the student-to-instructor ratios, research funding, job placement statistics, etc., and would be worth a lot more to a prospective law student or a prospective law employer.

[5] "Maclean's Law School Survey" *Maclean's* 6 October 1997 at 13.
[6] http://ring.uvic.ca/97oct03/Top_ranking.html.

Well, out of the blue, just before publication of this edition, Maclean's published a ranking[7] for professional programs, including law schools. At first, I was really excited to see that Maclean's was back in the game. However, the article was fairly short, and the criteria are still a little sketchy, but seem more reliable than the Canadian Lawyer rankings. Maclean's now base their rankings on four elements—Elite firm hiring, National Reach, and Supreme Court Clerkships (these three elements comprise student and graduate quality—50% weight), and Faculty Journal Citations (faculty quality—50% weight). There is a more complete explanation of the criteria used if you go to the article on Maclean's Web site. The ranking was completed by professor Brian Leiter, the Hines H. Baker and Thelma Kelly Baker, chair at the University of Texas at Austin Law School.

The rankings are below, followed by some brief commentary.

2007 Common law Schools Ranking

1. Toronto
2. McGill
3. Osgoode
4. Ottawa
5. Queen's
6. Dalhousie
7. Alberta
8. Victoria
9. UBC
10. Saskatchewan
11. Manitoba
12. New Brunswick
13. Western
14. Windsor
15. Calgary
16. Moncton

Civil Law Schools Rankings

1. Montreal
2. Ottawa
3. Laval
4. Sherbrooke
5. UQAM

There are a few consistencies with recent Canadian Lawyer rankings—Toronto, McGill, and Osgoode seem to be near the top across the board for rankings in both magazines. Dalhousie is consistently

---

[7] http://www.macleans.ca/article.jsp?content=20070924_109281_109281&source=srch

in the middle. But the rest move from rank to rank. For example, Ottawa, Queen's, and Calgary bounce around between years and between the two rankings.

As far as the criteria—I know that some sort of objective criteria are required, but I definitely don't agree with Maclean's criteria. "Elite Firm hiring" is not a good indicator of the quality of the education that a school is providing. Firms hire individuals—not the school name on your degree. Geographic proximity also will play a role in the hiring process.[8] Additionally, firms will take the cream of the crop from any school. Personality plays such an important role in hiring. "National Reach" is a mystery to me. I can't even provide commentary on that one. "Supreme Court Clerkships" follows the same logic as the Elite Firm hiring listed above. Individuals who are the cream of the crop at any law school who mesh with a Supreme Court Justice will get the available jobs. Finally, "Faculty Journal Citations" has absolutely nothing to do with the quality of a law school in practical terms. Being published or cited in a Law Journal means that you are a professor or instructor (or student) who is fairly smart, tenacious, and accurate in your writing and citations. It does not mean that you are a suitable legal instructor, or that you have the ability to produce successful law students. Also, I don't believe that this criterion acknowledges the fact that some faculties have some incredibly prolific staff who publish numerous articles in all kinds of journals each year. There are other professors that choose to focus on teaching or administration. The whole publish-or-perish concept of academia is a little different in a professional training program such as law school, although it does exist to a certain extent. I was disappointed to see that this last criterion was weighted so heavily. I didn't care how many publications my professors were writing, or how many citations they had published in legal journals. I cared about whether they were going to teach me what I needed to know—whether they were able to prepare me for my career. So who are these rankings for, the professors or the students?

Please do not put too much stock into law school rankings in Canada. They are not always indicative of the experience that you will have, or of the importance that a particular school will have on

---

[8] Note that Queen's offers data on this subject. Applicants chosen from Ontario for the class of 2008 was 81%, for 2009–76%, and for 2010–80%.

your employment chances. Law schools tend to be regional in terms of employment (despite the inclusion of a National Reach criterion in the Maclean's ranking). Clearly, not all law firms hire exclusively from Toronto, Victoria, or Calgary—it would not make sense. It makes much more sense to hire locally as much as possible, as those candidates will show much more loyalty to the city, and subsequently, the firm.

Be aware of those schools that consistently are at the bottom end of the ranking lists. Employers will perhaps consider more heavily the ranking of these schools than others. However, given the above arguments, this may be a cynical and superfluous approach.

Finally, I would reiterate my opinion that an above average to excellent law student from any Canadian law school will have an excellent chance at career success compared to an average or below average law student from the same school. Do not fret too much about which school you will attend. Pick the one that is the best match for you, and then concentrate on getting yourself as high as possible on the grading curve. The rest will take care of itself.

For a more grassroots approach to law school rankings (clearly not scientific), check out the "Weighing the Schools" section of the http://www.lawstudents.ca forum.

You can find some good commentary on this topic at the following sites:

Margot E. Young , Faculty of Law University of Victoria, LLBs and Compact Disc Players: Accountability versus Marketability
http://www.umanitoba.ca/faculties/law/LRI/Legal_education/you ng.htm.

Richard Moon, Faculty of Law, University of Windsor, Comment on Law School Surveys and Rankings
http://www.umanitoba.ca/faculties/law/LRI/Legal_education/mo on.htm.

Lisa Philipps, Osgoode Hall Law School, Comment on Law School Surveys and Rankings

http://www.umanitoba.ca/faculties/law/LRI/Legal_education/phill
ips.htm.

René Côté, Departement des Sciences Juridiques, University
du Quebec a Montreal, Comment on Law School Surveys and
Rankings
http://www.umanitoba.ca/faculties/law/LRI/Legal_education/CO
TE.htm.

Wesley Pue and Dawna Tong, Faculty of Law University of
British Columbia, The Best and the Brightest? Canadian Law
School Admissions
http://www.umanitoba.ca/faculties/law/LRI/Legal_education/Pue
Tong.htm.

Rising Tuition Costs!

When I started law school, I was prepared to pay about
Can$5,000 per year for tuition and fees. I felt very lucky, as this
number would be "grandfathered" for the next three years, which
means I would not see an increase in the tuition that I paid from year
to year, except for the usual university-wide increases. However, the
next incoming class would be charged a "differential fee" of about
$2,000, and the following class even more; so that tuition for them,
including differential fees, was $4,000 more than I paid during the
same year. It may not seem fair, but the argument is made that this
differential fee goes towards improving the faculty, and thus the opportunities and advantages for the law students. One or two law professors were hired during my second year, but other than that, I
never did figure out what the differential fees were being used for. I
was just happy that I did not have to pay so much!

The truth of the matter is, the cost of attending law school has
skyrocketed in the past few years. Incoming students for 2006/2007
are looking at anywhere between Can$3,000 to $17,280 for tuition
and fees, with an average of approximately $9,454. Add to that
amount the cost of living, gym fees, etc., and you are looking at a
very hefty total for a single year of law school.

It is not unheard of for a law student to amass a debt of
Can$100,000 or more. Although salaries for lawyers do go up over

time, especially compared to some undergraduate or graduate programs, prospective law students should be aware of the high cost and
the potential debt-load that they may have to carry. It is a significant
investment, and one that should not be taken lightly.

Fortunately, law schools are trying to increase the number of bursaries available to their students. One explanation for the differential
fee was that those who are able to pay carry more of their own costs,
allowing the school to assist those who are less able to pay. The fact
that provinces are increasing the amounts of the loans available to
law students, as well as the increased amount of re-mission available
to graduating students, feeds the differential frenzy.

University of Toronto recently raised their tuition to Can$17,280
and Osgoode Hall raised their tuition to $15,116 to be more in line
with American schools. These are very large increases and I wonder
how that has affected their students in the long run. Clearly, these
two schools are climbing the ranking lists (for whatever that is
worth), but the majority of their students are going to enter the
workforce with massive amounts of debt, stress, and wonder over
the practicality of their decision to go to law school. Except for those
who are hired by top-tier and top-paying firms, the significant debt is
going to haunt most of these students for years to come.

Considerations

As mentioned above, when choosing your law school, there are
many things to take into consideration. You might want to contem-
plate class size, your family needs, your proximity to friends, the cost
of living, available courses, job prospects in the geographical area,
the reputation of the school's law review, the reputation of the
school's instructors, tuition expenses, and many more things. Talk to
family and friends about the factors that pull you one way or the
other. It may be helpful to draw a chart, assigning number values to
various considerations, showing which are more or less important to
you.

Should I Look South?

Many prospective law students consider the possibility of obtaining a legal education and potentially legal employment in the US. There are some important factors to consider. The most obvious is tuition. Although tuition is rising dramatically in many Canadian law schools, most are still well under the average tuition cost in the US. Unless you can easily afford the costly tuition or can find some other creative way to pay for an upper-ranking law school, you may find that there is no advantage in obtaining employment, especially if you move back to Canada upon graduation. Tuition at US law schools range from US$8,200 per year at Brigham Young University (subsidized tuition for most of their students) to about US$40,024 at Columbia University. For most law schools of stature, a conservative tuition average is roughly US$15,000 per year. This is now in line with the tuition expense at the University of Toronto and Osgoode Hall at York University.

Most US law schools will consider an application from Canada., and all Canadian provinces will recognize a law degree from any ABA (American Bar Association) accredited law school—make sure that you apply to an ABA approved school if you are considering returning to Canada, or if you are planning to practice in the US.

If you are seriously considering practicing in the US, you should be aware that each state has unique entrance requirements for its own bar organization.

http://www.abanet.org/legaled/baradmissions/barcont.html has links to the Bar Admissions organizations of all fifty states. These Web sites set forth the requirements for bar admissions in their respective states.

Special Status—Mature and Aboriginal Students

If this section does not apply to you, please read on. For those of you who think you may be included in these two demographics, please pay close attention. This information is vital to your success. It will also interest those who may have been previously misguided or have been given false information regarding mature or Aboriginal applicants.

There is a misconception held by many that Aboriginal students get a free ride throughout their years in university, and subsequently in law school, and that they are somehow treated differently. There are rumours that Aboriginal applicants are guaranteed spots in law school if they apply, and that once accepted, they are also graded differently. This information is false. If you want the truth regarding Aboriginal applicants, read on. If you are an Aboriginal applicant who is seeking more information on the application process, or looking for a better opportunity to pursue your legal education, read on.

The truth is that the Aboriginal people are not properly represented in the Canadian economy. This under-representation is especially felt in law, an area where Aboriginal peoples require greater Aboriginal representation for all areas of law, including criminal, civil, and constitutional rights. More and more cases are coming forward and being heard in Canadian courts dealing with Aboriginal rights. Aboriginal peoples have unique rights entrenched in the Canadian constitution. As a result, there is a much higher need to have lawyers that are aware of, well versed in, and passionate about, the rights of First Nations, Métis, and Inuit. On the other hand, Aboriginal lawyers are needed to work for the Crown. Additionally, as more Aboriginal peoples are becoming involved in business ventures, there is a need for corporate and commercial lawyers who can be trusted and who have a good relationship with Aboriginal communities and individuals.

It is true that many law schools in Canada allot a certain percentage of spots available for Aboriginal and/or mature students. This percentage is often 10 percent. However, that does not mean that they always fill these spots or that the school is obligated to fill the spots with Aboriginal and/or mature students. The 10 percent number is a goal, not a rule. As such, not every spot set aside for Aboriginal or mature students is actually filled by Aboriginal or mature students.

Some schools seem to attract a larger number of Aboriginal applicants. The College of Law at the University of Saskatchewan and the University of Victoria both have a relatively large contingency of

Aboriginal law students. The University of Alberta does have an Indigenous Law Program, but the number of students was only fourteen in the 2004/2005 school year (out of a student body of about five hundred).

The process for applying to many law schools for Aboriginal students is a two-pronged approach. Aboriginal applicants have the option of attending a pre-law program at the University of Saskatchewan the summer directly preceding law school. Success at this program can lead to a conditional acceptance to some law schools. The program is aimed at preparing Aboriginal students for law school in terms of study habits and curriculum. Attendees take a course in property law. Successful students will get credit for this class, removing pressure during 1L. Acceptance is conditional on the student succeeding (in other words, passing) 1L. There are Aboriginal students who come out of the Saskatchewan program who do not succeed. However, the program is believed to help many students prepare and attempts to single out potential achievers among its attendees.

Aboriginal students can also be accepted unconditionally, and this is often the case. This means that the Aboriginal applicant is rated alongside every other applicant. This happens before a conditional acceptance is considered.

Now, here is the truth of the matter. I believe that if you are an Aboriginal student (I was one), if you show a sincere desire, and if you have a relatively decent GPA and LSAT score, then you stand a better chance than most applicants of obtaining acceptance to many law schools. Law schools that indicate that they encourage Aboriginal applications cannot say that they favour the idea of accepting an Aboriginal applicant. However, it is in their best interest to do so, as it looks very good for the law school when they can claim to have a decent contingency of Aboriginal students within their student body. However, remember this is the opinion of the author and that any reputable law school in Canada will never admit this idea. I just had to say it because I believe it to be true, and because I want to encourage any Aboriginal potential candidate to apply for law school because there really is a very high need for Aboriginal representation in law school and in the legal community.

For those of you who are not Aboriginal and who have read the above statements, please do not take a viewpoint that this is an unfair advantage given to Aboriginal students. The truth is that the number of applications from Aboriginal students is nowhere near what is needed to fill the 10 percent goal. It is also true that many Aboriginal people have faced extremely hard conditions in childhood and early adulthood, and the odds are against them gaining access to a university, not to mention law school. I will leave the issue at that and hope that it did not create too much fuss.

If you are an Aboriginal applicant, I highly suggest that you do thorough research on what each law school actually offers to its Aboriginal student body. Certain law schools claim to support their Aboriginal students in terms of counselling and study help. As much as possible, make sure that these claims are legitimate. Also, do some research into what course offerings deal with Aboriginal legal issues. Most schools do not offer much on this topic, but in order to practice in this area, it is a very good idea to be as exposed to as much Aboriginal law as possible during your time in law school. The Kawaskimhon National Aboriginal Moot (see moot section of this book) is an opportunity that is open to almost every law student across Canada and is a great opportunity to learn what it is like to research and practice Aboriginal law.

Mature students are defined as those who are 35 years or older. As with Aboriginal applicants, there may be a certain percentage of spots held for mature applicants. Special consideration may also be given to real-life experience. For example, if you have some connection to law in any way, you should emphasize this in your application résumé and statement of interest. Again, mature students are considered alongside all other applicants first. If they are not successful in this round, they may be considered in a mature student round. You should be sure to contact your law schools of interest to find out the specific mature student criteria and standards, if any.

Obiter Dictum

If you really want to go to law school, apply to multiple schools (I applied to eight). Apply the first day each school is accepting applications, and before you apply, connect with the head of the admissions committee at each school. Periodically check with the admissions coordinator at each school regarding your application. See if you can be placed on a wait[ing] list if you are not at first selected. Be persistent.

— *Shawn Davis, LLB/MBA Graduate, 2005, Associate, Shearman & Sterling LLP, Abu Dhabi, United Arab Emirates*

Apply broadly. Do not have your... [sights] set on only one school. Spend time on your application and letters. Proofread them. Have others proofread them. Communicate your intentions to your first-choice school.

— *Rob Nelson, Law Graduate 2005, Associate in Dubai, United Arab Emirates*

During my undergraduate degree, I was actively involved with my community through minor football and at school with the Students' Union. I think these extracurricular and volunteer activities definitely helped my application. As well, I worked really hard in my last two years of my undergrad to increase my GPA.

— *Lorne Randa, Law Graduate, 2005, Associate, Brownlee LLP*

LLB VS. JD

Most Canadian law schools award the degree of LLB (Bachelor of Laws), while law schools in the US offer the JD (Juris Doctor) degree. Toronto decided some time ago to offer a JD degree rather than an LLB They also increased their tuition dramatically, on par with US law schools. UBC Law students recently voted to switch to a JD (http://www.ubyssey.bc.ca/2007/03/06/faculty-of-law-moves-to-create-juris-doctor/). I heard recently that Western recently made the switch to a JD, but there is nothing on their Web site about it, and the class of 2007/2008 is still an LLB Ottawa has followed suit somewhat by offering a combined four-year LLB/JD degree in conjunction with either Michigan State University College of Law in East Lansing, Michigan or the American University (Washington College of Law) in Washington D.C. The JD is a US degree that enables the graduate to practice law in both Canada and the US. This seems to be a great idea, allowing for much flexibility for employment, and would be a great advantage to a prospective employer who does transaction work between Canadian and US corporations.

However, be aware that you will pay high tuition while attending Michigan State University or American University for two years of the four-year program. The University of Detroit Mercy and the University of Windsor, Ontario schools of law were the first to collaborate to create a joint American/Canadian law degree program. Students complete 104 credits in three years, and successful graduates receive both their JD and their LLB degrees.

Many other law schools have looked at the difference between the JD and the LLB There are many opinions on both sides; however, the predominant view at this time is that there is nothing wrong with the LLB in terms of gaining employment, especially within Canada. It is apparent that the combined JD and LLB would be an advantage if you wanted to work in the US and could not gain exclusive acceptance at a US law school, or if you think you might like to return to Canada one day. There is a long-standing tradition behind the LLB designation, and many people are not willing to exchange it for a JD designation easily.

I go on the record that if my alma mater were to switch to the JD designation, I would ask to turn in my LLB in exchange for a JD. I truly believe that the law program is at least equivalent to a master's degree program and that it should have a designation different from a bachelor's degree program. I am not a big traditionalist and don't care that in Canada we have traditionally called it an LLB I also don't care that this tradition comes from England. I live an hour away from the US border, and consider that my educational experience was at least equivalent to my neighbours south of the border. And I certainly consider that my experience was as gruelling as it would have been at U of T, Ottawa, UBC, or Western. I am a big fan of consistency, and expect that all Canadian law schools will make the change eventually.

COMBINED PROGRAMS

It is becoming increasingly popular to combine a second undergraduate or a graduate degree with your law studies. This may be a very viable option for you. More Canadian law schools are offering a combined program, including those listed here.

LLB/MBA [Business Administration] (Calgary, Alberta, UBC, Manitoba, McGill, Toronto, Victoria, Sherbrooke, New Brunswick, Moncton, Western Ontario)

LLB/MBA (MPA) (Osgoode Hall)

LLB/MEDes [Environmental Design] (Calgary)

LLB/MA in Asia Pacific Policy Studies (UBC)

BCL/LLB/MSW [Social Work] (McGill)

LLB/MES [Environmental Studies] (Osgoode, Moncton)

LLB/MA (International Affairs) NPSIA Program (Ottawa, with Carleton—The LLB is from Ottawa, and the M.A. is from Carleton)

LLB/National Program (Ottawa)

LLL/National Program (Ottawa)

LLB/MIR [Industrial Relations] (Queens), LLB/MPA [Public Administration] (Queens, Victoria, Moncton)

LLB/B.Comm (Saskatchewan)

LLB/BA (Saskatchewan)—5 years

LLB/B.Admin (Saskatchewan with U. of Regina)—6 years

LLB/MAIG [Indigenous Governance] (Victoria)

LLB/M. Environmental Studies (Moncton)—4 years

LLB/HBA (Western Ontario)—6 years

LLB/B.Esc [Engineering] (Western Ontario)—6 years

LLB/BSc [Science] (Western Ontario)—6 years

LLB/BA(History) [History] (Western Ontario)—6 years

LLB/ BA (Political Science) (Western Ontario)—6 years

LLB/BA(Kin) [Kineseology] (Western Ontario)—6 years

LLB/BA(Kin) [Kineseology] (Western Ontario)—6 years

LLB/BA (Media, Information and Technoculture) (Western Ontario)

Toronto offers a number of joint programs with their JD:
JD/Certificate in Environmental Studies; Combined
JD/Collaborative MA (International Relations); Combined JD/MA
(Criminology); Combined JD/MA (Economics); Combined JD/MA
(Russian and East European Studies); Combined JD/MBA.; Com-
bined JD/MISt.; Combined JD/MSW.; Combined JD/PhD (Eco-
nomics); Combined JD/PhD (Philosophy); Combined JD/PhD (Po-
litical Science).

MBA/LLB

The LLB/MBA joint program has become more popular in the
last decade. The popularity of the MBA soared in the 1990s and an
MBA became synonymous with success. The idea was that every
great business leader had an MBA to back them up, and that it was
impossible to reach upper management without one. Even successful
businessmen and businesswomen took leaves of absence, or began
part-time studying to obtain an MBA even if only for its status-
symbol significance. Definite distinctions exist in MBA programs
across the US and Canada. However, because more and more people
wanted to obtain MBAs, colleges and universities started accepting
more students into their MBA programs, smaller schools started offering MBA programs, and soon the workplace became rather di-
luted with MBAs.

Despite the rise in that number of people in Canada with MBAs,
there are some important considerations. Extremely valuable information and skills can be acquired in an MBA program, such as how
finance works and how to conduct yourself in business situations.
However, obtaining an MBA is not easy, even today, and employers
can look at this credential as proof that you have both dedication and

perseverance. The MBA is a challenging degree to obtain with high workloads and, for many, very difficult examinations and assignments.

So, how do legal employers look at the MBA? It really depends. If you plan to work at a major national law firm, or at a firm that specializes in corporate and financial transactions, an MBA can be a genuine asset that may truly set you apart from your competition. An MBA can open up opportunities to be involved in files that you might not otherwise get to work on as a junior associate, unless you have knowledge and skills that duplicate what is learned in an MBA (such as accounting, financial, or practical business experience). I have heard, although do not have anything substantiate this, that a LLB/MBA graduate has the potential to start at a higher salary, but that this salary usually evens out over a few years. More than anything, the MBA, along with your LLB, will set you apart from your colleagues during recruitment time, will give you some social status within your firm and with clients, and more important than anything, may provide unique opportunities to work with files that interest you, especially corporate and financial.

There seem to be widely differing experiences among those with a combined degree. I have heard from some who obtained this combined degree that they there are not many opportunities to utilize the skills from their MBA degree, and that those skills often go by the wayside. I have also heard that having the degree has contributed little or not at all to their salary. However, I know some individuals who claim to use their skills from their MBA every day in their legal work; anything from providing business information (lawyers cannot give business advice—only legal advice) to recognizing good business opportunities for themselves or for their firm.

One great advantage to the joint degree is the opportunity to have a backup plan in case you do not want to continue in law. For the extra year that it will take you to obtain the second degree, this may be good insurance for you as you ponder your career.

To be accepted into an LLB/MBA joint program, you will have to gain acceptance into both the LLB program and the MBA program at your university of choice. Once you have accomplished this feat, you will make a formal application to the LLB/MBA decision-making panel. I have heard that it is virtually guaranteed that you will be accepted to the joint degree program if you can successfully gain acceptance to both faculties within your university.

To apply for the MBA program, you will have to write the GMAT standard exam and apply directly to business schools where you are planning to attend law school. Make sure that you are fully aware of the MBA application deadlines, GMAT exam timetables, etc. The GMAT is drastically different from the LSAT, and it will require a very different approach in your preparation. The GMAT is scored using an adapting computer program that uses a unique point system. Basically, you gain more marks for answering early questions correctly. Getting those first few questions right can make a monumental difference to your end result. Make sure you are fully aware of this system, and come up with strategies to obtain as many points as quickly as possible at the beginning of the examination.

Obiter Dictum

I completed an LLB/MBA program. I thought doing the combined degree would give me an extra arrow in my quiver. For any person with aspirations in business, I suggest you start off in the MBA program [your] first year. ... Then at the end of the first year, if you decide that business is your niche, then you can opt out of the LLB portion and take only one extra year (or less) to complete the MBA. I would strongly consider that any prospective LLB/MBA students do some reading on two simple financial principles: time value of money and compound interest. There is a definite opportunity cost to being locked into a joint program and a cost-benefit analysis is absolutely crucial.
— *Shawn Davis, LLB/MBA Graduate, 2005, Associate, Shearman &*
Sterling LLP, Abu Dhabi, United Arab Emirates

I considered the combined MBA/LLB. I thought that it would give me an added advantage in the market place. I decide against it for financial reasons. I could not afford another year of school.
— *Rob Nelson, Law Graduate 2005, Associate in Dubai, United Arab*
Emirates

BCL/LLB

Students in the undergraduate programme at McGill obtain both a civil law (BCL) degree, which is used in Québec, and a common law (LLB) degree after completing 105 credits taken over three to four years.

You can take either the BCL program or the LLB program at the University of Ottawa.

A joint LLB/BCL is available from Osgoode, with the BCL coming from the University of Montreal. A joint LLB/BCL is also available from Queen's, with the BCL coming from Sherbrooke.

Victoria will potentially accept those students who have obtained a BCL degree from another school into its school to obtain an LLB degree. These students will have to complete three semesters worth of classes to meet this requirement. There are also other requirements that must be met. It also looks like Moncton does this as well. (http://www2.umoncton.ca/cfdocs/repertoire/1er_cycle/prog_droit_llb_lic.htm).

THE ACTUAL PROCESS OF APPLYING TO LAW SCHOOL

Admissions Information and FAQs

Rather than go through the individual process of each school, it is more prudent to provide links to the admissions sections for the Web site of each law school, along with a link to the Frequently Asked Questions (FAQ) section, if available. Please also refer to the appendices for school contact information and a complete run-down of GPA/LSAT requirements and other important information about each school. I provide this information in an easy to browse table.

The FAQ section is usually an excellent resource, and you should spend some time on the Web site for each of your prospective schools. You will find information on such topics as part-time options, re-application processes, requirements for recommendations and personal statements, how your undergraduate degree will be evaluated, courses completed after a degree, and more.

University of Alberta

http://www.law.ualberta.ca/LLB-Program/index.php

Apply online: http://www.registrar.ualberta.ca/ro.cfm?id=211

FAQ: http://www.law.ualberta.ca/LLB-Program/FAQS.php

What are my first round chances? 15.3%. There are 1,143 applicants for 175 available seats.[9]

University of British Columbia

http://www.law.ubc.ca/prospective/guides.html

Apply online: https://apps.law.ubc.ca/application/welcome.asp

Admissions Guide:
http://www.law.ubc.ca/prospective/files/pdf/booklets/final_LL.B.pdf

FAQ:
http://www.law.ubc.ca/prospective/llb/faq.html

What are my first round chances? 11.9%. There are 1,679 applicants for 200 available seats.

---

[9] Note that this percentage does not take into account the frequency of selections by the application committee for in-province applicants. Nor does it take into account the fact that many applicants will turn down an offer on the first round to go to another law school. It also, of course, does not take into account your LSAT, GPA, or application quality. However, this provides at least an initial figure with which to compare the schools.

University of Calgary

http://www.law.ucalgary.ca/law/programs/llb/admission

Apply online:
http://www.law.ucalgary.ca/law/files/law/UofC_appform_may200
7.pdf

FAQ:
http://www.law.ucalgary.ca/law/programs/llb/admission/faq

What are my first round chances? 8.5%. There are 843 applicants
for 72 available seats.

Dalhousie University

http://law.dal.ca/Prospective_Students/Bachelor_of_Laws_(LL.B.)
/Admissions

Apply online:
http://www.registrar.dal.ca/forms/Law_App.pdf

What are my first round chances? No data available. There are
161 available seats.

University of Manitoba

http://www.umanitoba.ca/faculties/law/newsite/faq.php

Application Material:
http://www.umanitoba.ca/student/admissions/media/law.pdf

Apply online:
https://aurora.umanitoba.ca/banprod/twbkwbis.P_GenMenu?name
=kssocas.p_StudMnu

What are my first round chances? 10.0%. There are 1,000 applicants for 100 available seats.

McGill University

http://www.mcgill.ca/law-admissions/

FAQ:
http://www.mcgill.ca/law-admissions/undergraduates/admissions/faq/

Apply online:
https://banweb.mcgill.ca/mcgp/hzskalog.P_DISPLANGUECHOICE

What are my first round chances? 11.3%. There are 1,509 applicants for 170 available seats.

University of Moncton

http://www3.umoncton.ca/templates/droit/imgs_demande/admission.html

University of Montreal

http://www.droit.umontreal.ca/baccalaureat_droit/admission.html

What are my first round chances? No data available.

University of New Brunswick

Application Guide:
http://law.unb.ca/admguide.pdf

Apply online:
http://mozart.its.unb.ca/etw/ets/et.asp?nxappid=GRA&nxmid=GetApplication&appprog=1090SNXH2

What are my first round chances? 9.5%. There are 845 applicants for 80 available seats.

Osgoode University

http://www.osgoode.yorku.ca/llb/applying.html

What are my first round chances? 11.8%. There are 2,500 applicants for 295 available seats.

University of Ottawa

http://www.commonlaw.uottawa.ca/index.php

What are my first round chances? (English) 5.8%. There are 3,456 applicants for 200 available seats.[10]

Queen's University

http://law.queensu.ca/prospectiveStudents/LLBProgram/admissio nInformation.html

What are my first round chances? No data available. There are 160 available seats.

University of Saskatchewan

http://www.usask.ca/law/prospective_students/program_informati on/admission_information/index.php

FAQ:
http://www.usask.ca/law/prospective_students/program_informati on/faqs_llb_students.php

---

[10] Note that Ottawa's website indicates that in 2006 they made 617 offers of admission to fill the 200 seats. In 2005, they made 670 offers of admission for those 200 seats. This just goes to show that the above percentages are not accurate portrayals of your chances of admission. This is why it is important to apply to multiple schools.

Apply online:
http://www.usask.ca/law/pdfs/Law_application_form.pdf

What are my first round chances? 12.0%. There are 965 applicants for 116 available seats.

University of Toronto

http://www.law.utoronto.ca/prosp_stdn_content.asp?contentID=4
41&itemPath=3/6/15/0/0

Apply online:[11]

What are my first round chances? 8.9%. There are 1,900 applicants for 170 available seats.

University of Victoria

http://www.law.uvic.ca/Admissions/about_admissions.php.

What are my first round chances? No data available. There are 105 available seats.

University of Western Ontario

http://www.law.uwo.ca/info-
prospective/admissions_first_year.html.

What are my first round chances? 6.9%. There are 2,400 applicants for 165 available seats.

---

[11] Check out http://www.ouac.on.ca/olsas/. The Ontario Law School Application Service (OLSAS) is a non-profit centralized application service for applicants to the six Ontario law schools: Osgoode Hall Law School (York University), University of Ottawa, Queen's University, University of Toronto, The University of Western Ontario, and University of Windsor.

University of Windsor

http://cronus.uwindsor.ca/units/law/lawtop.nsf/982f0e5f06b5c9a2
85256d6e006cff78/795e6935e3b3e76885256d870049b11d!OpenDoc
ument.

What are my first round chances? No data available. There are
1,600 applicants.

Strategies

Be sure to follow the instructions given in the admissions and
FAQ sections outlined above. Keep very close track of pending
deadlines both for the applications and for other necessary submitted
documents, such as reference letters and transcripts. Also, make a
note of what the specific criteria are for each law school and whether
there are allowances made for mature or Aboriginal students if this
applies to you.

Make sure that you send your application in on time and to the
right person. If it is a rolling admission policy (kind of like first
come, first serve), get your application in as early as possible. Make
sure that you address your package correctly, and that you check and
double check that you have included everything. Spell check everything, and have someone else go over your application packages to
look for errors. Submit everything on 20 lb. bond white paper. Nothing fancy. Do not give the admissions committee anything to set
your application aside. Make it perfectly clean, concise, and compelling.

Please see Appendix D for sample Statements of Interest.

Résumé

The résumé is probably not the most important aspect of your
law school application. However, it is vitally important to include it,
even if you are not requested to. This is because if it comes down to
the wire between you and another candidate, a strong, well-written,
and organized résumé could provide you with an advantage. It can

be a convincing and accurate look into you and your potential. Take time to prepare a strong résumé.

Wherever possible, include any experiences related to law. Also, be sure to include all volunteer positions. This résumé is not really like a résumé for a job interview—it is a chance to really put yourself forward. As such, you do not need to be so meticulous about what to include. However, avoid an overly lengthy résumé. Keep it concise and keep it correct! No spelling errors, typographical errors, or formatting issues. Keep it on 20 lb. letter sized paper. No fancy stuff— just the basics.

References—What Kind are Best?

Obviously, the best reference is a positive reference. Other than that motto, it can be a good idea to get a reference from somebody in the legal community. I got references from practicing lawyers whenever I could. Most schools will ask for a minimum number of academic references. You may also have to, or might want to, include a reference connected with community volunteer work.

Many people will be happy to work with you on the reference letter. You may want to provide a bullet list of things that you think are important to point out to the application committee. You might want to remind your referee of outstanding achievement in connection with the referee. Some referees will even be willing to slightly edit a pre-written reference letter. In any case, use tact and the proper respect when requesting reference letters.

Make sure that your referee is fully aware of the rules set out by each school. If the school requires the referee to mail the letter directly, provide the referee with a pre-addressed envelope with postage already affixed to the envelope. If the school requires a sealed envelope with a signature over the seal, make sure that this is done properly. You do not want one botched reference letter to mess up your chances. Let your referee know the potential consequences for going outside of the explicit rules.

If possible, get a copy of the reference letter. Put it in a file. The letter may come in handy later on. At some point in the future, for scholarships, summer jobs, and even articles, an old referee can be called upon again to help out. You can provide a copy of the letter with your suggested modifications and ask the referee to print off another copy for the new purpose. It can save a lot of time and effort for both parties involved.

Deadlines, etc.

Please refer to Appendix B for all deadlines. Be sure to also consult the school calendar and Web site to ensure accuracy. Absolutely do not miss a deadline. There are no exceptions, and no excuse will be accepted. Do yourself a favour and get your application in on time.

Where applicable, you will want to be aware of the rolling admission rule, where a school accepts candidates on a rolling schedule, or as they receive their applications. Where this is the case, get your application in well ahead of the deadline.

Deferral

Many prospective students do not realize that there is often an opportunity to defer your studies for up to one year. Note that not all law schools offer this option. However, it may be a good option for you. Some examples of good reasons to defer law studies for a year are:

1. Finishing a graduate degree. I know of one classmate who attempted to finish a master of arts degree concurrently, without joint-degree status, and ended up spending both summers tackling the issue. Had he taken a year off before studying law, he might have circumvented the high stress he experienced. He also would have opened up his summers to potentially work in the legal field. Another student attempted the same with a master of science degree and ended up spending her first summer doing something that she did not feel would help her directly with her law career. However, both of these individuals had made a commitment to finish their graduate degrees.

2. Getting an offer for a job that you just cannot refuse. I had a friend who received an offer to work for the federal government—something he had always wanted to do. He managed to get a deferral from some of the schools to which he had applied and was able to try the government job. It was a great résumé booster and a fantastic opportunity that he would have missed otherwise.

3. You need to save up for school. Now you can take up to a year to work full time, get prepared, and the pressure will be off because you have already been accepted.

Be sure that you apply for deferral in plenty of time, and that you put forward a very strong case. Do not just assume that a school will hold a spot for you once you have received an offer. Also check into tuition fee hikes or differential fees that your faculty may have scheduled. If waiting an extra year will add thousands of dollars to your cost, you should consider this in your decision-making.

CHAPTER 4:
FIRST YEAR (1L)

Make crime pay. Become a Lawyer.
— Will Rogers

HOW TO HANDLE THE LOAD

Time Management

MANAGING your time during law school can prove to be very challenging. This is especially true during your first year (1L), when you can have up to seven courses to deal with. In my first semester, I had Contracts, Criminal, Constitutional, Torts, Property, Legal Research and Writing, and Foundations to Law. All were full-year courses, except Foundations to Law, which was a half-year course. Most of these courses were 100% final exam courses, meaning that your final exam score, and nothing else, determines what grade you receive in that course. Legal Research and Writing included two written memos, a written factum, various assignments, and a moot. In addition to coursework I juggled a slew of extracurricular activities, interviews for summer jobs, social activities, Canadian Bar Association activities, a part-time job, and family responsibilities.

For someone coming right out of his or her undergraduate degree, law school can be a huge jump in time commitment. It can also be a huge jump in personal autonomy in terms of how you manage your time. Most classes do not have mandatory attendance and do not include scheduled assignments. However, some of your classes may include a participation portion in the evaluation breakdown. Many lecturers utilize the Socratic method, a method whereby the instructor may call upon you at any time to answer direct questions or postulate on a point of law. Lecturers usually expect students to actively participate during class.

Obiter Dictum

I have a love/hate relationship with the Socratic method. While I find it sadistic I always do better in classes that utilize the methodology. Fear is an excellent motivator so I tend to prepare more for classes I might be grilled in.

— *Carissa Browning, Class of 2008*

I enjoy the Socratic method. I noticed that a large proportion of law school students do not enjoy public speaking. The Socratic method uses embarrassment as a motivational tool and it's extremely effective. If you don't do the reading, you'll feel embarrassed... and no one wants to be embarrassed. Giving a wrong answer isn't harmful; it's not doing the work. And at the minimum, you have to learn to admit that sometimes you don't have the answer.

— *Ari Singer, Class of 2008*

How difficulty of your schedule will depend largely on your professors, your school's philosophy of teaching and evaluation, and the way that your classes are structured over the three years. However, it is likely that your schedule will be much more challenging than your undergraduate studies regardless of the specifics.

To do really well in your classes, most of you will be required to prepare for each class each day. Preparation can vary between students. However, those who really excel seem to read all or almost all of their cases, prepare briefs for each case, and actively participate in class. This is a monumental task!

Assuming a schedule of six courses, each consisting of three credit-hours, and one consisting of two credit-hours, you will be in class twenty hours every week. This may seem reasonable. You will not have any labs or tutorials in law school (at least there were none at my law school). You should, ideally, assume two hours of preparation time for each credit hour of class time. This is equivalent to fifty-eight hours every week. You can break it down however you like. I knew many students who worked seven days a week. Some chose to take one day off. Some took two days off. It will depend on your stamina, and on the importance you place on personal time and other commitments.

This description may scare you. If it does, that is good. You should not embark on this challenge if you do not feel up to it. If you add up the numbers above, you are looking at an eighty-hour school week, including preparation time and class time. If you have never done anything for eighty hours a week, this may not mean anything to you. If you have worked long hours at a job, you may have a better understanding. I will break it down for you. It is equivalent to 11.43 hours each day, seven days a week. If you take a day off, you would be working for 13.33 hours a day for six days. If you take two days off, it is sixteen hours a day.

OK, I have scared you. You can't imagine spending eleven hours a day doing anything, let alone sixteen, right?

Neither can most law students. The truth is that most law students do not spend this much time on their studies. There are a number of students who do, however, and I imagine that many of them are truly excelling in their studies and in their career. I cannot speak for these super-humans, as I consider them to be. I am well aware of their diligence, their commitment to their career, and their tenacity to beat everyone else.

Most law schools implement a very concrete grading curve, with rules about where professors and instructors must place students on the curve. What does a curve mean? It means that most students receive a grade of B, equivalent to a 6.0 out of a possible 9.0 or a 3.0 out of a possible 4.0. The important thing to realize about this curve is that it is a steep curve. The majority of students are right around the middle. A fewer number receive higher or lower grades. For most law schools, the grades look like this: A+, A, A- (for excellent work), B+, B, B- (for good work), C+, C, C- (for satisfactory work), D+ (for poor work), D (for a minimal pass) and F (for failing work).

You can see a good example of a bell curve at http://academics. hamilton.edu/biology/smiller/curve.html. You may also find the commentary on grade inflation interesting.

I would like to provide some of my personal experience, not as a map for what you must do to succeed, but so that you can learn from my experience and my mistakes. So, what did my schedule really look like? I can tell you that I did not spend eighty hours each week on law school. In my first year, I went to almost every class. I only missed class if I was sick or had family obligations that had to be attended to. This means that I spent about eighteen to twenty hours every week in class. I did most of my reading for most of my classes. This equated to about fifty to sixty pages on some days. Other days only included about twenty pages of reading. So, I would average it out to about forty pages each week. I was usually able to complete this daily task in about two hours, which I tried to fit in between classes and after my children went to bed. It was not always easy to fit in during the week, so I tried to use Saturdays extensively to catch up. On top of this, I spent about an hour for each class every week briefing and reviewing my class outline that I was building up over the term. This equated to a total of about forty to fifty hours a week spent on schoolwork.

I did not do nearly as well as I should have in 1L. My 2L grades were far superior. What was the difference? Well, I spent some time over the summer preparing for my second year. I collected every CAN and outline that I could get a hold of. I collected every practice exam that I could get a hold of. And here's the kicker: If I was not learning something that would help me in writing the final exam while in class, I chose to pack up my stuff, go to the library, and do something that would help me on my final exam. As well, I chose to write as many papers as possible, as I felt there was a greater level of control over my final grade than with final exams. This is not true for everybody, but was true for me. Papers allowed me to manage my time over the semester. I could read only those things that I thought were important, and work on my paper research over an extended period. The actual writing process could then be completed within a week of time.

I learned a lot from my first year exam experience. I learned this: Do not get bogged down in facts. Do not get bogged down in analysis. Spend your time extracting the main arguments and reasoning of courts. Spend your time practicing application of legal principles to new sets of facts. How do you do this? Here is what I did: Before the class got rolling, I prepared my CAN as much as possible. I did this by extracting information from CANS or outlines that I had collected, from the commercial CAN, and where necessary, from Quicklaw™ or other summary sites that I found using Google®. I then spent considerable time reading over past exams—right at the beginning of the semester. This allowed me to become familiar with the types of issues that were important to look for during the course, and allowed my mind to ignore issues that had not been brought up on past exams. Just doing these two things saved me loads of time! I spent slightly less time on schoolwork in my second year. I chose only to read those cases that had been emphasized in class, or which had been confusing to me when we went over them. I spent a whole lot less energy in creating class notes, as I only had to fill in missing information as we went along in class.

You probably think that I show laziness through these techniques. You might be right. However, these techniques resulted in a lot more personal confidence going into exams, and resulted in superior grades going into that very important summer of articling interviews. My grades were so improved that recruiters simply ignored any faulty first year grades.

I also had a whole lot more fun! These techniques freed up tons of time to pursue other activities, such as my family, friends, leadership roles, business opportunities, volunteer opportunities, and more, all of which were also valuable in getting a job, as recruiters often like to see exploration of interests outside of the law classroom or law library. This is not the sole way to receive good marks in law school. There are many ways to go about it.

With any endeavour, time and talent play the largest role in success. For those of us with less natural talent, we must put in more time. This is the argument behind the LSAT—that those with natural problem solving abilities, and high analytical reasoning will excel in law school. Here is the thing: as I said before, most law students are right around the median. Most of us are average in relation to other law students. However, even those who are average are arguably in the upper ranks of society, in terms of intelligence, talent, diligence, and potential to earn an excellent income. So, unless you are on the upper end of those with Type A personalities (by the way, this personality type is extremely common in law school), why sweat it so much? I have numerous colleagues who have landed excellent jobs with slightly above-average grades.

The Dean's List in law school is sparse. Those people deserve tremendous respect, and many of them will probably go on to achieve great things down the road. It is my opinion that there are really only two ways to get on that list: time and inborn intelligence. Beyond time and talent, there is a third element that I think may help as well: having a parent that is a lawyer. There seems to be a high ratio of children of lawyers among dean's list students. However, that is a personal theory.

So, to recap, there are many different ways to approach time management during law school. How you manage your time will depend on your personal goals, your inborn analytical talents, your recall ability, your interest in extracurricular activities or initiatives, your financial situation, etc. If you want to be at the top of your class, you should do your best to eliminate interfering activities as much as possible. If you want to be in the upper end of your class, make sure that you put in enough time reading, CANNING and practicing exam writing. Also, be sure to spend sufficient time building up your résumé in preparation for the upcoming job hunt.

Obiter Dictum

Prioritize, develop a routine, and plan ahead. You will know long in advance how many papers you have to write, their deadlines, and when your exams and midterms will be held. Look at your known commitments and make a plan. If you have two papers, a couple of midterms, and three exams, for example, you know you will not have anything due in the first month, so why not write one of your papers? Similarly, if you have five exams, prepare as you go through the semester and aim to have your course summaries completed when classes end. That way you are only brushing up your knowledge between exams, not desperately trying to relearn something you never quite understood three months ago.

— *Robin Penker, Law Graduate 2005, Risk Manager and Legal Counsel, Maple Trade Finance*

Expect to be very busy. It is important to find balance; however, you may need to eliminate some less important activities from your life.

— *Rob Nelson, Law Graduate 2005, Associate in Dubai, United Arab Emirates*

Work hard during the week by keeping up with your readings and reviewing your notes, but don't forget to enjoy life and take time for yourself during the week and weekends. For me, I also found that the busier I am the more organized I am. During down periods when I didn't have much going on, I started to slack and ignore law school and studying.

— *Lorne Randa, Law Graduate, 2005, Associate, Brownlee LLP*

Use CANS. Use a laptop in class to amend the CANS rather than printing them out and changing them after the fact. Stay away from people who like to gossip—you don't need your attention diverted.

— *Shawn Davis, LLB/MBA Graduate, 2005, Associate, Shearman & Sterling LLP, Abu Dhabi, United Arab Emirates*

THE SOCIAL ASPECT—JR. HIGH AGAIN

In my experience, shared by many of my classmates, it felt like I was going back to junior high school all over again when I began my first year of law school. I was assigned a locker, given a class schedule, told to line up for class materials and textbooks, and given a rather cheesy orientation and class photo. All of my classes were in one building. There was a 'club day' and student-union-type elections for law school executive committees; complete with speeches and a vote. Small groups and cliques began to form almost immediately. Social activities such as softball day, golf tournaments, and Friday Afternoon Beer Sessions [FABS] rounded out the first few months.

The atmosphere will be different at every law school, I am sure, but some things will make your arrival and survival a little easier.

First, **protect your stuff!** In a world with laptops and expensive textbooks, it is important that you keep track of your stuff. In my first year of law school there were over twenty laptops stolen from lockers and from the law library. You are in a school with many people; in some cases over five hundred students. Add to that many other students who use the law library to study. I made it a point to keep my laptop with me at all times. This can be cumbersome and inconvenient at times, but worth it. Another wise thing to do is to invest in a laptop lock so that you can secure your laptop to a table or some other unmoveable item. This is especially useful if you have to step away to the washroom or to the water fountain. I had a friend who lost his laptop while checking e-mail messages on the library computer. He turned his head for a brief moment, and whammo, his $1,500 laptop was gone, which brings up another point. Back up your computer files constantly—daily if possible. That same friend lost and entire semester of notes because he did not back up his files. He had to scramble to get notes from friends, which put him at a great disadvantage.

Connect with positive, well-balanced people. It is my opinion that you do as well as the friends you associate with. I found this to be true in secondary school, and the same holds true for university, and especially for law school. The competition is fierce, the path can be lonely, and having positive, motivated, balanced friends can be an excellent source of energy and motivation. It can also be helpful when you need to confide worries, anxiety, or problems with somebody with whom you can relate. Allies are incredibly important in law school. By aligning yourself with the right people, you can count on getting those missed notes that you need, sharing CANS or outlines, and finding necessary study partners when required. Further, having positive friends will make your law school experience a lot more fun. And when you finish law school, those friends will potentially become very important colleagues in the workplace.

Find your own space. It took me a while to learn this lesson. In preparation for my first-year exams, I spent a lot of time at law school studying in the law library and seeking out people for assistance. This really hurt me in many ways. Firstly, classmates seeking empathy for their academic problems constantly distracted me. Secondly, the anxiety level was super high in the weeks preceding exams. I felt tense all the time. The positivism that I needed was lacking, and I worried all the way through first-year exams. Further, the anxiety dragged on into the summer months and really drained me. I would suggest either establishing a comfortable study space in your living quarters, or seeking out another place away from the law school to study. I have successfully studied at the public library where I did not encounter another law student, at another library on campus, and most successfully at a café. It is up to you, but it is important to find your own space. I would recommend using the space regularly during study time. It has been proven that having a regular space and time to study can increase your endurance and concentration ability. Make sure that you have access to or bring plenty of food and drink. Most libraries do not allow you to eat in them, but going outside for a quick snack is a healthy thing.

Obiter Dictum

I was very conflicted. I didn't know if law was really for me; sometimes it seemed incredibly invigorating and other times it seemed highly mechanical and deathly dull. The first case I tried to read, I read three times, could not understand the obfuscatory language, and went to bed resigned to the realisation that not only would I be learning the law but also a new language. The case was only two pages long.
— *Robin Penker, Law Graduate 2005, Risk Manager and Legal Counsel, Maple Trade Finance*

I thought I had made a mistake and I was under qualified.
— *Gayle Hiscocks, Law Graduate, 2005, Associate, North & Company LLP*

My first impression of law school was somewhat correct: the fact that it is very cliquey. Like junior high school, there are the slackers, the over-ambitious types, the geeks, the cool kids, the LSA people, and even the jocks. To generalize more, the law school population seems to consist of three groups. One-third of the people here are really ambitious, a bit Machiavellian, very driven, and aiming for a top Calgary/Toronto/Vancouver firm. One-third of the people are here for the party, along for the ride, [or are here to] do some of their readings, but aren't too concerned about what the future holds. I find these are often the people who come from rich/lavish/spoiled backgrounds, and those who have parental expectations with regards to law school. The final third (which I strive to fit in with) lies somewhere between the two. They take law school seriously, but enjoy other social activities beyond the sphere of law school. Not every weekend means getting hammered at the bar with the law gang, but likewise, not every weekend involves passing up Friday night fun to hit the books. I realized this breakdown very early into my law school experience, and it has remained true throughout my 2nd year as well.

— *Michael Gunther, Class of 2008*

I found the first month to be very overwhelming because of all the orientations and because reading cases and learning about law was a very new experience. It took me a while to get my bearings. I essentially had to find what worked for me in terms of studying. I was impressed by the different backgrounds of the other students.

— *Kim Yee, Law Graduate, 2006, Associate, Brownlee LLP*

The first month of law school is quite overwhelming. I was not sure what to expect from the lessons and readings. There is a new language one learns in the beginning of law school, which at first seems confusing and hard to relate to. This definitely made lectures and readings hard to comprehend at first. I was also afraid of the Socratic style of teaching.

The amount of reading every night also seemed like a lot and also overwhelming, thinking "Will I have to read this much every night for the next three years?" I was also disappointed with the structure of what we were taught. The focus was mostly "This is what the law is and this is how one should look at things," while I thought law school would be more free thinking with room to explore options of what the law ought to be as well.

What impressed me was some of the great lecturers that I had during my first years (however, with that…came some really bad professors as well). I was also impressed with how open and accessible the professors were with students—most treated students like colleagues rather than students.

In terms of the atmosphere of law school, I found the social life of law school to be much like high school with cliques forming and some students' focus just being to party. I thought that law school would be much more of a focus on intellectual stimulation and challenges, but quickly found in the first month that this was not always the key focus. Being married, this aspect of school did not impress me.

— Lorne Randa, Law Graduate, 2005, Associate, Brownlee LLP

FIRST YEAR SUBJECTS (SCHOOL BY SCHOOL)

Different law schools in Canada have adopted various core subjects for their law programs. You will not have any choice over the subjects that you study or what section you are placed into. You will not have any control over your class size, or which professor you will have for any of your classes. This can be very frustrating and stress inducing. Nevertheless, it is just one of those pills that you have to swallow. The most important thing is to remember that you are in the same boat as the rest of your classmates, and that you are graded on a curve with the students in your section. Try to have patience with professors that rub you the wrong way. Look forward to 2L when you will have a lot more autonomy over your legal education.

Below is an outline of the first-year programs at Canadian law schools. Most have a core of the basic areas of law, along with a legal research and writing course. This core will introduce the Canadian legal system, and will teach you how to read law cases, and to analyze legal situations, scenarios, and problems. After 1L you will have many options, but some schools still have required courses for 2L and 3L.

Law schools have shifted back and forth over time between more theoretical legal education and more practical legal education. There seems to be a recent shift towards practical legal education, which is a great thing in my opinion. It may be fun to learn about the history, reasoning, and theory of the law, but having practical skills builds confidence. Learning to scrutinize the law well is important, but learning to write a good contract, negotiate, advocate, and so on, is equally as important.

University of Alberta

First year: Foundations to Law, Legal Research and Writing, Contracts, Torts, Criminal Law, Constitutional Law, Property Law

Upper years: Administrative Law, Corporations, Evidence, Jurisprudence or Legal History, Civil Procedure, Conflict of Laws, Professional Responsibility

University of British Columbia

First year: Contracts, Criminal Law and Procedure, Legal Institutions of Canadian Government, Legal Writing and Moot Court, Perspectives on Law, Real Property, Torts

Upper years: One class from each of five categories: Public Regulation, Private Regulation, Procedure, Law and Society, and Legal Research and Writing. Several available classes exist in each category.

University of Calgary

First year: Constitutional Law, Contracts, Legal Perspectives, Legislation, Administration and Policy, Property, Legal Communication and Research, Torts, Crime: Law and Procedure

Upper years: second year: Civil Evidence and Procedure, Interviewing, Negotiation and Counselling, The Administrative Process; **third year:** Advanced Legal Research, Trial Evidence and Procedure, Trial Advocacy

Dalhousie University

First year: Contracts and Judicial Rule-Making, Criminal Justice, Introduction to Law, Fundamentals of Public Law, Legal Research and Writing, Property in Historical Context, Tort Law and Damage Compensation

Upper years: Civil Procedure, Constitutional Law, The Legal Profession and Professional Responsibility

University of Manitoba

First year: Contracts, Criminal Law and Procedure, Constitutional Law, Torts and Compensation Systems, Property, Legal System, Legal Methods

Upper years: second year: Introduction to Advocacy, Evidence, Negotiation, Civil Procedure, Corporations I, Administrative Law; **either second or third year:** Trusts, Family Law, Introduction to Taxation; **third year:** Legal Profession and Professional Responsibility

McGill University

First year: Civil Law Property, Constitutional Law, Contractual Obligations, Extra Contractual Obligations/Torts, Foundations of Canadian Law, Introductory Legal Research, Optional Complementary (Administrative Process, Criminal Law, Family Law, or Public International Law)

Upper years: second year: Advanced Civil Law Obligations, Advanced Common Law Obligations, Common Law Property, Legal Writing, Mooting and Advanced Legal Research; **one of your upper years:** Criminal Law, Judicial Institutions and Civil Procedure

University of New Brunswick

First year: Contracts, Property, Foundations of Law, Fundamentals of Advocacy, Torts, Criminal Law, Constitutional Law.

Upper years: Civil Procedure, Commercial Law, Business Organizations, Evidence, Administrative Law, Professional Conduct and Law, Conflict of Laws.

Osgoode Hall, York University

First year: Civil Procedure, Constitutional Law, Contracts, Criminal Law, Property Law, Torts, Introduction to Canadian Public Law, Legal Research and Writing, a "Perspectives" Option

Upper years: Completely optional courses

University of Ottawa

First year: Alternative Dispute Resolution (ADR), Constitutional Law I, Legislation and Public Law, Contracts, Criminal Law, Property, Torts

Upper years: Civil Procedure, Constitutional Law II

Queen's University

First year: Constitutional Law, Contracts, Criminal Law, Property, Public Law, Torts

Upper years: second year: Appellate Advocacy—Moots;

Any Year: Civil Procedure course, a substantial term paper, and a practice skills course

University of Saskatchewan

First year: Contracts, Criminal Law, Property I, Tort Law, Constitutional Law (Division of Powers), Constitutional Law (Charter of Rights and Freedoms), Legal Research and Writing

Upper years: No courses are mandatory

University of Toronto

First year: Constitutional, Criminal Law, Torts, Property, Legal Process, Contracts.

Upper year: Perspectives course, moot requirement, and extended paper requirement.

University of Victoria

First year: Constitutional Law, The Criminal Law Process, The Law, Legislation and Policy, The Legal Process, The Private Law Process, Legal Research and Writing

Upper years: Civil Procedure with Drafting, Evidence, one major paper

University of Western Ontario

First year: Constitutional Law, Contracts, Criminal Law, The Foundations of Criminal Law, Legal Ethics and Professionalism, Legal Research, Writing and Advocacy, Property, Torts

Upper years: second year: Company Law, Civil Procedure, and *three* of: Evidence, Administrative, Income Tax, Public International Law, Trusts.

University of Windsor

(LLB program)
First year: Access to Justice—LLB, Property, Contracts, Criminal Law and Procedure, Legal Writing and Research, Constitutional Law

Upper years: second year: Civil Procedure, Torts I

(JD/LLB program with Detroit Mercy)
Law I: Property Law, Contracts, Criminal Law, Constitutional Law, Access to Justice (JD), Applied Legal Theory and Analysis, Taxation

Law II: Civil Procedure, American Constitutional Law, Evidence, Torts I & II, Commercial Law—Sales, Law of the North American Free Trade Agreement (NAFTA), Comparative Civil Procedure
Law III: Payment Systems, Secured Transactions, Business Organizations, Canada US Business Transactions

EXTRACURRICULAR ACTIVITIES

Law schools in Canada vary in terms of the number and types of extracurricular activities available to their students. I attended a law school that offered a myriad of opportunities. This section may not apply to all law students across Canada, but I feel I have something to say about this subject based on my own experience. Law school may be a lot like secondary school; opportunities can abound. Like a dessert buffet, it is tempting to want to try some of everything.

I joined Student Legal Services, both the Criminal Project and Civil Project. This entailed a weekly shift at the Student Legal Services house, along with work related to specific assigned files. I also ended up going to court as a principal for some clients. The experience was great, although at times taxing. Remember, I did not know much about the law, and was handed a great amount of responsibility right away. Nothing like being thrown into the fire!

I also was an editor for the law school newspaper, first-year rep for the Aboriginal Law Students' Association, Technical Director for the Faculty of Law Oratory Association, volunteer for a moot, and volunteer for the Environmental Law Club. Retrospectively, this was far too much to expect from myself. However, in the competitive environment of law school, I believed that I needed to do everything possible to set myself apart for the imminent summer job interviews. In addition, I was very interested in several areas of law and wanted a taste of everything—I had no idea what area of law would interest me the most.

Knowing what I know now, I would recommend getting involved, but keep your involvement to a few activities in which you are very interested and that are likely to add credence to your résumé. Be aware of expectations for time and keep meetings to a minimum, and try to maintain a regular schedule for those activities. My alma mater has reached a point where there are just far too many student groups, and people are stretched beyond reason. I have also heard from many classmates and recruiters that it is important to show involvement outside of the faculty of law. Do not limit your extracurricular activities to your faculty, but do try to develop your legal skills and interests at a level that is comfortable to you.

Balancing work, school, extracurricular activities, and family was nearly impossible for me in 1L. I did not achieve my potential in terms of learning or grades, and the stress that I felt was detrimental to all aspects of my life. My single biggest regret in law school was that I worked part-time during my first year. It allowed me to pay rent more easily, but retrospectively, I should have found another way to obtain the funds, perhaps with additional loans. However, I should have limited my other extracurricular activities before my part-time job. You know yourself the best. I only hold up a warning sign to you to monitor your time commitments carefully. More on this in a later section.

GRADES, GRADES, GRADES—OR, DOES IT MATTER?

Most of the literature that you will read about law school will tell you that grades should be the most important focus of your first and second years of law school. The competition is fierce for top jobs at law firms in Canada. Further, the competition is getting fiercer for jobs in general in Canada. I received better than average grades in law school, with improvement each subsequent year. I wish I had concentrated more on grades my first year, but at the same time, I have little regret, and am well pleased with how things turned out.

Grades can be very, very important in 1L if you are vying for a summer job at a legal firm, which can subsequently lead to a guaranteed article at that firm. As well, stacking up your law school transcript before your second summer can be important in distinguishing yourself for future employment. This is especially true in larger urban centres such as Toronto and Calgary. If it is your desire to work at a national or large city firm then make sure you put grades at the top of your priority list.

Although I believe grades are great indications of commitment, hard work, and intelligence, I do not think that they provide an entirely accurate portrait of the individual. This is why law recruitment committees also include such criteria as personality, experience, fit with the firm culture, and other personal definers in their recruitment material and information. Grades will definitely help you to get in the door of a law firm for an interview, but it is the interview that will ultimately determine your success in obtaining employment at a law firm. I am not aware of too many interviewers who would hire an individual on the spot without interviewing them even if they had a 4.0 GPA. Nor would they be likely to hire a law student with a 4.0 GPA who made a terrible impression at an interview.

So, get your grades up as high as possible. This may be increasingly important as each year goes by, as article positions decrease, and as competition increases. However, do not ignore development of non-law related interests, skills, and personality. It is important to come across as unique, while at the same time convincing a recruiter that you will fit into their particular team. This balance is difficult to achieve, and I do not have specific advice for you that will help you achieve this perfect balance. My advice is simply to work hard. Work harder than hard. Achieve your very best. At the same time, try to remain sane, fun, excited, and exciting. Bring passion to school every day, and bring passion to your interviews.

Grades are obviously more important at top law firms than they might be at smaller law firms. There seems to be a pecking order in the recruitment process. Top firms usually choose the top students. Many of those students end up choosing positions in top firms. However, it is not unheard of to have a very good law student choose a mid-size or small-size firm, or another legal setting altogether. I really admire those who choose for themselves, rather than going where they are expected to go. Some high achievers are afraid that they will not be challenged enough, or that they will not be sufficiently compensated unless they are at top law firms. I have done research that challenges this notion.

One example includes Justice Canada, or a provincial justice office. These environments can be extremely challenging and rewarding, and include a very decent and predictable salary along with very good benefits. The 'billable hours' are usually less demanding, which can lead to a much better balance. Another example is going solo in a small community. I am personally aware of such sole practitioner lawyers who bill between Can$300,000 to $400,000 a year. Even after paying their business rent, expenses, and support staff salaries, they make a very decent six-figure income, often while working a very regular nine-to-five type schedule. A third example is corporate counsel positions. Often, people who work as lawyers for corporations can earn very high salaries, be highly challenged, and yet enjoy very regular and decent schedules.

All of these examples require a lot of planning. They are not something that is necessarily achieved immediately upon graduating, or even soon after graduating. My point is that it is possible to be very happy as a lawyer outside the big firms.

Obiter Dictum

Grades in 1L and 2L are critically important because they are the grades firms see before summer and articling hires.
— *Shawn Davis, LLB/MBA Graduate, 2005, Associate, Shearman &*
Sterling LLP, Abu Dhabi, United Arab Emirates

I worked equally hard in all my years, although I did slow down a little in my last semester.
— *Rob Nelson, Law Graduate 2005, Associate in Dubai, United Arab*
Emirates

EXAM WRITING STRATEGIES

Law school classes do not teach you how to successfully write exams. The best thing that I ever did in terms of gaining an advantage in writing law school exams was to read the book *Getting to Maybe* by Richard Michael Fischl and Jeremy Paul. This book changed the way I prepared for and wrote law school exams, and is considered to be the preeminent resource on the topic of law school exam writing. I do not think that I could add much more to what these excellent authors have outlined on the subject.

You can find their book at http://www.amazon.ca/exec/obidos /ASIN/0890897603/canadalawstud-20/701-3675836-3447539 or on www.CanadianLawSchool.ca.

The only advice that I would add is to follow your instructor's or testing supervisor's instructions closely. Ask the instructor what colour pen they prefer, if they prefer single or double spaces in the test booklet, and if they will give marks for an outline written by you in the test book. I have received partial marks in the past for points made in a quick outline written in response to a question even when I did not complete the answer or write out my full answer. Any extra marks you can gain are worth scrounging for!

If you decide to attend review classes, prepare for them by doing practice tests first so you know what you do not know, and then do not be embarrassed to ask questions.

LEGAL RESEARCH AND WRITING STRATEGIES

Legal research and writing proved to be the most stressful and frustrating part of my first year in law school. Although I had a very competent instructor, this was a brand new way of thinking and writing for me. If I could go back, I would have done a few things differently.

First, I would have asked my instructor, as well as other instructors, for copies of legal writing that was good according to their standards that I could use as examples. I would have asked for copies of memos and factums. As it was, I wrote these documents cold, without ever having seen a decent example of either. This would have helped me greatly to get into the mode of legal writing.

Second, I would have asked more help of the librarians in the law library. I was too proud to do this, and was afraid to bother them. In my upper years, I realized that this is what the law librarians are paid to do. They will not give you the answer all the time, but they will do what they can to point you in the right direction. This would have saved me hours and hours!

Finally, I would have sought out more direct feedback, both from the instructor and from my classmates. This would have helped me to make improvements that would have added a certainly cogency to my legal writing and legal arguments based upon the law that I was researching. It is often hard to see through stacks and stacks of cases, but it is necessary, and it is a very good idea to learn this skill at the outset. In the case of 1L, the most difficult obstacle is not ignorance, but pride. It is hard to describe the pervasive fear of being discovered to be at the bottom of the heap. It is so real and so frightening that it becomes an impediment to asking for help, and thus learning.

You may find the following books helpful, although I have not reviewed them personally. They can all be found at http://www. CanadianLawSchool.ca.

Writing to Win: the Legal Writer (Dec 1999)
by Steven D. Stark Can$14.47—From a master teacher, a results-oriented approach to powerful legal writing that communicates, that persuades—and that wins.
http://www.amazon.ca/exec/obidos/ASIN/0385495927/canadala
wstud-20/701-3675836-3447539

The Legal Writing Handbook: Analysis, Research, and Writing
by Laurel Currie Oates, Anne Enquist, Kelly Kunsch Can$61.14
http://www.amazon.ca/exec/obidos/ASIN/0735524874/canadala
wstud-20/701-3675836-3447539
Only available used on Amazon now, starting at Can$11.63

The practical guide to Canadian legal research
by Jacqueline R Castel Can$53.80
http://www.amazon.ca/exec/obidos/ASIN/0459554301/canadala
wstud-20/701-3675836-3447539
Only available used on Amazon.ca

You might also find this Web site helpful: *Doing Legal Research in Canada*
by Ted Tjaden—http://www.llrx.com/features/ca.htm

In addition, this one: *Best Guide to Canadian Legal Research*
by Catherine P. Best—http://legalresearch.org/

SEEK OUT A <u>REAL</u> MENTOR

Some schools offer formal mentorship programs for first-year students. This may link professors together with law students, practitioners with law students, or even lower-year with upper-year law students. My experience with this was abysmal. It may have been fantastic for other classmates or colleagues at other law schools, but for me it was useless. The practitioner to which I was assigned was extremely over-worked, overstressed, and overcome with emotion about his own career. He signed up for the mentorship program with very good intentions, I am sure, but bit off much more than he could chew. As a result, the time that I was able to squeeze out of him was comparatively futile for both of us. Scheduled appointments were postponed, invitations to attend court were cancelled, and the relationship quickly deteriorated and eventually disappeared by my second semester of law school. I have heard similar stories from classmates.

I would highly suggest seeking out a formal mentor of your own choice. A practitioner is great if you can find one. A family friend or colleague of someone that you know is ideal, as they will feel more inclined to follow through with their commitment that they make to you, and may feel more accountable for the relationship. Seek out someone who you perceive to handle stress well, to be on top of their game, and most importantly, who shares some of your interests, both in and out of law school. Try to strike up a professional relationship, but do not be afraid to be friendly.

In my experience, a golf game or coffee with a chosen mentor is worth more than almost anything in law school. A small word of advice from a veteran of the law school and practical legal worlds can save you tons of time and stress, and can really help you in your goals to succeed. A good mentor can also be invaluable when it comes time to apply for a summer job or an article. A practitioner can be an excellent 'in' at the law firm that they work for, but also at other firms. Remember, they were once law students and likely have maintained friendships with their past classmates or coworkers. The legal community is relatively small, and having an ally, or more than one ally, can be like gold when it comes to obtaining employment in your field of choice.

TO WORK PART TIME OR NOT?

I worked part-time during my first year of law school. I did not get all of the scholarships and bursaries that I was hoping for, and so felt pressure to pay all the bills that were trickling in within a few months of starting classes. I worked between ten and fifteen hours a week, which probably doesn't seem like much. But for me, it was the difference between feeling sane and running at the red line. It meant that I lost a day and evening each week to studying. Even though I only worked one day on the weekend, by the time I got home I was exhausted, and the last thing that I wanted to do was crack open a book to study.

I have known others who have been able to comfortably maintain a part-time job throughout law school. Most of those people really minimized extracurricular activities to accommodate working. Many people do not have a choice. They either do not receive sufficient scholarships, bursaries, or student loans to cover their tuition, books, rent, food, and the rest of their expenses. This is especially true to-day, as tuition costs have risen dramatically with deferential fees popping up all over the country.

If you can, I advise that you avoid part-time work during law school. If you do have to work, try to obtain flexible employment. Many people are able to maintain a research position for professors, which comes with a decent salary, and most importantly, flexible hours. However, be aware of your ability to avoid procrastination. It is easy to push work that does not have a deadline into tomorrow. The saying goes, "I have been thinking about writing a book on pro-crastination...but I never seem to get around to it." Try to get firm deadlines from the professor that you are working for.

THE BILLS ARE COMING—HOW DO I KEEP UP?

There are a few options to consider when your wallet starts get-ting too lean. The first is to obtain part-time work. Although it is not recommended, it is possible. I had a part-time job selling computer hardware and software in my first year of law school. I also had a part-time job as Editor-in-Chief of the Alberta Law Review in my third year. Lastly, I built Web sites on the side during all three years, and this really helped ease the financial burden of law school. I knew many students who had part-time jobs. It takes real discipline to pull it off, but it is possible.

The second option is to obtain a student line-of-credit. There are certain banks (Royal Bank being the favourite of professional students) who give preferential treatment to professional students, especially law and medical students. I was able to obtain a significant line-of-credit (Can$17,000) without a consignor. Many of my classmates met with the same success, often with even higher amounts. However, I caution you to be careful with this new financial power. Remember, you begin paying interest the day that you withdraw from a line-of-credit. One nice thing about a student line-of-credit is that you only need to pay the interest during your stay in school (revolving credit). However, be aware that this line-of-credit will convert to a loan upon graduation, and the bank will freeze the loan at the last amount of the loan. You will begin paying regular monthly payments, and your interest rate will increase. One piece of advice is to withdraw the full amount of the line-of-credit before graduating. It is a very easy way to qualify for a loan without really having to qualify. The line-of-credit will automatically convert to a regular loan, and will be amortized over a relatively long period. This is a good way to ensure that you have a little backup cash during your first few months of articling, if necessary.

Third, check your school for supplementary bursaries or access fund bursaries. Depending on your situation, you may qualify for some assistance.

Fourth, appeal your student loan. If you have not obtained the maximum allowance from the government, you may be eligible for further loans. As well, if you reach the maximum allowance, you may be eligible for certain bursaries and grants, such as the Millennium Bursary or Canada Study Grant. Further, you may qualify for remission on your loan upon graduation. I maxed out my student loans each year, and as a result, was credited $16,000 towards my National Student Loan upon graduation. However, be sure that you maintain a strict budget and avoid the temptation to go and spend all of your loan money prematurely. It will bite you back when you graduate.

Fifth, live off credit cards, family help, and whatever other legal sources you can think of. Put your energy into your studies and put yourself in a position to win scholarships and/or bursaries from your faculty and university. Most schools have an abundance of these, and you may be better off staying away from part-time work to give yourself a better chance at winning one or more of these. I often wish I had avoided working part-time during my first year, as I believe my GPA would have been higher and I would have made a lot more from scholarships and bursaries.

Obiter Dictum

I paid for law school from personal savings, a small contribution from my parents, financial support from my wife [for]...living expenses, part-time and summer work during the year, and a large part from scholarships—particularly in my last two years.
— *Lorne Randa, Law Graduate, 2005, Associate, Brownlee LLP*

AVOID LAW SCHOOL TUNNEL VISION

Law school can be overwhelming for some people. It is easy to be consumed by the intensity of your coursework, moots, exams, and job applications. It is easy to get overzealous in your extracurricular activities in an attempt to beef up your résumé. You may feel an overactive desire to make contacts in the legal field. All of this can lead you to feel that you must attend every activity, every meeting, every open house, and every social event announced. I was overcome with a desire to do everything and be everything related to law school, and it was not until about midway through my second year that I realized that I was trying to do too much. I also came to realize that recruiters were not going to expect me to be Superman, involved in every activity or opportunity under the sun. In speaking to various mentors in the legal field, I came to realize how important it is to have some variety in your life; to have a life outside of law school. This was a major revelation for me, and I quickly adopted this mentality.

Recruiters will be interested in various activities that you are involved with in the legal field. However, they will also be very interested in non-legal activities that you spend your time on. For example, are you involved in sports? Sports involvement can mean that
you are a team player, or that you have a certain drive or ambition
that will be important in your legal career. Are you involved in your
community? Are you be willing to reach out to the community and
offer pro bono work? Do you have connections or potential connections in the community? Are you taking yoga or a quilting course?
Involving yourself in these types of activities tell recruiters that you
seek to control stress, and are attempting to have balance in your life.
Are you involved in entrepreneurial activities? This type of activity
can indicate a certain drive and self-motivation. I'm not suggesting
that you do every activity mentioned here, but choosing one or two
that suits your personal needs and interests will set you apart from
others in a very large pool of competitors. It can also provide opportunities to connect with a recruiter. Perhaps you share a similar interest, or perhaps you are involved in something that a recruiter has
always been interested in and would like to know more about. Sometimes you receive an invitation to an interview because you seem
interesting to the job or articling committee and they want to meet
someone who is involved in the particular activity in which you participate.

To recapitulate, do not feel that you must focus all your energies
on law school and law-related activities. I have known classmates
who have been involved in amateur sports at a high level, political
communities, their children's school or sporting activities, volunteering at geriatric units and advocacy groups, and many other things
during law school.

Looking outside the walls of your law school can also provide an
outlet for you, or an opportunity to just give it a rest. Your mind is
constantly working out legal problems, trying to remember important principles from various cases. Your mind will appreciate the opportunity to routinely forget about these things, even if only for a
brief moment each day or each week.

You will find that it is important to achieve balance once you enter the practical field of law. Working on this aspect of your life in

law school will equip you with good habits and aspirations once you are working as a lawyer.

1L ATTITUDE AND BEHAVIOUR TIPS:

I got a simple rule about everybody.
If you don't treat me right—shame on you!
— Louis Armstrong

In-Class Comments

One of the things that shocked me about law school was the Socratic method of teaching employed by many law professors. You have to be prepared to answer questions in front of your classmates on demand whenever called upon in the classes that employ this type of education. It can be stressful if you are unprepared.

This type of teaching style does not work for everyone. Some people buckle under the pressure. Some lose their cool and get lost. Unfortunately, some professors choose this type of student to pick on. One of the things that bothered me most in law school was students who could not keep their thoughts to themselves in such situations. If a classmate appears to be struggling in this type of stressful situation, snickering behind them or whispered comments about them only adds to their struggles. Keep your thoughts to yourself. Who knows when you will be in a similar situation without an adequate answer? Or perhaps you will have had a bad night the night before and been unable to properly prepare for class. Remember that before you make comments about or take pleasure in the unfortunate situation of your classmate. Law students are supposed to help each other through the grind, not grind each other down. Do unto others … remember the golden rule.

On the same note, it is important to be humble in a law classroom. It does not take long to identify the student that just will not shut up or the one who cannot help but to provide a full and unannotated answer to a professor's rhetorical question. This type of behaviour does nothing but irritate classmates who are there to learn about the law from the professor.

If you have something useful to say, or rather if you have a question that you think will be useful to the entire class, feel free to share with the class and with the professor in a succinct, professional manner. If you feel that you want to have further discussion about the subject matter being discussed, arrange a private meeting with the professor. If the professor thinks that he should share something about your discussion with the rest of the class, he will usually bring it up in a subsequent scheduled class.

Do not present yourself as a know-it-all. You may know the subject matter inside and out. You may feel the need to prove this to the professor and to the rest of the class. You are well advised to save your genius for the exam. You will keep more friends this way, and will make life a lot easier on yourself.

Sense of Humour

Congratulations, you have a sense of humor.
And to those who didn't: Go stick your head in the mud.
— Jesse Ventura

Law school can be a very serious place. With the high levels of competition, the ceaseless discussion of articles, summer jobs, grades, and exams, it can become a rather depressing place for some people. That is why it is important to remain calm and have a sense of humour about things. Remember to sit back occasionally and look around you. You are all in the same boat. Most people succeed. Very few people actually die from law school.

Laugh about the way that your law professors conduct themselves using silly nineteenth century mannerisms. Take joy in the junior high school antics that go on around you. Marvel at how seriously people take themselves. For example, I had one fellow two years behind me who wore a suit to school every single day of his first year of law school. He might have been trying to make an impression, or trying to keep himself serious, but, in my opinion, it ended up doing him more social harm than good. Do not sweat things too much. You have succeeded in making it to law school, and that in itself is something to celebrate each day you are in law school. You really are among the elite. Tell yourself that you belong, and that you have the intellectual, emotional, and physical tools to battle with the best of them.

Ask yourself often, "What is the worst that can happen?" It is relatively difficult to fail out of law school. Further, no one has ever died from failing in law school—this much I know. You might have to challenge a particular exam and then rewrite it, or even have to repeat a year. I have one colleague that did this and succeeded the following year. Although this may be a big disappointment (and costly), it is hardly fatal. The most horrible thing that could happen is that you may have to choose another career, and there are probably more reasons for this alternative than simply failing your exams.

Be sure to celebrate your victories. A victory can be finishing your first year moot, getting through midterms or final exams, or completing that first-year memo. Celebrate every step of the way, and you will be a lot happier. I found it helpful to give myself rewards, even for the small stuff. For example, if I could read for an hour straight from a law textbook, I would treat myself to a cup of tea or hot chocolate. The next time, I got the reward if I could sustain two hours. Law school, like any big challenge, is a series of baby steps. Build on your successes and soon you will reach the finish line.

Obiter Dictum

The first assignment is always stressful. Nobody really knows what is going on and how much work to do. Inevitably, people stress too much and work too hard on the first memo.
— *Rob Nelson, Law Graduate 2005, Associate in Dubai, United Arab Emirates*

With the memo, I tried to brainstorm all the possible issues that might be involved in the fact scenario given. I then researched those issues extensively in textbooks, Quicklaw™, the Canadian Encyclopaedia Digest (CED) and Canadian Abridgement. I also spoke with classmates about the topic to see if I had missed any issues or key cases. With all this info obtained, I then pulled out the relevant cases needed and wrote the memo following the outline provided to us as close as possible. Lastly, I edited my memo several times to make sure it was logical, coherent, and cohesive.

— *Lorne Randa, Law Graduate, 2005, Associate, Brownlee LLP*

Share Your Notes!

There is nothing worse than beginning your exam preparation and finding that you have gaps in your class notes. Perhaps you were sick one day—it happens to even the best of us—or you were caught in a meeting, or you just plain did not feel like going to class. Losing one class worth of notes can be devastating, depending on the professor or the class. The easiest way to fill these gaps is to get notes from someone else. Share your notes back and forth (and freely) with others at every possible opportunity.

What is unique about law school when compared to most undergraduate programs is that exams are not, for the most part, testing your ability to memorize facts, figures, numbers, or events. They are testing your ability to read a situation, analyze it, and come to a logical conclusion that is compatible with the law. As such, even if you have the very best notes in your class, it won't really do your classmates much good if they haven't been able to comprehend the material and form their own opinions about it. In other words, sharing your notes does not put you at a great disadvantage when it comes to exam time. Chances are that you will have grasped the knowledge better than your classmate who missed the class anyway, and you will be better be able to recall things from your notes than they will be able to. On the flip side, if you have gained a reputation for not sharing notes, there would be no note-sharing gesture to reciprocate, and you would not be able to easily fill in the gaps if ever faced with an emergency that caused you to miss a class.

In short, work with the system rather than trying to hoard information. It will pay off in the end.

Obiter Dictum

I shared my notes without reservation anytime I was asked. If you're so worried about other people getting your notes, then you're too competitive and need to relax. If someone never attended class and then they wanted all your notes or your CAN, then that's something different. But the learning is through writing the notes and understanding the issues. Helping...someone who missed a class should be a good deed....Law school shouldn't be cut throat....And I've noticed that the people who are cutthroat are not the ones who do the best in law school.

— *Ari Singer, Class of 2008*

Don't Share Grades—Period

With the exception of your mom, dad, husband, wife, and maybe your best friend (who isn't in law school), do not share your grades with anyone. It does not help anybody, including you. It leads to negative emotions, either on your part or on the part of your confidant. It leads to unnecessary gossip, unnecessary stress, and ultimately does more harm than good most of the time. Assume that everyone else is getting great grades, and work hard to keep up with the rest of the class. Remember, everything is graded on a curve (the most common grade is a B), and that your goal is to stay on the right side of that curve. Also, remember that it is more important to show improvement, dedication, and perseverance when it comes to recruiters. True, some recruiters will have a bias towards those who receive top marks. However, do not count yourself out if you have received some low marks your first year. Recruiters look things other than grades, contrary to popular opinion. More on that later.

Keep Your Opinions to Yourself

I mentioned that it is important to keep comments to yourself during class time. It is equally important to keep negative thoughts, opinions, or gossip to yourself while at law school. Because law school is inherently competitive, stressful, and often full of pessimism, do your best to curb those trends. You will be much happier in the end, as will your classmates. Keep opinions about professors, exams, deans, and classmates to yourself. Everybody already knows if a professor is incompetent. They already know if a classmate is irritating. These things do not really need to be pointed out. If you have a problem with an individual, confront them individually, not through a group.

1L MOOT

The first-year moot, which is a required element of most Canadian law schools, can be the most rewarding experience or the most regrettable and terrible experience of your law school career. Classmates of mine have been brilliant in their moot, and others have absolutely bombed. There are many urban myths flying around about the first-year moot. Don't be surprised if you hear of former mooters fainting during their moot, swearing at the judges panel, going absolutely blank, being forced into submission by a overbearing moot judge, or even peeing themselves during their moot. No doubt about it, the moot is a challenging and often intimidating experience for many.

The solace comes in the fact that almost nobody, if anybody, fails his or her first- or second-year moot. Along with the urban legends listed above, you will hear about how that same person who fainted still passed their first-year moot. The moot has a pass or fail portion, usually combined with the legal research and writing or constitutional class in your first year.

Along with the moot, you will likely be required to write a formal factum that you will submit before the moot. You will be marked on this document, so treat it very seriously. Check out http://www. CanadianLawSchool.ca for an example of a factum.

For your moot, you will be paired with somebody, so be prepared to drop any pride or selfishness. It truly is a team effort, as you will write your factum with your partner(s) and will present alongside them. The moot is meant to simulate a court proceeding in every way possible. You will submit your formal factum, dress up in formal robes, sit in your proper place within the simulated court room, and follow all formal court procedures throughout the moot.

Teams will be separated into the Appellant and the Respondent, or the Defendant and the Prosecution, depending on the case you are given. You may also have the opportunity to represent an Intervener, which is a party that has an interest in the case at hand, but is not a direct party to the action. The Intervener is more like an advocate of a particular cause. The Intervener will also be responsible for submitting a formal factum, and will have an opportunity to address the court. This address will also be formal, and will follow the rules of the court.

Strategies to Prepare for the Moot

Once you have written your factum (your researched and written concise submissions) in preparation for the moot, which is the usual protocol, most of your work will be done in preparation for the moot. By now, you have worked extensively with the given case, and you probably know a lot more about it than you realize. There are some things to be aware of as you prepare for your oral presentation or moot. There is no way to fully prepare for the questions that the judges may pose to you. Each of the four students (or more if there are interveners involved) will have an opportunity to address the court. Your presentation should be in line with your co-counsel, and during this you should avoid overlapping issues; however, the judges can ask you about any matter that you may be representing on your side.

Your presentation will have a time limit, and a timekeeper will probably keep very strict track of the time. Your presentation will include time to introduce your position along with opportunity to answer questions posed to you by the judges. Depending on the judges assigned to the panel, you will either spend most of your time presenting, as with a speech, or answering their questions. It is not unheard of for judges to jump in with questions before you can get two sentences out. Some students are very intimidated by this prospect. However, in my experience with mooting, this should be a welcome opportunity to show what you know. It is hard to feel that you have caught the attention of the judges if they just passively listen to you.

Given the information outlined above, it is best to prepare for anything that may come your way. You should prepare an introduction, which you should memorize as much as possible to avoid actually reading a prepared speech. Many students prepare an outline with as little detail as possible in order to avoid reading straight from their paper. Other students have found index cards to be very valuable for outlining their ideas. The key point is that judges are not impressed (nor are instructors) by verbatim reading. All of the judges and your instructor will have read your written factum and will be aware of the arguments that you have presented in your factum. The oral presentation is an opportunity to put forward fresh ideas or to clarify what you have said in the written submissions. It is also an opportunity to showcase your personality. Now is your chance to live out your litigation dreams (or nightmares).

Focus on the law, not on performance. Do not sweat it too much. You will make it through your first moot. The advice in this section of the book is provided in hopes that you will be able to cope with the stress of the moot more easily. It is not meant as a formula for success, or a formula to avoid failure. Failure, in my opinion, is not really an option because it is not possible.

You may decide that you never want to get involved in mooting or litigation after your first moot. You may find it exciting like I did. Many people decide their career direction as a result of their first moot. Take it as an opportunity to learn about yourself and your potential.

I do suggest that you practice your moot. Practice with your co-counsel partner, practice with your girlfriend, boyfriend, spouse, brother, or sister. Practice in front of the mirror. Even practice in front of your competition. Practice in front of practice judges, who are often available—usually upper-year students who can give very valuable advice.

I would avoid talking to too many upper-year students about their experience, as this can do more harm than good, especially if they tell horror stories. Save the war stories until you are finished with your moot. Keep your focus on understanding your case, your position, and potential hang-ups. One last piece of advice—before you go into your moot, write a list of as many possible questions that might be asked about your case or your position and practice answering them. Practice this repeatedly, and you should not fail. I mean, you will not fail.

Obiter Dictum

The main thing I did to prepare for the first-year moot was to talk to different students in upper years. I found that they were much more helpful in the practical hints than my instructor was in the course.
— *Jamie Johnson, Law Graduate, 2005, Associate at a major Canadian municipality*

For my first-year moot, I reviewed my team's factum many times to get a strong understanding of all of our arguments and cases. I also made sure that I understood our opponent's case and possible arguments they.... [might have made] towards my position. I then wrote out a very structured and logical speech. This speech I practiced in the car, in front of a mirror, and in front of my wife in order to be comfortable speaking about the issues and arguments. I practiced my arguments in front of my partner who would challenge me with questions related to my case.
— *Lorne Randa, Law Graduate, 2005, Associate, Brownlee LLP*

I really enjoy public speaking, so I was really not concerned about my moot. I spent a couple hours with my moot partner going over arguments and questions. Our moot opponents realized that our moot was essentially a performance; our mark was not dependent on who "won." Thus, the four of us got together before the moot (without our prof) and had a dress rehearsal. This helped us see the weaknesses in each others' arguments and prepare for the nasty questions posed by the judges.
— *Michael Gunther, Class of 2008*

How to Compose Yourself

First, get to the moot location in plenty of time. Make sure to bring your factum (tabbed with any helpful notes in margins or on sticky papers), your presentation outline (including your main points or arguments), and some concise notes to help you answer potential questions. Once you have gowned, make sure that your notes are in order and easily accessible, and then sit back, take some deep breaths, and relax. Wait patiently for your turn. If you are not first, then take the opportunity to listen to the others and the questions posed by the judges. If helpful, make some notes to yourself in your materials based on the previous presentations and questions posed. You may also find it useful to take note of any important answers given if they are pertinent to what you want to say.

To the best of your abilities, stick to the rules of etiquette, which you will hopefully learn from your instructor. Address your class-mates as your friend. Address the judges in the appropriate manner, as taught to you by your instructor. Avoid personal opinions and frame all arguments or comments as a submission on the part of your party (e.g., "I submit" or "I respectfully submit" or "we sub-mit" or "we respectfully submit", etc.).

Listen very carefully to questions posed by the judges. If neces-sary, ask the judge to repeat the question (however, avoid doing this too often, as the judge can get irritated or think that you are stalling). If necessary, paraphrase the question for clarification. Also, do not be afraid to take a moment or two to collect your thoughts or to flip to the appropriate spot in your notes. If you require more time than this, ask the judges to give you a few moments. Once you have calmed your nerves or thought of a smashing response, dive in. If you have done your homework, you will be able to come up with some answer to almost every question. If you cannot, then find something to say. Avoid going too far down a road if you think it feels dangerous. Moreover, if you feel that you just have nothing to say, admit it and move on. A good response for this may be, "I do not readily have information on that particular issue or matter and would have to take the matter back to my office for consideration before answering your question. May we move on to another ques-tion or matter?" Try to stay composed. Do not let the judges fluster you, although they may test you. Usually where people get hung up is when they keep being attacked by a judge on a particular matter. Stake your position, and do not flinch. It is better for you to admit that you cannot answer a question and move on than to be caught floundering.

Show as much respect for each of the participants, especially the judges, and you will make it through your ten or fifteen minutes without too many hitches.

The Debrief

Good moot coordinators will provide an opportunity for feedback to the mooters from the judges. This can be very intimidating, especially the first time. For the most part, you will receive positive feedback. However, be prepared for some criticism. You may be critiqued on the content of your arguments, but more comments will centre on your presentation style, your ability to address questions, and your general impression you made on the judges. Your instructor will be the one critiquing your arguments, so do not sweat the judges remarks too much. Your written factum will carry far more weight in most instructors' eyes than the oral presentation. The moot is simply an opportunity to practice oral advocacy skills, to introduce you to the world of litigation, and to give you a taste of what may come in subsequent moot opportunities in your upper years.

Be sure to try to get a debriefing session with your instructor if possible, or if desirable. The moot is a great opportunity to grow personally, and any feedback that you can get will help you gain a position on upper-year moot teams, and hopefully to excel at competition.

As well, try to get together with your moot partners and/or opponents to discuss what you could have done better. Be sure to provide constructive criticism that will truly help your colleagues become better mooters and litigators. Do not harp on personal style issues. Focus on how arguments could have been stronger, how a point could have been better made, and how to better handle questions. You should expect the same, so do not feel that you have to sit and listen to someone banter about your personal style. Ask for courtesy if necessary.

FINDING A SUMMER JOB

The race for a summer job begins on first day of law school (if you want to ride on that track). Find out if you want to ride on that track later in this section.

What do I mean by "the race begins on the first day"? I have indicated previously that law school is a very competitive place. I am going to repeat this fact with some emphasis here. The number of summer jobs available at law firms to first-year law students is very few. This is especially true in some cities where law firms tend to hire second-year summer students over first-year summer students. Read this portion of the book carefully—it can be rather complex.

In some cities, law firms are anxious to identify potential articling candidates as soon as they can. They are also anxious to find students that will be loyal to their firm, and equally as important, to the city where the firm is located. This is true for some of the not-so--major cities, such as Edmonton and Regina. Summer employment allows firms a great opportunity to 'interview' an articling candidate for four whole months. It also allows them to get some of the less-attractive tasks done at a relatively low wage.

However, summer jobs are not about the summer alone. They are about recruitment for the all-important article. Normally, firms cannot recruit or offer a student an articling position outside a specific period during the second summer of law school. These dates are set in stone in the various jurisdictions, and there is no deviance from these rules without consequences. The rules are there for both the firms' and students' well-being and fairness. I will speak about these rules in the articling section of this book. However, a firm can get around the usual articling rules about recruitment through the summer job program. A firm can offer a summer student an articling position at the end of the summer employment.

So, a classmate can gain a great advantage early on in their law school career by landing a summer job as soon as possible. By doing so, they will potentially avoid the article competition later on, and can rest easy during their second and third years. It may sound preposterous, but a student can potentially have their career laid out before them as early as January of their first year. Perhaps you can see why I said that the race begins the first day of law school.

If this route sounds attractive to you, there are some things that you will have to keep in mind right from the starting line.

Get to Know the Different Firms. For summer positions, do they generally hire first year or second year students? How many summer positions do they offer? Do they normally offer articling positions to their summer students at the end of the summer term? Are you interested in the firm? If they ask you to eventually article with them, is that a decision you would be comfortable making?

Attend Open Houses Held by Firms. Many firms will make visits to your law school to get to know potential candidates. This can act as a pre-screen interview process, so take it very seriously. Although you may be one face in a rather large crowd, if you are able to make even a slightly positive impression at this type of function, the recruiter may remember you at interview time. Make sure that you dress well for these functions. They are usually formal, so here is an early chance to break in that new suit that you bought before law school. Do not show up in khakis, jeans, or other informal wear. The general rule is to overdress. Nobody will ever think ill of you in this situation if you dress better than the rest of the crowd.

Make as Many Contacts as Possible in Law Firms. You may be able to make contacts through your assigned, found or chosen mentor, friends, professors, and your career officer. It does not matter, as long as you can make some contacts. You will utilize these contacts in both your résumé and your interview (discussed below).

Be Very Aware of Application Deadlines and Interview Times. The application process will vary from school to school and from city to city. Know the dates as early as possible and make note of them.

Get Your Résumé and Cover Letter in Order Quickly. You will want to update your résumé as soon as possible. Do not leave this until the last minute. You will be too busy with classes and exams to take care of this stuff when it counts. You can always add to these documents at the last minute.

Get Feedback on Your Résumé and Cover Letter. This is a tricky one because you may not want to show it to classmates who will be competing with you for the same positions. Look to career officers, contacts who are already lawyers, upper-year students who have already been through the process, and where possible, professional career consultants. Résumés come in many different formats and sizes. There is no one way to write a résumé or cover letter. However, there are some guidelines to follow that will assist you in your drive for a summer job. Some of these are listed below.

Keep it Concise. For those of you who have jumped from job to job, you may want to cut some of them from your résumé, especially if they were short-lived or are not skills and abilities that will be required in the law field. On the other hand, be sure to emphasize jobs where you have shown dedication and loyalty. These two items go a long way in making an impression.

Start Focussing on Law. Wherever possible and feasible, make connections to the field of law. Include any volunteering related to law that you have done or are doing. You will probably have opportunities to get involved in your first semester. Include these activities.

Set Yourself Apart. This probably seems obvious. However, candidates often overlook this idea. The truth of the matter is that recruitment is more about finding a good fit than in finding the perfect candidate. The résumé and cover letter process is the first step in getting yourself to the top of the pile. The pile is often large, so setting yourself apart early is very important. How can you set yourself apart? It is really a personal thing, but perhaps you could highlight your passionate reason for applying for law school, or highlight unique personal interests and hobbies such as involvement in sports or travel. What worked great for me was to create a professional personal Web site. I highlighted the URL address for this site in both my résumé and Web site. At the time, personal Web sites were rare, and many recruiters went to the Web site simply out of curiosity. When they arrived, they found all kinds of things about me that would never fit into a résumé, including photos, lists of awards and accomplishments, a more detailed résumé, etc. Often, I received positive feedback about my Web site at the time of the interview. Whatever your gimmick, make it unique, and if possible, fun. It is my opinion that if you can get yourself past the résumé cull, you are in fantastic shape, as you have already put yourself in the top 10 or 20 percent. I would suggest avoiding fancy paper, fonts, or colours. I am not convinced that any of that makes a difference. That opinion is based upon a tradition of stodginess. As I said, most recruiters are younger associates. You will have to use your instincts. If you feel that you are best represented on pink paper, then use pink paper. If you think you want to incorporate a modern, stylized design in your résumé, then do it. However, most people still use the old 20 lb white paper with a Times New Roman or Arial font. If you want to get extreme, you may not want to work for a law firm that will reject you because of your personal style as represented on your résumé. Again, this is a grey area, and I do not feel qualified to tell you how to go about setting up your résumé. I am convinced, however, that unique = interview. Understand that *unique* is not synonymous with *weird*. Be aware of the style of the firm to which you are applying. Show that *you* are unique, not just your résumé itself.

Do Not Make Mistakes. Check everything over twice, then three times, then four. If possible, have others edit every copy of your résumé and cover letter that you send out. A misspelled firm or lawyer name can result in your résumé and cover letter being filed away in nearest garbage can. Also, be very sure that you have the properly addressed the documents, and that the enclosed documents correspond with the correct envelope (Firm B is less likely to take your cover letter seriously when they discover it was clearly intended for Firm A). Be sure that you have included sufficient postage, and make sure that your application arrives in plenty of time. If necessary, use an express service or other timely courier. A late application is a missed opportunity.

I discuss suggestions for interviewing in greater detail in the section on the articling recruitment process.

For many of you, the opportunity to get far, far away from the law will be a welcome prospect upon completion of your first year final exams. You will likely feel a need to break free and try something different for four months. This is a very healthy thing. Contrary to many opinions, recruiters do not look down on students who seek opportunities outside the law, and will not, for the most part, punish them for doing so at articling recruitment time. However, be sure that you can account for this time away from the law, and be able to explain why you did what you did. I had a classmate who went surfing all summer. I would be curious to hear the interview conversations that he had with recruiters. A non-law summer job can be a great opportunity to refresh your body and your mind. It can be a great opportunity to assess your first year, away from the crowd, competition, and stress.

For others, you may want to explore areas or opportunities in law that are not a part of a law firm environment. There are many excellent opportunities in public law, legal research, and advocacy. As well, there are some awesome opportunities in the corporate realm. I will share my experience with you here, as this is what I chose to do with my first summer.

After failing to make the very competitive cut for summer positions at law firms, I decided to exploit any other legal contacts that I had. I applied for many positions posted with the career office at my law school. I also sent out emails to almost everybody that I knew indicating that I was looking for a summer job experience connected to the law. After many inquiries, one of my former friends put in a good word and my résumé to the legal services department of the multinational oil company where he worked. This was a non-publicized position, and as a result, I was in a group of about ten applicants. This was pared down to three after the résumé sort, and I was eventually able to successfully gain an offer for this summer position.

The legal services department consisted of sixteen well-seasoned lawyers with a large variety of expertise and interests. I worked at least once with each of these lawyers on a large number of files. I wrote over forty memorandums (many of them very concise) on at least twenty different areas of law, including employment law, labour law, Aboriginal law, contract law, oil and gas law, corporate governance, securities law, property law, municipal law, administrative law, privacy law, real estate law, international law, and more. I was able to attend some labour arbitrations, a hearing, and attended a number of legal consulting and client group meetings. I was the only summer student in the legal services department, and so was given a lot more attention than many of my classmates who were working at law firms. I was paid generously for a summer law student. As well, there was little to no expectation to work overtime, so my summer was very manageable and enjoyable. Colleagues at law firms were often in the office long after the clock hit 5:00 p.m. I know some that even spent Saturdays at their firms—not me. I was home every weekend, enjoying the summer rays.

You may think that if you do not get a summer job at a big or mid-sized law firm that you will be at a great disadvantage when it comes to articles. It is true that students who are hired for summer jobs who make a good impression can avoid the articling process, thus enjoying less stress in their second year. However, these students are only filling a relatively small portion of the total article positions available to your particular class. As well, these students will not have the opportunity that you will have to explore the whole field. They will have interviewed only with those firms offering summer positions, which are usually few in number. For your article, you will have the opportunity to submit applications to many other firms and establishments, which ultimately might be to your advantage in gaining employment at a firm that is just right for you. Summer students often feel pressured into accepting an articling offer because they do not want to gamble in the articling recruitment period. They would rather take a less-than-best article than no article at all.

By not summering at a big firm, you have a great opportunity to explore non-firm law related employment, such as research, advocacy, corporate, or academic. Or in turn, you can explore other interests, pursuits, and opportunities.

Another great option for your summer is to study abroad. There are a number of fantastic chances to study an area of law of your choice in a destination of your choice, often with an excellent bursary attached. These programs are usually quite expensive, but you usually get credit for your work there, which can take a big load off in your upper years of law school. The following are some examples of programs.

Montreal Summer Study Abroad
Villanova University School of Law—Study abroad without travelling too far from home.
http://www.law.villanova.edu/shared/montreal/montreal.asp
Note that this program no longer exists. Villanova now has a summer Rome program. See http://www.law.villanova.edu/academics/studyabroad/

Queen's International Program
Britain (In a castle!)—(The Law of International Trade and Investment, International Commercial Arbitration, International Business Transactions)—http://www.queensu.ca/isc/

The University of Pittsburgh School of Law and Semester at Sea
Offers you an incredible opportunity to travel to the Pacific Rim, studying the cultures and legal systems of seven countries. Departs from Vancouver. http://www.semesteratsea.com

Widener University School of Law—2003 Summer International Law Institutes.
Four Summer International Law Institutes offered by Widener University School of Law—Nairobi, Kenya; Sydney, Australia; Geneva, Switzerland; and Venice, Italy—enables students to experience foreign cultures while learning from the different perspectives of students and faculty in foreign countries. These institutes offer a variety of courses and educational opportunities often unavailable in the United States. Students can earn up to six credits that may apply at their home law school. Both Widener Law and its summer programs are ABA-approved. Visit www.law.widener.edu, and click on International Program for more information.

As of the summer 2004, **Osgoode** hopes to provide special access to three summer programs:

(1) Mini-term of Monash University at its villa in Prato (just outside Florence)

(2) University of Montreal's China Law Summer Program in Beijing

(3) Trilater (Bologna, Osgoode, Monash) summer school in International Business Law in Bologna, Italy.

Note that when I went to update this information, I could no longer find it on Osgoode's Web site.

THE CANADIAN BAR ASSOCIATION (CBA)

As a law student, you have the opportunity to be a member of the Canadian Bar Association (CBA). For a nominal membership charge, you have the opportunity to attend numerous CBA events and lunch-hour seminars put on by the CBA sections that focus on a many different areas of law. Often the lunch is provided free, and the sessions prove to be very informative. These sessions can also be a great opportunity to network with practicing lawyers in a field of interest to you. As well, they are chances to explore different areas of law to see if they might interest you once you begin to practice. Another benefit of purchasing a student membership with the CBA is that you receive their publications, which are well written and often informative about contemporary legal issues and issues facing Canadian lawyers. There are also opportunities to act as a student representative for the CBA. For more information go to http://www.cba.org.

EXECUTIVE POSITIONS IN LAW SCHOOL

Every law school will differ somewhat in their law student association or society. Our law school had a very robust and active Law Students' Association (LSA). There were many positions to fill for students in each year of law school. The LSA provided many useful and fun activities as well as information throughout the school year, including social events, commercial CANS, lockers, a student lounge, and a formal dinner and dance. Many students decide to get involved in this group to gain leadership experience, beef up their résumé, and to have fun during law school. Law school does not have to be all study and no fun, and our LSA made sure of this.

The process of elections for executive positions may intimidate you. It is not unlike elections in junior high or high school for the school executive. It can be a mad rush of getting nominated, putting up signs and photographs, preparing a speech, and doing any other type of self-promotion. This is not everyone's bag. This is especially true for first-year students. You are facing many strangers in a strange and new environment.

As I was a bit shy, I looked for opportunities that did not involve speeches or elections, at least not the typical election process. I ended up volunteering as a first-year representative for a couple of student groups, which led directly to me being elected for executive positions for my second and third years. For me, this was a more safe and comfortable way to get involved. Recruiters looked very favourably on this type of activity, and I was able to be very involved with classmates and often with the community at large.

For many of us, law school will be the last formal post-secondary school that we go through. Why not have fun, get involved, and create some memories for yourself, all while polishing your résumé for those upcoming recruitment interviews?

REGISTERING FOR 2L COURSES WHILE STILL IN 1L

Your first year of law school is pretty much laid out for you. But once you make it past that first year, you will be given more freedom when it comes to choosing your courses. Some schools have certain required courses for upper years, and some even require certain courses your second and third years. See the Course Requirement section of this book for details.

Even if you do have some required courses in upper years, for the most part you will have a lot of flexibility in your course choices. There are a number of considerations when choosing courses. This can be difficult sometimes because you will have to register for second-year courses in the waning months of your first year. You may still be unsure about what type of law you are interested in, what kind of firm or legal setting you want to end up in, or in a worst-case-scenario, what type of law you will do poorly in come exam time.

There are very different schools of thought regarding course choice in law school. One school suggests that you should stack your schedule with courses that will give you an edge for bar ad or CPLED courses. These often include the staples such as family, trusts, wills, and real estate. These areas of law will usually be covered on the bar exam or in your CPLED modules. However, you will cover these areas to such an extent that you should be well prepared for the exam or assignments, regardless of whether or not you took all these classes. It would be unreasonable to expect every student to have taken all areas covered on the bar exam or in your CPLED courses, as this would negate the concept of a flexible course offering in your upper years. However, if you feel that there is an area of law that will intimidate you, and you want to get a jump-start on the subject area, you may want to consider registering for that class. Otherwise, I suggest that you do not sweat it too much.

Another school of thought, similar to the one mentioned above, believes you should stack your schedule with courses that firms will find attractive. There is a belief by many that you should have all the staples mentioned above, and corporate classes if you are thinking of going into corporate law, criminal if you are thinking of going into criminal law, and torts if you are thinking of going into personal injury law. Some classmates may feel it necessary to take land titles, judgment enforcement, or other types of classes, but my experience during articling interviews was that it is not necessarily that important to have taken all of these courses that are considered to be staples. Recruiters realize that there simply is not enough time during your three years of law school to take every ideal course. They also realize that there are scheduling restrictions, and that you may not always have a choice about taking certain classes. When I have asked about this problem in the past, most recruiters have told me not to sweat it, and that the firm would ensure that I received instruction on any area of law during my articling year if they thought it was required.

A third school of thought suggests that you should take what you enjoy learning, and take a whole range of classes. You never know—you may discover an area of law that completely fascinates you. For example, I have a colleague who discovered the area of international commercial arbitration. He had never even heard about the concept until he took a class on international business transactions, something he had no intention of taking, but because of a scheduling obstacle, it ended up on his course list. Now he is fully pursuing the field. In any case, I believe that you should take at least some courses that are enjoyable, mind-expanding, or just because you love the style of the professor teaching the course. Law school should not be all about business. It is a wonderful opportunity to grow as an individual. Treat it as an extension of your liberal undergraduate education and you will end up much happier in the end.

Be sure that your course choices fulfill all the credit requirements. There have been nightmare stories of those who realized that they were one credit short when it came to convocation registration time. Even more frequently, people enter their last semester and discover they have to take an extra class in order to meet credit requirements. This can be a real strain on what would have been a more relaxed or even pleasurable end to your law school career. Also, if you get educated in an area that interests you, you are more likely to practice in an area of law that interests you.

Most schools offer a number of paper-based courses, or research projects. These courses can provide variety and offer an opportunity to fine-tune legal research and writing skills, which will be valuable when you begin practicing. They can also ease exam-time strain, as you will already have completed your work before exam week arrives. However, if you have a tendency to procrastinate, have a hard time putting your thoughts down on paper, or if a thirty-page-or-more project seems like a daunting task, you may want to avoid this type of course. Ironically, many people prefer to get the course over with in a two- or three-hour exam, even though there will be plenty of preparation time required for that exam. I have always preferred paper courses because they often do not involve as much lecture time, and they allow me to design a more flexible schedule, which can be very handy if you have a part-time job or other commitments. A research project also allows you to gain a thorough understanding in a particular area of law, which can ultimately earmark you as someone who has expertise in this area, which will come in very useful down the road. For example, I wrote a research paper on foreign corruption and bribery, and the appropriate responses by Canadian multinational corporations. Who knows, this may be very valuable knowledge for a client someday down the road.

The timetable will indicate how each class section will be evaluated, so you can choose a mix of courses based on more than the time of day. If you love to write, but classes that have finals that make up 100 percent of your grade scare you, then look for options that have paper-based marks. Or, choose a mix so you don't have five papers or five finals.

You will also find a variety of pass-or-fail courses, along with courses that involve presentations, role-playing, or even internships. It is a good idea to take one or two of these types of courses to round out your experience. This will introduce you to a variety of skills such as negotiation, client interviewing, court procedure, and more.

ADVICE FROM 2LS AND 3LS

You will find many upper-year students willing to share their knowledge and experience with you. Take advantage of this opportunity whenever you can. Often you will gain exposure to upper-year students through volunteer experiences. This is a great chance to get the goods on various things such as the moot, which professors are best, and what it is like to work at a firm or a non-profit organization. This is also a great opportunity to ask them for course recommendations, about their study habits, for tips on legal research and writing techniques, and for whatever else you can think of to give you an advantage in your law school experience.

I caution you to take the advice and opinions from more experienced students with a filter in place. Remember that we are all individuals and react differently to various professors, classes, and situations. Try to canvass more than one person about any given topic, especially if you need to make a personal decision related to that topic. Avoid upper-year students that show an unmistakably negative outlook on law school, individual professors, or specific areas of law. As I have said, a positive experience at law school is most easily obtained by surrounding yourself with positive people.. It will be challenging enough without someone painting a dismal picture for you of something that would otherwise prove to be a very positive experience for you. From personal experience, I can share with you that even though an upper-year student told me that a moot competition would practically kill me and would leave me with a very bad taste for litigation, I persisted and participated in a moot anyway. That moot ended up being one of the most positive experiences of my law school years. I never would have known how much I enjoy the courtroom setting and preparing for litigation had I not experienced a competitive moot for myself. You really owe it to yourself to try as many different experiences as possible in your three years of law school. I was also told that there was no good alternative to working at a national law firm for a summer job. I ended up working at a multinational corporation one year, and acting as Editor-in-Chief of the Alberta Law Review the next summer. I was not hurt in my own capacity when it came to articling offers. In fact, the opposite was true. On top of that, I gained incredibly valuable experience, enjoyed myself immensely, and was able to do something that many of my colleagues could not. Stretch your mind and embrace the opportunity to learn and grow. Do not limit yourself to what others say or do just because it was said or done by one individual. Ask for advice, listen to it, put it all together and process it—but trust yourself to come to your own conclusions.

STUDENT LEGAL SERVICES

In my first year, I signed up for a shift at Student Legal Services along with a huge number of classmates. This is a non-profit, student-run, legal assistance program that provides legal services to low-income, underprivileged people both on and off campus. There are a variety of similar organizations at various law schools in Canada (listed below). My experience with this was excellent, so I will take the opportunity to make a plug for these organizations. I volunteered for both the criminal and civil sections, and they were very different experiences. The criminal section required you to attend one shift every week at the SLS house with a small group of other students and two upper-year student day-leaders. The office was open during this shift, and at any time, principals (clients) could come off the street to ask for legal advice. We were also responsible for answering the telephone and any questions asked by clients during those calls.

Law students are prohibited by law from providing legal advice. However, there is a monumental amount of *information* that can be provided, which will save the principal loads of time and, more importantly, money. You can also make referrals to Legal Aid, low-income legal programs, legal information hotlines, and other services. Where appropriate, we were also responsible for assisting the principal in preparing for court. Law students (or anyone) are able to rep-

resent principals in summary proceedings for issues like traffic viola-
tions and bylaw tickets as their agent, but are not permitted to represent principals for indictments including assault, robbery, or other
high-level charges.

I was able to assist principals in preparing their files for their upcoming court dates. This involved interviewing the principal, getting
complete information into their file, obtaining any evidence that
would be in the principal's favour, filing and submitting any necessary legal documentation to the court, and meeting with a lawyer to
discuss the matter. Lawyers volunteered their time to discuss these
matters with students on a weekly basis.

When it came time for court, I was able to assist the principal in
walking through the procedure (i.e., where to sit, what to say, how to
address the court, and how to bow when entering and exiting). I
spoke to the court on the principal's behalf, indicating that I was a
law student with Student Legal Services. For the most part, the judge
and the lawyers representing the prosecution were very kind and gen-
tle with me, and walked me through anything with which I was unfamiliar. It can be very intimidating as a first-year law student to
stand up in court and try to advocate something or represent information in such a formal setting. However, it was one of the most
rewarding and learning-rich experiences of my law school career. I
would recommend it to anyone, whether or not you are interested in
litigation. For me, the experience confirmed my desire to be involved
in litigation in some way.

Those who really like their Student Legal Services experience may
have the opportunity to apply for a full-time summer position. If you
have an interest in criminal law or civil litigation in general, this is an
excellent opportunity to learn, gain experience, and make good contacts. It can also lead to a day-leader position for Student Legal Services, which is an excellent opportunity to gain further practical experience.

The civil law section differed somewhat in that I spent most of
my time on the telephone. Similar to the criminal section, I was responsible for providing information. However, with this section, a
seasoned day-leader who was either a law professor or a practitioner
was available each shift. If an answer was too difficult to answer my-

self, I could put the client on hold and ask the day-leader for the answer. Most of the time, we were able to point the principal in the right direction. Every once in a while, a principal would come into the office and we would help them prepare documentation. During my civil law service, I encountered principal matters involving small claims court applications, landlord and tenant issues, and separation and divorce matters. We were able to write and send demand letters on behalf of the principal, which in many cases was very effective in getting the desired result. SLS also conducted do-your-own-divorce clinics, which we would encourage telephone callers to attend.

It amazed me how much more easily I was able to address questions by the end of the school year than the first time I answered a phone call at SLS. Downtime also provided an opportunity to talk about the ins and outs of law school with 2L and 3L students, opportunities that 1Ls rarely have. Again, I learned a ton and had a lot of fun. I cannot recommend this experience enough!

Alberta—Student Legal Services (Criminal and Civil sections)
(http://www.slsedmonton.com/)

UBC—Law Students' Legal Advice Program (LSLAP)
(http://www.lslap.bc.ca/)

Calgary—Student Legal Assistance
(http://wcm2.ucalgary.ca/law/legalassistance/SLA /)

Dalhousie—Dalhousie Legal Aid Services
(http://law.dal.ca/Institutes/Dalhousie%20Legal%20Aid%20Service/)

Toronto—Downtown Legal Services
(http://www.dls.utoronto.ca/default.html)

Osgoode—C.L.A.S.P—Community and Legal Aid Services Programme
(http://www.yorku.ca/osgoode/clasp/claspgen.htm)

Ottawa—Legal Clinic (http://www.uottawa.ca/associations/clinic/)

Queen's—Queen's Legal Aid
(http://law.queensu.ca/students/legalAid.html)

Western Ontario—Community Legal Services

DO I NEED A LAPTOP?

More and more students are using laptops in law school. In my last semester, I took a random count near the end of the term, and counted 54 percent of the class with laptops during a lecture. In comparison, the count was about 25 percent at the beginning of that semester. UVic did a survey in 2003, and about 72 percent of their incoming students had laptops and just over 50 percent of those laptops were wireless. Many of my classmates came to realize the advantages of having a laptop in law school, and decided to bite the bullet and get one.

I had a laptop throughout law school. The reasons for me were plentiful. I can type far faster than I can take notes by hand. It also allowed me to keep my head up, so I could look at the professor during the lecture. This in turn allowed me to keep tabs on him or her, which can be very important in a Socratic-style lecture. I could read the professor and better anticipate when I might be called upon to provide an answer.

All students should prepare notes for their upcoming lectures. Those with laptops can have some advantage over their laptopless counterparts during the lecture. With a laptop, you can quickly scroll to information to which the professor is referring. You can use the search function to find in your personal notes the facts of a particular case by typing in a keyword. Further advantages come when the lecture is over. I also kept numerous CANS that I found on the Internet that I collected from classmates or that were sold commercially by our Law Students' Association. With my laptop in front of me, I was able, to do quick searches for cases being covered in class while I was in class, and many times incorporated what I found in that search into my class notes. Or when I was totally stumped, I could refer to this myriad of information with a very quick search function query. It saved me more than once. On one occasion, I even did a quick search on the Internet during a lecture, as I had been less prepared than I would have liked.

While I was attending, my law school had high-speed Internet access at most seats in the lecture halls. Now they have wireless Internet access throughout the law faculty, so if you have a wireless card for your laptop, you have Internet access anywhere. This is great for lectures and invaluable for studying or writing papers.

There is further advantage to having a laptop post-lecture. I was able to swap notes with classmates many times immediately after the lecture. I also spent many hours right after a lecture going over the notes that I just completed, filling in the gaps using my collection of CANS, the Internet, and textbooks or class materials if necessary.

Having a laptop for research or writing papers is invaluable. This allows you to do your work in the law library at your school, providing great convenience and saving you time. You will spend a fair amount of time searching through the stacks of books, and it is great to avoid having to sign books out to take home, or to have to write your research notes by hand.

I purchased a used laptop during my first year, and it was more than sufficient. As long as you have a word processor and access to the Internet (high speed is preferable), you are off to the races. Later on, I purchased a very good new laptop for Can$999, and it is what I used to write the first edition of this book. I would not be without a laptop in law school if I were you.

I balance this advice with some words of caution. Not everyone can afford a laptop, and some people cannot type very fast anyway. If this describes you, please ignore the above. Many of my classmates made it through law school just fine without a laptop. As well, I have heard many times that exam writing can be compromised if you only write things using a keyboard. Law exams are brutal endurance writing experiences, and if your hand and wrist are not accustomed to writing at lightning speed for up to three hours at a time, you may want to come up with a plan to wean yourself from your laptop for a while prior to exam time. I utilized this technique in my third semester as my wrists killed for a week after my first-year finals. I also took notes by hand for one class each semester just to keep my wrist in shape. This was not on purpose. There were no plug-in outlets in that particular classroom, and my laptop would always run out of power before the lecture ended. But I found this to be a valuable exercise for exam time.

Another caveat—if you think you will be prone to play solitaire or surf the web during class, avoid a laptop. Unfortunately, this includes many people. I always marvelled at how many people spent their classes playing solitaire, knowing how much those people paid in tuition to attend that particular class. If you think you might have a problem with this, delete solitaire or any other distracting material from your computer. Likewise, you may want to keep your wireless card or Ethernet cable at home or in your bag.

I also purchased voice recognition software for my computers. This saved valuable time, because it allowed me to 'type' the equivalent of 140 words per minute with this software. I had to go back and edit for errors, but the errors decrease the more one uses the software. I used this technique for writing papers, and for preparing my final CANS. It was great to have my hands free to flip through textbooks, class materials, and other sets of notes, and to simply speak into the microphone headset. This may be the ticket for you if you are a seek-and-peck typist.

Obiter Dictum

Did I use a laptop? Yes and no. I brought a laptop to school to make my own notes and work on papers, but I didn't use one in class. I would only recommend using one in class if you type fast.
— *Mike Kariya, Law Graduate, 2005*

I purchased a laptop about 3 months into law school and feel it was a great purchase. I can type much clearer and faster than I can write and therefore it has improved my notes considerably. Before purchasing a laptop I would take my notes home after classes and type them into the computer so I would be able to read them easier in the future. I would recommend to anyone to purchase a laptop for school.
— *Jaime Johnson, Law Graduate, 2005, Associate, major Canadian municipality*

I did not use a laptop in law school. If you are a strong typist, then a laptop may be helpful in taking notes. I, however, found writing my notes and then coming home and typing them was a great review of the lecture and what I had just learned. If I had a laptop, I don't think I would have had such a regular review of the materials.
— *Lorne Randa, Law Graduate, 2005, Associate, Brownlee LLP*

TEXTBOOKS—USED? NEW?

Why would you pay retail price for something that you could purchase for 50 percent less? Until my third year when I received a sponsorship for textbooks and materials, I bought as many textbooks as possible in lightly used condition. I had no difficulty in obtaining textbooks with relatively little mark-up in them. When there was highlighting or underlining, I usually found it useful to my studies, as it helped me locate important information quickly during my first reading. I tried to avoid textbooks that were heavily marked, and I flipped through each book to get a sense of what type of student owned the book before I bought the book.

You may argue that you like the feel of a nice, crisp textbook, and that you like to make all your own mark-ups to the textbook. If that is your bag, go for it. However, for most of us, saving a few bucks (or a few hundred in this case) is very desirable. Most law schools provide some method of obtaining used textbooks. Some have used textbook sales each fall. Some sell used textbooks through the regular university bookstore. If these methods do not work for you, do not worry—there will be plenty of signs on bulletin boards around the law school.

If you can, try to find someone who took a lot of the same classes as you and see if you can buy a set of textbooks from them for a package price. They will probably be glad to get rid of them all at once, and may give you a discounted price.

PRO BONO WORK

Pro bono work is something that a lawyer, or in your case a law student, offers free of charge. Many practicing lawyers have a pro bono component to their practice offered as a good faith service to the community, and pro bono work can be requisite of being a professional. A lawyer may take on a particular client, or will do pro bono consulting work for a non-profit organization.

Many Canadian law schools have some sort of pro bono law student organization. Some of these organizations are very well organized and provide a prolific amount of volunteer services to a large number of non-profit establishments and individuals. According to the Pro Bono Students Canada Web site, work can range from "research[ing] legal issues relevant to the organisation or their clients, contribut[ing] to advocacy work on behalf of the organisation, produc[ing] reports and policy papers, re-draft[ing] board policy and manuals, review[ing] new materials (Internet, recent case law, periodicals etc), update[ing] resources, perform[ing] legal education, such as writing brochures or presenting workshops, provid[ing] legal support and information to clients or an organisation, [and] assist[ing] in intakes and assessments."[12]

Doing pro bono work is a fantastic opportunity to get involved in the community. It is also great practice in legal research, writing and education in a practical situation, and is a great way to build up your personal résumé with practical legal experiences. For more information, see http://www.probonostudents.ca/ en/?pg=toronto.

STUDY HABITS

The only reason some people get lost in thought is because it's unfamiliar territory.
— Paul Fix

---

[12] http://www.slsedmonton.com/pbsc/org.html.

Reading Textbooks

In an ideal world, all law students would complete all of their assigned readings. Preferably, law students should keep up-to-date on all cases that are being discussed in a subsequent class, as this would allow one to follow the instructor more easily and feel confident when called upon. I have to admit up front that I am a poor spokesman for completing all law school readings. I would like to tell you that I diligently read the forty to seventy pages assigned each day in law school. I would like to tell you that I then diligently briefed all of the cases that I read, went to class the next day, summarized and revisited my notes after class, and then began the cycle again. I have read some books that have recommended this practice. I am sure there are some students who are able to achieve this monumental feat. However, I believe these students to be quite rare indeed. A colleague of mine who attended a relatively small law school once did an informal survey of classmates in his third year and found only one individual who could claim to have achieved the above description. It should not come as a surprise when I tell you that this individual received exemplary marks.

I also must tell you that those who achieve something resembling the above description often are at the higher end of the grading curve. I warn you that most students in law school do not regularly succeed in completing all readings assigned. Nor do they successfully brief all of their cases in time for the next class. Nor do they regularly go back to modify their previously prepared notes based on their classroom experience. The truth is that many law students scramble all semester long, cramming in their efforts at the end of the semester, collecting as many CANS or outlines as they can, and meeting with classmates in a last-ditch effort to comprehend the information that will help them to write the final exam.

I can relate to you in a retrospective manner about the experiences that I had in my three years of law school, and share with you what worked for me and what did not work for me. Beyond that, there are some other good sources out there that may be able to increase your ability to organize yourself during the semester, and to increase your chances for success on law exams. I have the benefit of being able to reflect upon three years of law school and its corresponding examination schedule. Hindsight is 20/20, and so theoretically, I should be able to share with you some wisdom that may help you, especially through the toughest times.

If there is one thing that I can relay to you as a law graduate, it is this: BE CONSISTENT! In all capital letters. I cannot emphasize the importance of those two words enough. In your undergraduate studies, you probably had one or two midterms, some assignments, some lab work, a presentation or two, all depending on your faculty and semester. You probably had a mixture of multiple choice, short answer, and occasionally an essay question on your exams. Well, for the most part, these things do not exist in law school. You now face, in your first year especially, 100 percent written, long-form exams. Often, they are closed-book exams. Those that are open-book tend to be more challenging, so do not think that you are getting off easy when you read in your syllabus that your exam is open-book.

This new regime of 100 percent, fact pattern-based examination can be a complete shock to the uninitiated. It can also be extremely intimidating—it was for me. But I survived, and I learned a lot along the way. The first thing that I learned was that this method of testing requires absolute and resolute self-discipline. There is just no way that you can cram an entire semester's worth of information into one session, or even one week. You will not feel very confident going into the exam room if you choose to take this route. There is a reason why I found a direct correlation between those individuals on the dean's list and those individuals who I routinely found studying long hours in the law library. They were consistent. They had self-discipline. They had a plan and they stuck to it. As a result, they were prepared when it came time to write the exam.

So, for how long should you study? For how long should you read? There is no formula out there that lends itself towards success. From my experience, the more important consideration is the quality of your study sessions and the consistency of those study sessions. To achieve your best results, you need to plan your attack the first day of each semester, and lay out what needs to be done in order to fully comprehend the vast amount of information before you.

So, in relation to doing all of your readings, even if you are unable to complete all of your readings (likely), you should aim to have an adequate number of regular and consistent study sessions each week.

Do not deviate from this plan. Even if you don't get everything read, at the very least you will be working throughout the semester on building concept upon concept into your arsenal, and you will find that come cram-time, you will be largely prepared. Don't get bogged down and frustrated that you never seem to complete your reading assignments. Do your best to meet this goal, but be more concerned that you at least spend a consistent amount of time EVERY DAY of EVERY WEEK. Give yourself rewards if you like. Here is the bottom line: you cannot make up lost time in law school. There just is not enough time to spare in any given week. Stay consistent, and you will improve your chances for success in a very big way.

The above advice assumes that you will not be able to get all of your reading done. So, what reading should you be sure to get done, and what should you do with that information once you have read it? I found that in almost all cases, I learned a great deal, or the information stuck much better in my brain, if I prepared for class. That means that I at least skimmed the head note (summary) of each case or chapter that I was supposed to read BEFORE I attended class. It also meant that at the very least, I recorded the basics of each case or concept beforehand as well. Now, I did not always achieve this. I am just saying that when I did, the benefits of attending class were much enhanced. Equally, if I spent even a marginal amount of time each day going over the pre-class notes that I prepared and the notes that I took during class, and filled in any gaps in either of these, the information stayed with me much better, I was able to make important connections between legal concepts as we went along, and I was a lot less stressed as the end of the semester approached.

Reading cases will take up the majority of your reading time. Cases tend to be very long, sometimes poorly written, and most often do not come to the point quickly. They are advanced legal analyses, often written after much study, research, and deliberation. You will find that it takes a lot of practice to be able to read between the lines and to find the important stuff quickly. The more you practice, the easier it gets.

Fortunately, many tools out there can help you cut through the loads of information. Get a hold of the best quality CANS or outlines that you can. There are also online services such as Quicklaw™ or Westlaw™ to find case summaries. These are especially useful if you find that you have run out of time. However, I encourage you to prepare to the best of your ability and time constraints for each class. Again, BE CONSISTENT. Your brain works best if it has time to digest information and to make as many connections as possible. Don't fall into a trap of just reading other people's CANS or outlines and never reading cases. It is important that you practice transferring what you read in fact patterns and legal analyses to the practical application of the law.

My second piece of advice for readings is to regularly annotate the information that you have learned into your own CAN or outline. Readings, or for that matter, summaries or case briefs, are worth nothing if you cannot integrate the information and summarize it in a manner that is understandable and meaningful to you in the most concise manner possible. This will also take a huge load off you when it comes time to really hit the books in preparation for those exams.

Obiter Dictum

I did not do all my readings. I skipped the really long cases and read summaries instead.
— *Rob Nelson, Law Graduate 2005, Associate in Dubai, United Arab Emirates*

I did do all my readings in law school and found it very helpful. If I didn't get the readings done before class, or if I was struggling with finding the main points of a case, I would put the readings aside, read the CANS summary of the case, attend class, and finish my readings after the lecture. This was helpful because while I was reading difficult cases after we discussed it in lecture, I would already have an idea of what the important issues were so I could find them and spend my time trying to understand the analysis. As for techniques, I'm fairly good at speed-reading so I would typically spend a day or two during the week and zip through my readings. I would sit down with a grande coffee, highlighter, and my CANS. I would highlight the major points in the casebook and add notes in the CANS if I felt it was necessary.
— *Carissa Browing, Class of 2008*

In first year, I did most of my readings. Since then the extent of my reading has declined. I think that when you are reading a case one must remember that they are chosen by the professor to illustrate a specific principle, so try not to let yourself get bogged down in extraneous aspects of the case. Remember the principle of the case and the basic facts but don't stuff your mind with all the twists and turns of the case because you will not have the time to explain them on the exam anyway, unless of course the professor says that you may have to write a case comment. Also it is worth pointing out that over time, some cases have come to stand for certain principles, which on closer reading are not exactly what the case says. If you come across this, don't twist your mind into knots trying to logically reconcile two irreconcilable interpretations; just remember the principle that the case is supposed to stand for.
— *Robin Penker, Law Graduate 2005, Risk Manager and Legal Counsel,*
Maple Trade Finance

I usually start out in September (and January) with the best of intentions. However, by the time November rolls around, I usually end up skimming most cases, reading and summarizing the most important cases, and then doing a hardcore review the two weeks prior to the exam. I often carry my books with me, so if I am waiting around for a few minutes (LRT) I will read a case or two. I am a big fan of textbooks, however. Even if a text is not assigned, I will generally read one. If a choice exists between reading a textbook and a case, I will often read the textbook. Often the textbook will explain the case better than the case itself.
— *Michael Gunther, Class of 2008*

I only know one person who completed all readings. I usually did the readings in smaller classes where there was a strong likelihood of being called upon.
— *Shawn Davis, LLB/MBA Graduate, 2005, Associate, Shearman &*
Sterling LLP, Abu Dhabi, United Arab Emirates

In most of my classes, I kept up with all the readings. If I was unable to complete the readings, I would at least try to read a case summary or head note in order to get a basic understanding of the case and its relevance.

In terms of selecting readings, if a professor recommends a case as being important, I would at least read that case in its entirety. If the course was a paper-based course, I tended not to read anything unless it related to an assignment that I had. As well, I would skip reading a case if I had already read it in a prior class.

— *Lorne Randa, Law Graduate, 2005, Associate, Brownlee LLP*

When it came to crunch time, I skipped all course readings related to "historical" or "US approach" or "UK approach" etc., and just focused on what would be directly relevant for exams.

— *Mike Kariya, Law Graduate, 2005*

Generally, the two weeks prior to the exam are the most intense for me. I know they say it is best to start really early, but so much of the information needs to be fresh, I find. So the two weeks beforehand, I finish my CAN, then make a "Reader's Digest version" cheat sheet with the most important points. I do this even for closed-book exams; it helps me to study. If past exams are available, I will generally go over them. Twice, I have actually sat down and timed myself with the old exam. Both times, I have done well in those classes, so maybe next year I should find more old exams.

— *Michael Gunther, Class of 2008*

I didn't do all my readings for class. I generally decided by starting a course doing as much of the readings as was possible. As a course went on I generally continued the readings that were more beneficial when accompanied with lectures and less reading on concepts that were being explained fully without as much need for the readings. Alternatively, I read most of the material that was required for classes where professors would ask specific students questions during lectures.

— *Jaime Johnson, Law Graduate, 2005, Associate, major Canadian municipality*

I didn't read absolutely everything but I liked to read as much as possible. If I didn't have time to read everything, I used the professor's lectures as a guide as to what the important cases were and then I read those.

— *Kim Yee, Law Graduate, 2006, Associate, Brownlee LLP*

APPLY FOR 1L SUMMER JOB

Please see Chapter 6 for a full outline on what to consider for your 1L summer job. What I want to say here is that you need to be prepared in advance. Get your résumé and cover letter prepared very early in the school year. As well, do your research on firms as early as possible. Get help with interviewing skills. Interviews with law firms are somewhat different than interviews elsewhere. You should be able to get help from your career office and from colleagues (especially in upper years) through mock interviews. Take every opportunity to make contacts in the legal community. These can be made through organized events, conferences, etc. You may also consider asking firms that you are interested in for the opportunity to have a tour of the firm, and to conduct a survey interview. You may also find an opportunity to shadow a lawyer from that firm.

CANNING!

No doubt, you will hear all about CANs during your first weeks of law school. Professors will ward you off them. Upper-year students will tell you to get a good one. You will scramble to find them. What is a CAN, you ask? CANs are Condensed Annotated Notes. Some people call them outlines. Basically, they are the particular law class in a nutshell.

Most CANs or outlines follow a set skeleton or standard: Facts, Ratio, Analysis (or Reasoning), and Conclusion (or Held). The facts provide a brief description of what transpired in a case for both the plaintiff and the defendant. They describe the most important facts related to the problem in the case. They do not usually include extraneous facts that do not lend themselves to the decision to be made by the trier-of-fact (judge or jury). The *ratio* is a Latin concept that means "The principle or rule of law on which a court's decision is founded, or the rule of law on which a later court thinks that a previous court founded its decision; a general rule without which a case must have been decided otherwise" (Black's Law Dictionary). The Analysis is a quick summary of the reasoning of the court. In some cases, it may be more detailed, depending on the complexity of the facts. The Conclusion is the outcome of the case.

Do Your Own CAN!

As I said above, if you find the very best CAN in the world for a particular course, you will want to create your very own from scratch; CAN before you hit the exam room. You may think that you can get away without this step (and there may be a few of you out there who can do this), but for most of us, this is a necessary step in the learning, synthesizing, and memorizing process. By physically writing your own review notes, you will most likely be able to recall information more quickly and efficiently. This is especially true for closed-book exams. For open-book exams, writing your own CAN will allow you to be more familiar with the information, and you will be able to flip more quickly through your notes during the exam.

I have always found writing a CAN from scratch after studying my class notes and other materials to be an invaluable exercise to help me see where I am. I start with a fresh piece of paper or computer screen, and simply write out as much of the course as I am able to in as little space as possible. I include all relevant cases, statutes, and supplementary information as possible, all the while trying to make as many links in the information as possible. I try to remember why a particular case or statute is important in the big picture, whether it has altered or developed the law, and what the potential problems or solutions might be as a result of the reasoning of the case or statute. I may include some personal comments about where I think this case or statute may come up in an exam question, or write myself little notes that will help me to readily recall a piece of information come exam time. Whatever helps, I include it. I try to keep it as concise as possible, while trying not to omit potentially important information. This is a tough balance to strike, and it may take you a few times to get it figured out. The important thing is to avoid relying upon other people's work in hopes that it will get you by. The truth of the matter is that it usually will only just get you by, or slightly less. To succeed, there is no better alternative than to put in that effort and make it happen for you.

Obiter Dictum

Unless you have a very bad and disorganized professor and you have to teach yourself the course, other people's CANs are not the best or most efficient way to learn a course because it is actually the creation of the CAN that helps you learn the material much more than simply studying someone else's. That said, it is better to read a commercial CAN or someone else's CAN than nothing at all.

— *Robin Penker, Law Graduate 2005, Risk Manager and Legal Counsel, Maple Trade Finance*

I do not make my own CANs. I would always try to find CANs from upper years or from other students in the class and start with that as a basis. Some people found making their own CANs worthwhile as a studying tool but I found it a waste of time since you have to spend so much time on formatting and preparing. I would always start with a copy from an upper year student...[and] compare it to the class syllabus to see if it was missing any cases or sections. Then I would add my class and reading notes into the original CANs.

— *Carissa Browing, Class of 2008*

To prepare for law school exams I would go through my notes and create my own CAN. Once that was finished, I would compare that to the commercial CAN and look for discrepancies. The next step was to create a list of cases from the course with a one-line explanation of the *ratio*. When I started, I would spend less time organizing and more time trying to study by reading the notes repeatedly. As school progressed, I found it more effective to spend much more time organizing notes and continuously revising them as I studied.

— *Jaime Johnson, Law Graduate, 2005, Associate, major Canadian municipality*

Generally, I will buy the LSA CANs. If they are not great, I will make my own. I always make my own CANs for the exam, however. Generally, these CANs consist of a hybrid between the LSA CAN, a textbook I have, and any notes from class that differ from the LSA CAN. This has generally worked well for me. Profs hate regurgitation from the LSA CANs, so adding in some additional analysis from outside sources is often viewed favorably if the prof is looking for more than just points. The only time I used the LSA CAN exclusively was this spring for Civil Procedure, and it was a huge mistake (since there were several errors in the CAN that I didn't catch). Don't do it.

— *Michael Gunther, Class of 2008*

Three Kinds of CANs

Every law student will develop their own way of compiling information for exam purposes. Because most law courses will have a 100 percent final exam, or something almost as substantial, it is a very important skill to be able to compile a lot of information very efficiently. This can be a difficult chore, as you will read loads and loads of very dense cases and statutes, and will be thrown tons of information during lectures. You will work hard to have enough information at hand to be prepared for class, but will then want to pare that information to the bare bones concepts so that it is easy to recall and easy to apply to the problems in your exams. There are many ways to compile a good CAN. I have come up with my own strategy that has worked for me, so I share it with you here as an example.

I often created three sets of CANs for each class. The first, which I call Papa Bear (I have kids, obviously), is a complete set of notes that includes information that I gathered from other CANs, notes that I made while reading cases in preparation for class, information that I gathered at the lecture, and any subsequent thoughts or information that I added after each class. This ended up being a very dense, very thick document. It is not an appropriate study tool in itself, and it is not an appropriate document to bring into an exam if it is an open-book exam. However, it is a great tool for weekly review sessions, and it was the first thing that I read at the beginning of exam preparation time. It provided a lot of detail, and was usually free of gaps if I had done all of my preparation and post-class work. It was also a useful document for sharing with classmates who had missed a class or two, or who did not understand a particular concept. They could then sift through and make heads or tails of the information themselves.

The second CAN that I prepared, which I called Mama Bear, is a pared down version of Papa Bear. It included only the very relevant facts, reasoning, *ratio*, analysis, and conclusion for all case law studied. It also included the most important statute law, any important definitions, and any key thoughts from the professor. It included enough detail to jog my memory while I was studying. I brought this CAN to open-book exams, not as a primary tool, but as a back-up tool.

The CAN that I relied on for open-book exams, and which I used for the last days of studying before a closed-book exam, was the Baby Bear. This was basically a fact sheet that provided the bare bones information, key links between cases, key definitions in short form, and key statutes. I usually did not include more than two to three lines of information for each case; less if possible. I often only included key words that would jog my memory. If I was struggling to remember something, I could always pull out Mama Bear.

So, why all the work? Actually, it ended up being a lot less work than it would seem. The Papa Bear is like the encyclopaedia for the course. It has everything. Creating Mama Bear is simply a matter of culling the information in Papa Bear. This process is great because it really forces you to decide what is most important, and prompts you to make key links in the information. By the time you get to Baby Bear, you should already be so familiar with the information and concepts that you are really just creating a sort of cheat-sheet for yourself.

Everyone has their own way of dealing with the vast amount of information presented to them. This way helped me to deal with it.

Another technique that I used is to design a flowchart that includes every important concept or rule taught in a course. I tried to fit this onto two or three written sheets of paper. I then had written that information more than once, and as with the three bears, forced myself to write as much as possible by memory before copying the rest. I did not stop this rewriting and memorizing process until I had fully learned by heart all of the information contained in those sheets. On some closed-book exams, I wrote out the entire two or three sheets during the exam as a tool for myself. I have even handed that information in along with my exam (in the exam booklet), not necessarily because it answered the exam problem, but because it demonstrated my mastery of the information. This may not be advantageous to you, and not all professors will appreciate this technique. But for me, as I have a relatively poor memory, it helped me to get my bearings during an exam, and to feel more confident about being able to tackle the legal problems on exams.

Other people create case flowcharts, where they will chart out the entire course on a large single piece of paper. This can be very useful for seeing the development of the law in that area of law.

Commercial CANs

If your Law Students' Association or Society is a good one, they will produce and sell commercial CANs at your law school. These CANs are usually solicited from upper-year students or graduates. Usually a modest amount of money is offered by the LSA for the best CAN submitted. In turn, these are edited and formatted for consistency and then sold to students for a nominal charge, which includes the printing cost and a little bit more. The sale of CANs is often used as a fundraiser for student activities later in the year.

The quality of the CANs can differ greatly from class to class and author to author. My advice is that it cannot hurt for you to purchase a set of commercial CANs like those described above. I have had ones that mimicked the lecturer almost word for word. Others have included far too much information, others not enough.

You will receive fair warning from most professors that you should not rely upon commercial CANs, and that they can be a real detriment to you. If there is one thing that all professors DO NOT like, it is regurgitated CANs information on exams. Do not rely solely upon commercial CANs. I have heard some urban myths about students who did not study for an exam other than reading the commercial CAN the night before, and who met with success. But this is a rare story, and one that is hard for me to believe.

Obiter Dictum

Feel free to share my unfortunate story about "commercial" CANs. I usually make my own CAN, but didn't for Civil Procedure, because *I thought* that the CAN was bang-on accurate. Unfortunately, it wasn't correct on a key point regarding formal offers for settlement. I ended up losing 3 marks on the question, and my exam had written on it "STOP RELYING ON INCORRECT LSA [Law Students' Association] CAN." Obviously I wasn't the only one...

—Mike Gunther, Class of 2008

A commercial CAN, for the most part, can give you a good over-all perspective on the course material, especially case law. They can also help greatly in preparation for those Socratic method lecturers who will drill you on facts, conclusions, and everything in between. The best thing to do is to use the commercial CAN as a beginning place, and use it to augment your own prepared CAN and your class preparation.

Obiter Dictum

I did find the commercial CANs generally useful for two purposes. I would use them to find what material was missed when I was absent from a lecture, and to compare to my own notes for accuracy before an exam.

— *Jaime Johnson, Law Graduate, 2005, Associate, major Canadian municipality*

Online Resources

I include these resources with caution. I have found many out-lines from schools other than my own extremely useful in my studies, but it can be easy to get bogged down by the vast number available, and it can be time consuming to go through each looking for useful information. However, I found it useful to download as many as I could for each subject I was currently studying and then using my search function on my laptop to look for particular cases. This would bring up each CAN that was relevant in a window; I could quickly open each of them and scan for the best outline of the case at hand. I do not recommend doing this process in class. You may find yourself overwhelmed, confused, or not paying attention. It is best to do this preparation before class.

These outlines can also be useful in gauging your own CAN that you SHOULD be building yourself, and will give you a good idea of what works for you and what does not. Some people like a lot of detail; others only want the fundamentals when it comes to exam preparation.

Below are some good sources for obtaining CANs from various schools. You can also access all of my CANs, along with others that I have collected along the way, at my Web site www.Canadian LawSchool.ca/cans.html.

UVic Law Student Resources—Student Outlines
http://outlines.law.uvic.ca/
Lots of first year and upper year CANS, updated yearly

Queen's Law Students Outlines Site
http://qsilver.queensu.ca/~lss/outlines/
This was by far the most comprehensive site, with the best quality CANs, in my opinion. However, as of this second edition, it can no longer be found on the Internet. You may want to do some work to track it down, because it was so great when I was in law school

University of Calgary—Women in Law
CANS—http://www.fp.ucalgary.ca/womeninlaw/
A large selection of first, second and third year CANs

UBC Law Students' Association CANs
http://faculty.law.ubc.ca/cans/
CANs used to be provided on an as-is basis. This was a very good site. However, as of this edition it no longer exists. Perhaps you can track it down with some work

Ed Chan—Outlines
http://www.edchan.ca/outlines.htm
Intended for University of Manitoba Students, but some very useful
CANs for every law student

Melanie's Law Notes
http://www.geocities.com/melanie_lawnotes/
A few good sets of notes here

Duhaime Law
http://www.duhaime.org/
This is not an outline site per se, but is a great resource for various
courses. I used it extensively for contract law. It also has a great legal
dictionary

I am sure that there are others out there. If you find any, please let
me know and I will post the link on my blog, Law Eh?
(http://canadalawstudent.blogspot.ca) and my Web site, http://
www. CanadianLawSchool.ca.

PRACTICE EXAMS

It wasn't raining when Noah built the ark.
— Howard Ruff

There has been no other single thing more valuable to my success
in law school than doing practice exams. Get a hold of as many as
you can. Try to get past exams given by the professor that you have,
along with exams from other professors or instructors. Exams from
other schools can be useful as well. Often, you will be able to access
these exams online at your school, or from your law library where
they are kept in bound editions. Find out where you can access these
exams as soon as possible and start collecting them. You may like to
try taking an exam midway through the course just to get a feel for
how the professor will try to test you. It will also provide an oppor-

tunity to see your weaknesses in content and analysis. Doing a practice exam early on will open your mind to particular questions or problems, and can cause you to ask better questions of your professor in class or out of class, and will bring attention to the more subtle aspects of the cases that you read.

In preparation for exams, complete as many practice exams as possible. For open-book exams, write using your personally prepared CAN. This will show you where you have gaps in your CAN, and where you need to augment information or analysis skills. At least once or twice (especially before first-year exams), simulate the exam-writing environment. Keep strict track of the time, and, if possible, write it at the same time of day as you will be writing the actual exam. Bring the same snacks or drinks that you plan on bringing to the exam. This will help you better prepare for your physical needs, and will help you to relax when you enter the examination room on exam day. You will already be familiar with the process and the demands that will be placed on you.

Many professors are willing to review your answers on past exams. They may help you identify where you have gone wrong, provide exam writing suggestions and strategies, and will usually illuminate a particular fact, reasoning, or analysis from a case that you have studied. Remember, it is their job to teach you the law, not only to test you on the law. You are not just paying tuition to enjoy the luxury of listening to a lecture and to be examined. You are in law school to learn the law, contrary to the belief of many rather egotistical legal academics. Since you are the future of the law system, the responsibility falls upon the law professors and instructors to develop the best lawyers possible. Be sure to schedule times to meet with professors or instructors well before the exam. Provide yourself enough time to tackle the problems you are facing, and to go back to the exams you have written to see where you have gone wrong. If possible, try writing another practice exam after you have met with the professor or instructor.

You may be intimidated by the prospect of writing a bunch of practice exams. However, in my experience, this step of the learning process is crucial to your success. It took me two years to learn this lesson. My results in 2L were far superior to my results in 1L, and the thing that contributed most was writing numerous practice exams.

By the time that I wrote the actual exam, I was already a pro at identifying issues in a problem and in analyzing and coming up with an intelligent conclusion.

STUDY GROUPS

Study groups can be very helpful or they may be a large time sucker.

I personally did not find study groups to be useful, with some exceptions. For the most part, I found study groups to be disorganized and difficult to schedule. Many times, members of study groups would show up unprepared, bogged down by other pressures. Conversation tended to veer from exam content to professors, job stuff, other students, what was on TV the night before, and so on. This was the last thing that I wanted to subject myself to with the already stressful exam time drawing near.

That said, I did find a few students who were very focused on exam preparation, and who were very accountable in their preparation for study group meetings. I tried to meet at least once before exams each semester. In some cases, I met two or three times. Meeting once a week for two to three weeks before exam time seemed to be appropriate and manageable.

During study group meetings, write a practice exam question for the other person, and then both answer it right there during the meeting. Then compare your answers and fill any gaps that you can identify in the other person's answer. Also do this exercise with past exam questions, if available.

Another technique is to describe to the other person the entire course in about ten minutes, linking one concept to the next, mentioning key cases along the way. This is a great technique for synthesizing the information from the course, locking key concepts, case names, and facts in your mind. It has also been proven that teaching someone else results in far superior personal retention of information.

The key thing during study group meetings is to prepare, focus, and to have purpose. If what you are doing will not help increase your score on the final exam, you should be doing something else. Your time is far too valuable to waste on idle chitchat or gossip.

That said, you should definitely make some time for socializing during your exam preparation period. By doing so, you will provide yourself with a potential reward for diligently studying the rest of the time. It will act as a great outlet for stress. Try to keep conversations light. Do not get bogged down in details, and stay away from negative talk. Conversations should be full of encouragement for each other. Keep these appointments brief, and during a time when you find that your attention often dwindles, such as 3:00 p.m. to 4:00 p.m. Another option is to hit the gym, go for a run, or do some other entertaining activity with a friend to let off some steam.

Obiter Dictum

I used study groups in my first and second year, but not so much in my third year. I used them mostly around exam period and found them usually quite useful. I would definitely recommend them because they usually help to clarify things and help in getting a full analysis of hypothetical exam question[s] (everyone sees things differently, and hopefully that brings out all the issues in a question). I would assume that a study group throughout a term would also be beneficial and time-efficient in reviewing course material.
— *Lorne Randa, Law Graduate, 2005, Associate, Brownlee LLP*

I had more of a study-buddy than "study groups." The only class I used a group for was 1L Constitutional, and I ended up doing not as well as I'd hoped in that class. For me, the best strategy is to find someone who you get along with, is intelligent, and stays on task. I find explaining concepts to someone else helps me learn; moreover, it is nice to have someone else to explain concepts to you.
— *Michael Gunther, Class of 2008*

Small study groups are very effective. If you get two or three friends and go through the course after everyone has prepared, you will discover those areas that you missed or those areas that you are weak in. The one danger of study groups is that if they get too big, everyone

wants to have his or her say and it takes forever to get through the material. The period before exam time is precious so don't waste it!
— *Robin Penker, Law Graduate 2005, Risk Manager and Legal Counsel, Maple Trade Finance*

I find study groups difficult to work in since study habits vary immensely. However, I do sign into IM while I am studying and if someone in my class is online during the same time we might work together on an item we are both studying. IM can be lifesaver during studying.
— *Carissa Browing, Class of 2008*

EXERCISE—SO IMPORTANT!

You may think that this section does not apply to you. You may think that you do not have time or energy now to exercise, so why would you have time during law school, when you will already be so busy. If you really, truly believe this, then skip this section and read on.

Making time for exercise, even if it is very moderate exercise, will do wonders for you during law school. I am a huge advocate of making exercise a priority. I cannot speak for all of my classmates, but I know that for myself, my productivity with schoolwork went down dramatically when I did not make time for a workout on a regular basis. Exercise can help you in a number of ways. First, it allows you to take some time for yourself, to feed your body something that is good for it. It allows you to get away from the stress of case briefing, study groups, and the general mêlée of law school. It allows you to see another part of the campus, which is rare because you will be taking your classes all in the same building during law school. Exercise also gives you stamina and energy later on, especially during exam preparation time and during exams. As well, because you will be forced to sit in a desk chair for so many hours every day, establishing some muscle base will allow you to continue to burn calories, even while you are stationary.

I chose to workout three to four times every week for one hour a day during my first two years of law school. I tried to go with a friend as often as possible. This kept me accountable, and provided some much needed social interaction, which I felt deeply deprived of. During my last year, I chose to train for a triathlon, something I had wanted to do for years. I felt I had more time to concentrate on this due to my lighter course load during my last year, and I was less anxious about finding a job.

There are many other opportunities to be active. Our law school had a running club. They also had a rugby club a yoga club, and quite a few intramural teams. Many of my classmates worked out at the gym, got involved in intramurals on their own, and some even joined a modern dance class on campus. The school that you choose will offer many opportunities as well.

What I saw too often during law school were people who said they did not have time to exercise. They spent hour upon hour in the law library, trying to tackle the mountain of material in front of them. You could almost see them begin to wilt by early afternoon, and many of them were head-down on the desk by early evening. I think that if they had chosen to take a break for an hour and go move their body a bit, they would have enjoyed a much better rate of return for their study time later on in the day.

Exercise also sets good stress-relief habits that will be needed throughout your career, so you may as well start the habit in law school, if you haven't set it already.

ACCOMMODATIONS—RESOURCES

I didn't know where else to put this information, but thought that you would find it useful at some point. Who knows, it may save you a bundle of time and money. Good luck.

UBC—Off Campus Housing
http://www.housing.ubc.ca/other_housing/offcampus.htm; Housing—http://www.housing.ubc.ca/

Victoria—Off Campus Housing
http://housing.uvic.ca/offcampus/index.php; On Campus Housing—http://housing.uvic.ca/

Alberta—U of A Student Union Housing Registry
http://rentingspaces.ca/search.htm?ref=2; On Campus—
http://www.hfs.ualberta.ca/
Information on "Law House" and "Health Law House", the U of A's 2 new Law students residences at:
http://www.law.ualberta.ca/LLB-Program/Academics/Learning-Environment/Law-Residences.php

Calgary—Student Union Off Campus Housing Site
http://www.su.ucalgary.ca/ooch/listing.php; Residence Services—
http://www.ucalgary.ca/residence/

Saskatchewan—USSU Housing Registry
http://www.ussudb.usask.ca/housing/default.htm; Housing & Residence—http://explore.usask.ca/about/housing/

Manitoba—Off Campus Housing
http://www.umanitoba.ca/student/housing/off-campus_living.htm;
On Campus Housing—
http://www.umanitoba.ca/student/housing/on-campus_living.htm

Windsor—On and Off Campus Housing
http://wilu2003.uwindsor.ca/ENGLISH/Accommodations.html

Toronto—Off Campus Housing
http://link.library.utoronto.ca/StudentHousing/index.cfm?fuseaction=category&category=6; Student Housing Services—
http://link.library.utoronto.ca/StudentHousing/

Ottawa—Off Campus Housing
http://www.uottawa.ca/students/housing/OCH/; On Campus
Housing—http://www.uottawa.ca/students/housing/
Queen's—Apartment & Housing
http://www.queensu.ca/dsao/housing/ah1.htm

McGill—Off Campus Housing http://www.mcgill.ca/offcampus/;
University Residences—http://www.mcgill.ca/residences/

Dalhousie—Living Off Campus
http://www.housing.dal.ca/default.asp?mn=1.9.51; Residence &
Housing—http://www.housing.dal.ca/default.asp?mn=1.8

EXAM WRITING STRATEGIES

There are some excellent resources available to help you specifically with the art of law school exam writing. I strongly advise you to
seek out these resources as soon as possible to gain an early advantage.

I will provide some very basic (but essential) information here
about how to increase your chances for success on a law school
exam. However, remember that none of this information is of any
use unless you have been consistent in your readings, note taking,
and annotating.

Law school exams are gruelling experiences. If you thought that
the LSAT is or was a monumental challenge, wait until you experience a law school exam. That said, there are some very basic strategies and ideas that can help you to succeed. Before I begin, let me
just make some brief comments about law school examinations.

First, I absolutely do not agree with the methodology used by law
schools in examining their students. 100 percent finals DO NOT
make better lawyers. They do not and should not act as filters, weed-
ing out those who will not succeed as lawyers. What they do, however, is create a significant amount of stress and anonymity between
law students, and fashion an atmosphere that is not conducive to

creating better lawyers. They do not emulate in any way, real life as a lawyer.

Can you imagine a scenario like this: You are a first-year associate and have been called in by a partner. He tells you that you must read the facts that have been given to him by a client in relation to a business deal that the client has been involved in which has gone sour recently. The facts are very convoluted, often unclear, and inconclusive. Unfortunately, you will not be able to access any of your notes, any textbooks, any Internet search or research tools, or any legislation. Oh, by the way, you must have a complete, coherent, and legible answer that indicates all legal issues and any potential pitfalls or concerns, both for and against the client, making sure that you cite all relevant legislation, history, public policy, and case law that might be pertinent. Now, you have three hours—GO!

This is just not real life, people! I know that I cannot change this madness with a few paragraphs in this book, but I think that it is appropriate that I make my opinion known to you so that you can realize that you are not alone in your frustration with this system of evaluation. However, on the other side, I do realize that from an administrative standpoint, there are some arguments to be made for this type of examination, especially in law schools with larger student bodies. There are, in my opinion, many other alternatives to this scheme, but I will save those for another book or essay. Or, check out what other students are saying at www.CanadianLawSchool.ca/surveys.html.

The truth is, this is the methodology used in most classes by most instructors in law school. As such, we must work with it. Here are the most important considerations that you must take with you into the examination room.

IRAC (Issue, Ratio, Analysis, Conclusion)

Law students writing exams often overlook this strategy. Not unlike the KISS (Keep It Simple Sweetheart) principle, the IRAC principle can help keep your focus pointed in the right direction. Your job in most law exams is to be able to identify the key legal issues at the very minimum. If you can find more subtle legal issues, all the better. Many professors will tell you that if you can identify the relevant legal issues, half of your battle is over. Big points are given for this skill. It is not always easy to identify all of the issues that are being presented in a given fact pattern. This skill takes practice, and you should be sure to prepare beforehand by going through old exams and checking your answers with the professor or at the very least, a fellow student.

The next step is to be able to provide a reason or miniconclusion about why you think a particular issue will be treated in a particular way. Some students like to think of this step like a minihypothesis. Usually, you are not expected to come to a hard-line conclusion at this point. You are to identify that the issue could go in two or more directions. Identify clearly what those directions are and what the possible outcome could be.

Then comes the important part. Now it is time to put on your lawyer hat, along with your legal academic hat and hit the problem with full analytical force. Now is when you must put yourself in the lawyer's shoes, taking into account relevant legal theory, case history, and legislation to fully consider the hypothetical problem with which you are faced. Legal analysis proves to be the most challenging aspect of a law exam for most people. What happens too often is that the student will start down a particular thought path and get stuck on it, trying to flesh it out to the nth degree, forgetting that other possibilities remain, only to look up from their exam paper and realize they are running out of time. In my experience, and from what my classmates have shared with me, it is much better to fully organize your analytical thoughts beforehand (perhaps in outline form), and then to weigh the possibilities as you go along. One key aspect of the analysis process is to try to hook your *ratio* to a rule of law, whether it is common law, case law, statute law, or public policy. Once you have established this, your job is to find all of the possible exceptions to the rule, analyzing what might happen in the case of each exception. You may find that you have to go through this sort of analysis numerous times for each relevant legal issue.

Although not always worth the most points on a law exam, a sound and compelling conclusion can go a long way towards succeeding on the exam. Now is your chance to pound it home—your opportunity to bring it all together and come to some sort of deduction about what the best options are, in your opinion, for the hypothetical client. Remember, you are pretending that you are a lawyer. You are supposed to analyze all of the potential liabilities, risks, and potential outcomes. You will want to show that you are aware of all of these, and that you can potentially identify the best scenario available and what that scenario might look like.

Law exams are very practical, pragmatic exercises for the most part. As I mentioned above, they involve a mixture of lawyerly thought mixed with scholarly theory. With the exception of a few courses that you might come across that deal heavily with legal theory, you will find that those who are able to conduct legal analysis, as when actually practicing law will have the greatest success.

You should not limit your law exam strategy to what is written above. There are some excellent books written on the subject, including *Getting to Maybe* by Richard Michael Fischl and Jeremy Paul. This book changed the way I prepared for law school exams, and how I approached writing the exam itself, and is considered the preeminent resource on the topic of law school exam writing. You can find their book at http://www.amazon.ca/exec/obidos/ASIN/0890897603/ can adalawstud-20/701-3675836-3447539 or at http://www.canada lawstudent.ca.

Don't Be Too Eloquent

A law exam is a fine balance between showing everything that you have, and showing a mature ability to cut to the chase. In my experience, when my writing waxed too eloquent on an exam, I lost the most points. First, writing ad nauseam about something that I learned over the term wastes valuable time. Although you will be encouraged to write legibly and cogently, there really is very little value in using expressive or flowery language. You do not need to explain anything more than once. You do not have to explain it in new or novel ways. The key is to make your point, make it quickly, logically, argue it well, and then move on. Go for the points. Get it all on the exam booklet in a rapid-fire fashion. Then, if time permits, go back and flesh it out, explaining more fully to show that you have a better grasp of the material than your classmates do. It is better to put yourself into the middle of the marking curve as quickly as possible, and then fight for those marks that will put you higher in the distribution. Too often, I have heard of students who have gotten caught up on a particular legal issue, only to run out of time before they can even identify all of the other issues, let alone analyze them and come to a conclusion.

Approach Your Instructor

Again, this is the key to success in preparing for an exam. Approach your instructor about ANYTHING that you feel you are weak on. I felt intimidated early in my law school career about doing this. It is not easy to admit that you feel lost. However, remember this: If you are paying $10,000 in tuition, and you take fifteen credit hours a semester, you are paying $1,000 for every course. That is approximately $25.64 for a one-hour lecture. So, you are paying $25.00 an hour to be in a group session with up to one hundred other students. Surely, given this very crude analysis, you deserve more for your money. I think that you can feel entitled to ask a little more time of your instructor for some one-on-one instruction on material that you feel you need help with.

It's All About Getting as Many Points as Possible

As I mentioned above, law school exams are a race against time. Even if you have complete mastery over one of the topics that you have covered, you cannot count on impressing the instructor by answering a single question on the exam in full essay form. You are far better served to survey the exam as quickly as possible and look for the big points and bag them. This will ensure that you get the maximum advantage out of your knowledge garnered while studying and preparing.

This can be a rather schizophrenic exercise. Many students have difficulty with organizing their writing to meet this challenge. I would suggest reading the entire exam before even setting your pen to paper. You may want to make very brief notes in the margins of the exam question paper, or on one sheet of your exam booklet. However, *force yourself to read everything once before proceeding with any answers*. It is amazing how this exercise can allow you to better see the forest through the trees. In some cases, you may even find that one question can help you to formulate an answer for another question, or trigger an idea. Also, you can see better how the marks are weighted and tackle the most valuable ones first.

Once you have read the exam, it is prudent to write a very brief outline for each question. Given your time constraints, you will want to keep these outlines very brief. The advantages of doing this are twofold. First, it allows you to keep everything straight while you are madly writing away on your long-form answers. Secondly, in the event you are unable to get everything done for a question, you may be able to grab some points within the outline itself. I have often gained points for simply stating a legal issue, a ratio, or a conclusion within an outline. Remember, the big points are gained for getting all the issues in the first place.

Stay organized, focussed, and calm. Those who can do these things will have the greatest advantage. Ride the proverbial law school B-curve and surf your way towards an A.

I cannot emphasize enough the importance of consistency throughout the term. Even if you use all of the exam writing strategies mentioned above, without attention to detail and a good working knowledge of the material, you will limit yourself to the land of the average. Take every advantage that you can.

Obiter Dictum

For exams, first I reread my class notes and then I skim at least the materials covered in the first half of the course. Once that is done, I make a condensed summary of the course, which should be no more than eight pages. This usually includes each case name, one sentence giving the principle of the case, and one or two words to remind me of the facts. It will also include a list of important definitions and the names and section numbers of any important legislation along with a one-sentence summary of each section. When this is completed, I try to commit the summary to memory, even if the exam is open-book. This saves time during the exam and allows you to organize more efficiently.

— *Robin Penker, Law Graduate 2005, Risk Manager and Legal Counsel,
Maple Trade Finance*

I would read my notes and as I went through. I would create a handwritten list of case names with a very quick (one or two sentence) summary of the cases. It's important to remember the key facts and not rely on any notes or superfluous facts. You want to remember the issue, the reason (ratio) for the decision and some facts that will help you remember the information, nothing more is really required. I then went over my notes a few times. I noticed a lot of my peers would spend too much time in exams regurgitating useless information. The key to preparation for the exams is recognizing that it is an exam and the professors are looking for specific answers... Don't give them things they don't want—you won't get marks for it.

— *Ari Singer, Class of 2008*

My typical preparation for a law school exam was to begin reviewing my notes about a month to two weeks before the exam and then to prepare my own CAN for the course. Depending on the course, preparing a CAN may take up to a week to do. I would then review my CAN and refer to any textbook for areas that I might have had difficulty with. Then I tried to answer questions on old exams to get myself into the mindset of applying the law to facts. This I usually did a couple days before the exam. The night before the exam, I continued to review old exam questions and tended to review my CAN at least twice. In some classes, I also spent time with other students in a study group to review exam questions. This is how I studied for exams all three years.

— *Lorne Randa, Law Graduate, 2005, Associate, Brownlee LLP*

I always attend the review class before exams so I have an idea of what the professor is going to be looking for in an exam. Then I typically use what I affectionately termed the "Goldilocks technique" to prepare for exams. I start with CANs from an upper year student and add notes into the CANs based on lectures and my readings. Because of the additional notes, it is ominously big near the end of the semester. To prepare for exams, I take my large ominous CANs ("Papa CANs") and prepare it for exams. First I take the class syllabus and make sure all sections, cases, statutes, etc., are in "Papa CANs." I add what I feel is missing, highlight analyses/decisions and generally try to summarize issues, analyses, and decisions so I can find the major points fast in an exam. Then I print out "Papa CANs" and tab it so I can find the major points, decision, analysis, statutes, etc., quickly during an exam. After "Papa CANs" is done I work on a quick outline called "Baby CANs." I take a copy of the class syllabus and add in the major points/analysis/decision of cases and relevant statutes/regulations under each section that I require for the class. Example: in Contracts, a class syllabus might include promissory estoppel and include *Hughes v. Metropolitan Railway and Central London Property Trust Ltd. v. High Trees House Ltd.* as readings. I would put in "Baby CANs" the main points to meet the requirements of promissory estoppel that came from each of the cases and then cross-reference it with "Papa CANs" so I can find additional information quickly. While "Papa CANs" is typically around eighty pages I try to keep "Baby CANs" around ten pages. I print out "Baby CANs" and tab like "Papa CANs." Then I work on "Mama CANs" which is a case review. I make a spreadsheet with the columns: Case Name, Topic, Facts, Ratio, Judgment and fill in the information from "Papa CANs" and the class syllabus. I print it out, then I have a reference to find all related cases for a particular topic (e.g., promissory estoppel).

— *Carissa Browing, Class of 2008*

1L EVALUATION

*Inside yourself or outside, you never have to
change what you see, only the way you see it.*
— Thaddeus Golas

You did it! You made it through your first year of law school. Exams are over; perhaps you have a week or two before you need to start your summer job. Now is a great time to look back and evaluate what contributed to your success and what did not. If you aced your exams, good for you. Make notes of what types of questions or types of issues challenged you on exams. If you achieved average grades, assess why you think this is. Remember that most of your classmates are near you on the curve. The important thing is to think of ways that you can push yourself higher on the curve next year.

Ask yourself if you need to spend more time on school and less time on extracurricular or leadership activities. Perhaps you need to change the balance of your time spent on different things. Perhaps you need to reassess working that part-time job. Avoiding debt now may have a very negative impact on your ability to make income in the future. If your grades are suffering too badly because of a part-time job, you might want to consider a higher student loan, a student line of credit, or some other means of allowing you more time to hit the books. Theoretically, you can pay off that money much faster making $30.00 or more an hour as a lawyer than you can at $7.00 or $8.00 an hour working at a café. However, do not take this to the extreme and create a situation where you have more debt than you can reasonably manage. It is just something to consider.

You may find that you wished you spent more time in study groups, more time briefing cases, more time consulting with instructors, or more time conducting daily reviews of the material. You might want to make certain resolutions for 2L, such as getting to bed at a certain time each day, or deciding to only go out one evening each weekend. You might want to reduce the time that you spend in the gym (however don't cut it out—three times a week is totally justifiable). You might want to talk to your significant other, your best friend, or family and let them know that you just cannot be quite as available in the coming year.

All of these are examples of considerations that you may want to make going into the next year. The next year will be crucial towards you gaining your articling position. You will want to find as many ways as possible to improve your chances for success. The end of the first year is the best time to do this assessment, to make strong resolutions for the following year, and then to let it rest for the next four months. Enjoy your summer experience, learn from it, and get ready for the next round.

Obiter Dictum

While the sirens can easily lure students into the pub for a jug of beer and greasy nachos it's better to find a healthy alternative to cope with stress. You won't have to study while sluggish from greasy food and a hangover if you take a break to walk the dog, take a bubble bath, or attend a yoga class. Off the record, I also read celebrity gossip on the Internet.

— Carissa Browing, Class of 2008

To cope with stress in law school, I was lucky to have an understanding fiancée/wife, and a friend in another law school to talk to about common concerns.

— Shawn Davis, LLB/MBA Graduate, 2005, Associate, Shearman &
Sterling LLP, Abu Dhabi, United Arab Emirates

Running, exercising, playing guitar, hanging out with NON-LAW friends, who are not going to spend Friday night debating the merits of s.7 of the Charter—all these helped me to cope with stress during law school.

— Michael Gunther, Class of 2008

CHAPTER 5: SUMMER JOB

The law is not so much carved in stone as it is written in water,
flowing in and out with the tide.

— Jeff Melvoin, Northern Exposure,
Crime and Punishment, 1992

OPTIONS

CONTRARY to popular belief, there are many fine options for summer employment as a law student. The following examples are certainly not exhaustive. Go into your first summer with an open mind, considering carefully how your summer experience might affect your future career choices or chances.

Firm

As soon as you begin your law school career, you will be inundated by both students and faculty members about the importance of spending your first summer working at a law firm. You will start hearing rumours and announcements about on-campus interviews within the first month of law school. I remember coming home one day from school during first year and sharing this phenomenon with my wife. We were both dumbstruck at how quickly the fracas had begun. I had barely cracked open a textbook and I was being told to prepare my résumé and to purchase a suit for the upcoming interviews. I could not believe this for a few reasons. I had no idea if I wanted to work at a law firm during my spring and summer break. I did not know if I wanted to stay in the city where I was attending law school—why would I want to jump into a firm in a city at this point without being sure? I didn't know a thing about law firms when I entered into law school—what was a good firm, what type of law do different firms practice, what were firms looking for in a first-year law student? All of these questions swam around in my head, and I admit that I felt quite lost.

I wish that someone had taken me aside and explained to me what my options were, and provided advice for landing that coveted summer job with a firm. A few application deadlines went by, along with some interviews before I clued in.

A job at a law firm in pretty much any city in Canada is an exceptional opportunity. By that, I mean that these jobs are rare. You will hear repeatedly that they are imperative towards getting a good article. My experience tells me otherwise. However, it *is* a much easier way to get an article, if you happen to land one of these jobs. The number of these positions, like articling positions, declines during economic hard times. It is common to have your class fighting for ten to thirty law firm jobs within the local community. That number may not be accurate, given that most major firms recruit across the country. At my school, that meant many students were left high and dry. Unfortunately, there seems to be a stigma placed on not getting a summer job at a law firm. To me, it seems ludicrous, given that the chances of landing one of these jobs are very low indeed.

Law firms come sweeping into the law schools, often sending representatives across the country, looking for the brightest and the best law students to come join them for a summer internship with the possibility (some go so far as to almost make a promise) of an offer for an articling position at the end of their summer employment. Many of the major law firms incorporate this recruiting technique. Their goal is to get the best first—they want to scoop the competition. Firms also benefit from being able to interview you over four months during this summer job, giving them an opportunity to really find out if you are a good fit. This recruiting technique is also an opportunity to find very cheap, very eager help. The truth is that summer interns do almost as much work, although often more menial, as articling students at a relatively low wage. These are all logical reasons for firms to use this recruiting method.

So, where does this place you? The first thing to consider is your overall plans after law school. Do you feel driven to get the most prestigious, best paying law job available? Do you consider this the only way to justify the monstrous tuition that you are going to pay over the three years of law school? Or, on the other hand, do you want to get a better view of the landscape of the law?

These are important questions to ask, and can be answered in numerous ways. If you feel driven towards prestige, you will want to be sure to get your applications in and do your best to impress in interviews. Please read the sections on résumés and interviewing included in this book to better prepare yourself. However, remember that you are competing against the very best. The funny thing about this recruitment period is that impressions are based upon what you did during your undergraduate degree, which may have been totally unrelated to the law. It will also take into account your LSAT score. So, really, your application for a summer job is an extension of your law school application. Firms will try to predict who will be great lawyers based on these criteria, in addition to the impression that you make on them at an interview. Read the section in this book on being your own person carefully. Most of your chances will be based on the first impression you make, as recruiters have little else on which to base their opinion.

On that point, if you can find any form of contact with someone at a recruiting firm, this can be hugely advantageous to you. As with all jobs, networking is imperative and often lends itself towards success in landing a job. You will want to sweep your list of personal contacts to find anyone and everyone that works for, or knows someone who works for a recruiting firm. I know, I know—this seems like too much to think about right off the bat. I agree, but I must give you a taste of the reality of law school and your legal career.

Now, I have had many classmates who had great experiences during their summer job at a law firm. They had opportunities to be exposed to new and exciting areas of law and the courts, honed their research and writing skills, and extended their personal network of contacts in the legal field. However, the majority of students that I have spoken to about their summer law firm job have indicated that they worked very hard, wanting to impress partners and recruitment staff, that they felt a large amount of competition between themselves and other summer students, and that they felt significant pressure to work long hours and even weekends in some cases—all for $2,000 a month. Many students do express a sense of relief when that articling offer comes at the end of summer, leaving the student to relax in their upper year(s) of law school. However, I have also seen students wish that they had the opportunity to test other waters out there, feeling trapped by a firm that has shown confidence in them. These are all things to consider before deciding to apply or accept summer firm positions.

You are not really trapped if you happen to land a summer firm job. You can always say no to an articling offer. If you feel that you have what it takes to find another article, and if you consider that this firm has shown confidence in you, you may feel that you can take a chance. However, realize that if you say yes to an articling position at the end of your summer employment, you are now bound to that agreement, and that it would be considered bad form to go back on that agreement later.

If you happen to luck out and get a job during your first summer and are not attracted to the firm, you can decline any offer they might make and you can also try to gain employment at another firm during the second summer. However, you are once again playing the odds. That said, you do have a summer of experience to put on your résumé, and you can tell a subsequent firm that you feel you would be better suited at their firm based on what you learned from your previous summer experience.

Some firms like to hire students in their first year of studies. Others prefer second-year students. There does not seem to be much logic to this. However, it seems that firms in less attractive cities (i.e., not economic centres) like to scoop students early to convince them that their firm and their city is a great place to practice, or in turn, to find students who are of this mindset already.

I did not work at a firm either of my summers. However, I had friends who did. I feel that I had better summer experiences than they did, but everyone will have their own opinion about this.

Regardless, it never hurts to get your applications in early, do as much homework as you can on the specific firms, and give it a shot if you are accepted. If you decide against it after you have learned more, or decide to go a completely different route, you can always change directions later on. In any case, practical experience will make you a better student in your subsequent year(s) or will make you a better lawyer in the end.

Please note that not all job advertisements for positions with firms come out during the school year. Many pop up at smaller firms near the end of the term or even during the summer months. There are often cases of firms looking for help on a part-time or short-term basis. Keep your eye open for these opportunities, as there might be an opening to a perfect-fit career choice for you.

Obiter Dictum

Get involved in extracurricular activities. Take a hit sometimes in not doing all your readings so you can meet with firms and adequately prepare your applications.
— *Shawn Davis, LLB/MBA Graduate, 2005, Associate, Shearman & Sterling LLP, Abu Dhabi, United Arab Emirates*

Internship

Many of the summer jobs that come up are internships at various organizations. These can include non-profit organizations, government agencies, advocacy groups, community foundations, international organizations, etc. There are also opportunities with various levels of courts. Jobs of this nature will be posted on a periodic basis. These can be excellent opportunities to expose yourself to new areas of law, to gain practical experience, and to increase your knowledge in a field in which you are interested. A summer internship can never hurt you in terms of gaining an article.

Corporate

Not very many law students consider this option. One of the reasons is that most corporate legal departments do not readily advertise summer internship positions. However, students (including myself) who have taken advantage of this opportunity often have great things to say about it.

As I said, most legal positions for corporate entities are not advertised. Some are often small departments who do not always know their budget until the last minute, while others simply do not have a need to advertise to get that small but worthy applicant pool. There are corporations that regularly hire summer students. However, even these corporations rarely advertise, but usually hire based on current employee or other personal recommendations, or on résumés sent to them directly by interested students who heard from this person or that person that they might have an open position. This is where your networking skills can be particularly useful, as they proved to be for me.

After some consideration, I decided to apply for a position at a multi-national oil firm in Calgary for my first-year summer job. This was an unadvertised position, but I did have a friend who worked at the company. I sent my résumé to the friend and asked them to pass it on to someone in the legal services department. I had to wait until almost the last minute, as the company did not know if it would be hiring until late March. I was very glad that I waited and that things worked out.

As I said in Chapter 4, my first summer was fantastic! As I was the only summer student, I was able to receive a lot of attention from the sixteen lawyers in the department. I covered about twenty areas of law, wrote many brief but worthwhile memos, and was able to attend a number of hearings, arbitrations, and conferences. I was able to meet directly with a large number of company client groups, and generally improved my legal research, writing, and advocacy skills. I was well paid compared to my colleagues at summer law firm positions. Best of all, I worked regular hours, five days a week, with an hour lunch every day. Unlike many law firms, they had no expectations of summer students, or of lawyers for that matter, to work crazy overtime hours.

During my summer, I was also able to work many hours at a local big law firm, which was partnered in a way with the corporation where I was working. This allowed me an opportunity to see what it was like to be in a firm, to see what other summer students and articling students were doing, and to get an idea of whether this option would be right for me. I was able to do research in their law library, and to consult with a number of their lawyers.

Some of my classmates also took advantage of a summer position at a corporation. They experienced a wide variety of work, relatively good pay, and relatively fewer work hours when compared to classmates who were working at law firms.

When it came time to interview for articles, this experience was obviously appreciated by recruiters. It was unique and offered the recruiters an inside perspective on a major potential client. I found that they were also impressed with the knowledge I had obtained during my summer, both of the law and of corporate matters. I highly recommend this option either for your first or second summer.

Research for a Professor

This option for summer employment is a great one. Some people look at this option as a last-resort, but it can be an excellent opportunity to increase your knowledge of a particular area of law, can improve your research and writing abilities, and best of all, is often very flexible. These positions usually come up at the end of the school year or the beginning of spring, so be sure to keep your eye open for them.

Many law professors are awarded research grants, part of which can be allocated to student researchers. Work can vary from researching particular legislation or case law to historical information. It can also involve compiling casebooks for the upcoming year.

Schedules are usually accommodating, with a fixed-term contract. In other words, as long as you get the job done, you can do it however you want. Try to get an after-hours access card to the law library to allow you even more flexibility.

Many students take on research positions in conjunction with another part-time job. Research work usually pays relatively well (around $15 an hour), but the hours are not always full-time.

A research position can be a great asset to you when it comes time to apply for an article. Showing that you have excellent research and writing abilities will be very attractive to an employer. As well, if you are able to improve your expertise in a particular area of law, this can also be appealing to a potential employer.

Be sure to be honest with the hours you report. You absolutely do not want to tarnish your reputation within the Faculty of Law. Reporting is usually done on an honour basis. Remember, you are training to become a lawyer, so conduct yourself accordingly.

Student Legal Services

This is an excellent opportunity for those of you who are interested in any type of litigation, and can be equally useful to those interested in civil matters. These positions are coveted, and competition can be stiff. If you are interested in this type of summer job, you will want to volunteer during your first year of law school. Applications for summer jobs occur early in the year. Interviewers often make their decisions based on commendations from your day-leader during your first year.

There are usually opportunities on both the criminal side and the civil side. The criminal section deals with summary convictions, including traffic laws, possession of recreational drugs, and similar offences. The civil side deals with small claims issues, landlord tenant law, and family law.

Working at Student Legal Services (or its equivalent) can lead to further work in your second summer as a supervisor or director.

You can expect to go to court often, especially on the criminal side, as a representative of clients or principals. You will spend a lot of time on the telephone providing information on the civil side, but you may have the opportunity to go to court as well. You will spend time interviewing clients regardless of the side you choose, and will hone your letter writing skills as well.

Articling interviewers usually look very highly on this type of experience, as it shows that you have a high interest in a particular area of law, that you have practical experience, and that you have had exposure to clients.

WHAT ELSE CAN I DO WITH MY 1L SUMMER?

There's more learning than is taught in books.
— Lady Isabella Augusta Gregory

Study Abroad?

As mentioned earlier in this book, an international law study program may be a very good option. I had one colleague who attended the international program put on by Queen's University in England. He had a fantastic time, went on some amazing field trips with the program, and gained some fantastic credit towards his LLB By doing this, and by increasing the number of courses that he took in a couple of semesters, he was able to finish law school in 2½ years, and was able to start his article earlier than his classmates. This is definitely a viable option. Depending on what school you attend, you may be eligible for funding for certain programs. Check with your school.

Get Away from Law? Travel

I have often found a tinge of jealousy in my heart towards those classmates who chose to avoid a summer law job and instead chose to embark on a travel adventure. I know of students who have gone surfing, over to Europe, or down to the United States. They did not learn anything about the law, and they did not increase their legal network. However, and this is why I feel some jealousy, they were able to unwind after a gruelling year of study. They were able to recover and rejuvenate.

You might think that this option would be tantamount to career suicide. However, from what I have heard from recruiters and from students who have travelled instead of worked during their summer, this option can be equally advantageous. However, it is important to spin your story to your advantage. Let the recruiter know why you took the summer off to vacation. Let them know that you learned a lot about yourself, about another part of the world, and about another culture, if applicable. If you travelled to a non-English speaking country, tell them that you wanted an opportunity to improve your second or third language skills. You should also feel free to tell the recruiter that you needed an opportunity to gather energy for your all-important second year so that you could put your best effort into getting good grades, and more importantly, learning the law.

NETWORK!

Your summer job is a great opportunity to network. First, you will potentially have an opportunity to meet practicing lawyers at your workplace, depending upon where you work. Meet as many of them as possible. Find out what kind of law they practice. Take the opportunity to share a bit about yourself, but also try to find out what their lives are like. You can learn a lot about the firm this way, and it will be much more revealing than the firm Web site! Your summer job can also be a good opportunity to meet lawyers from other firms or establishments. If you have time, take every opportunity to attend firm functions and conferences. Get your name out there!

Obiter Dictum

My first summer after law school I did landscaping. I had done the same throughout most of the summers in my undergrad and knew what to expect.

My second summer of law school I worked at ATB Financial in its legal department. It was a good chance to experience aspects of the legal profession and created a number of connections for the articling process.

— *Jaime Johnson, Law Graduate, 2005, Associate, major Canadian municipality*

My 1L summer was spent traveling and working at a summer camp. My 2L summer has been spent doing research for two profs, doing research for a sole practitioner, and doing applications/interviews for my article.

— *Michael Gunther, Class of 2008*

HOW TO WRITE YOUR FIRST MEMO

Chances are that you will be asked soon after starting a summer legal position (especially at firms, corporations, or other organisations with a legal team) to write a legal memo or document of some kind. My first memo assignment was really quite terrifying. I was given a rather complex set of facts and was asked for a legal opinion outlining the law, an analysis of the law, and a statement of the available options. I was given no other instructions. So, where was I to begin? I had only written one formal memo before this, and it was rather contrived because it did not deal with real people or a real legal problem. It had been based on a hypothetical situation. But now my work seemed to count, and I wanted to get it right.

Start first with the lawyer that asked you to complete the assignment. Let them know what background you have in the area of law, ask for clarification on the facts, the questions that are placed before you, and about what resources might be immediately available in the law library or through other lawyers in the department. That first step will be a massive help to you. Without this first step, you may be scrambling throughout the rest of the memo! Then go to other lawyers and ask them some clarification questions. Ask them where they would look first for the answers. Fill them in on your background in the area—they should know it is your first real memo and that you feel rather green. By doing so, the lawyers may take some pity on you and be willing to help. You might find the response somewhat different from firm to firm, but I think that most sane lawyers would not expect you to be an expert the first day of your first legal job! If you do get dissention or attitude, be humble, ask questions kindly, and if you still do not get reasonable answers, try another source. Too often, people get intimidated, try to do everything on their own, and end up hurting themselves and disappointing the other party when they do not produce a satisfactory product.

Next, get your hands on as many textbooks and articles written on the given subject. Do a quick survey of that area of law and try to find key words that will help you find information. Search the online legal databases for any cases that might help shed light on the subject. Finally, do a comprehensive search online using search engines. It is surprising how much information this last step can produce. Although I personally did not use this information as my basis for analysis, it was a great tool for familiarizing me with the issues and the basic law.

Once you have gathered enough information and have taught yourself at least the very basics, start to tackle each issue individually. If you can think of sub-issues, write them down and try to find answers. If you stumble over something that requires clarification, go back and start the process over for that issue. Make yourself an outline of all of the issues, all the relevant law that you can find (both case law and legislation), and then proceed to fill in the blanks.

Write that first draft several times over. In retrospect, I wish I had consulted the lawyer throughout that first-draft process. It would have saved considerable time on the second draft. Nevertheless, I let pride get in the way—I wanted to impress the lawyer! Again, humility goes a long way when you are a *greenie*. The lawyer, in my case, reviewed my draft and had me do it again. Then again, and again. I went through seven drafts altogether. At the end, the lawyer asked me what I thought of the final product. I admitted that I had not thought it would be so arduous to write the memo, but that I had learned a significant amount through the process. The lawyer said that this was a good thing, and that it would take progressively shorter times and less effort as I went along. Her prophecy was accurate; each subsequent memo built on the knowledge gained from writing previous memos, saving me both time and effort.

I think the important thing is to be sure to get help sooner rather than later, and to ask for feedback throughout the process. Many of my classmates told me stories about how they tried to do their research work assignments on their own, and of then ended up having to redo the entire thing because they went down the wrong path. Remember, your summer job is a training opportunity, not an opportunity to show that you already know everything. Briefly, be humble and take help whenever it is offered.

WHY AM I DOING DELIVERIES?

This was the first thing that a colleague mentioned when I asked her how her summer job was going at the law firm where she was working. She couldn't believe that after completing an undergraduate degree, gaining entrance into law school, and excelling in her first year of law school, that she was being asked on a regular basis to deliver documents all around the city, both to courts and to individuals. She could not figure out why couriers could not be used, or why other support staff could not take care of this menial work. She was much more interested (and showed this interest to her superiors) in legal research, practical application of the law to specific files, and legal questions.

I have kept this thought in my mind for a couple of years now, and I still do not think that I have an answer to the question. The truth is that almost every summer student (and sometimes every articling student) ends up having to make deliveries for stretches of time (often a day a week) during their summer employment if they are working at a major firm. Summer students will also end up doing more photocopying, collating, and general office work than they anticipated. There are some cases where a good principal will avoid giving you this kind of work. But, most students express that they spent much more time on these tasks than anticipated or wanted.

There are arguments that it is part of "putting in the time." It could also be a "test" to see if you are willing to do the mundane when requested (not all law is fun). There is also an argument that this is part of the practicality of being a lawyer.

These arguments do not fly with me. It seems to me that this is an opportunity to exploit eager and easily moulded individuals. Often, associates and partners are much more interested in doing other forms of legal work, are under the gun for deadlines, and the summer student seems the obvious answer to doing this menial work for them, leaving time to bill other work. On the point of billing, it is possible that your delivery is being billed to a client, perhaps at a cost to them that would boil both your and their blood.

The reason I bring up this topic within the confines of this book is to warn you of the possibility that you may end up doing this type of work for at least part of your summer. And I caution you that it is best to avoid railing against the machine on this one. You do not want to jeopardize your chances at a firm just because you think that they are not treating you fairly and underestimating your value to the firm. Truth is, you are a summer student and therefore subject to the mercy of the members of the firm. They will all joke that they had to go through the same thing. Just treat this as part of the initiation of becoming a lawyer. A summer only lasts four months, and you will only end up doing deliveries between ten to fourteen times. Moreover, do not fret about photocopying or collating—take it with a grain of salt, and try to enjoy the downtime.

A word of caution: a number of students have shared that they wished they had been warned of the number of deliveries and other extraneous duties. Often, students will face serious deadlines given to them by a partner or associate, perhaps for an important legal memo or contract draft, and are still expected to courier or collate documents or make photocopies. Try your best to coordinate deadlines on days when you know you won't be asked to do a bunch of deliveries or photocopying. Further, let your principal know clearly what other expectations are on you and let them know that you will do your best to complete all of your duties and meet all of their expectations. Many students fear they will look bad, but my experience is that it is best to fully communicate your scenario and ask for help, concession, or mercy. Most principals will listen to your situational assessment and will try to accommodate you. However, be prepared for lawyers who are up against huge deadlines themselves, and who do not want to hear about your problems as a summer student. Try your best to anticipate peaks in deadlines and expectations, and do

your best to meet them early, leaving room to breathe when necessary.

MAKE AN IMPRESSION

On the point of making impressions, I cannot stress enough the
importance of this. However, making an impression does not mean
brownnosing. It means portraying yourself as a professional or future
professional. There are a number of points of advice that I would
like you to think about.

Dress the part—your physical appearance does not stop being
important once your interview is over. Often, students will wonder
what they should wear the first day on the job. Wear a suit. Period.
The cardinal rule is that you can never dress up too much. However,
you can dress down too much. Avoid embarrassment and dress up.
If you find that other lawyers at your firm or establishment dress
down, ask your supervisor if it would be all right if you did the same.
Find out if the organization has a casual Friday or other casual days.
For casual days, do not dress down too much. Stay dressy. Imagine
meeting a client—what impression would you want to leave?

In terms of working impressions, leave the very best one that you
can. Meet all deadlines whenever possible. If you cannot meet a
deadline, be sure to let the lawyer know as far in advance as possible.
Let them clearly know why you require an extension, or if you think
the task can be modified to meet the deadline. If you are working
hard, the lawyer should make some breathing space for you. The first
legal memos that you write will be extremely challenging. You will
end up spending a long time on them. However, do not think that
you have to produce a perfect memo without blemish. No sane lawyer can expect a summer student to produce the same calibre of
work as a lawyer or articling student. Ask for feedback on your work,
perhaps at stages along the way before the deadline. This is especially
important for anything going to a client, as you want it to be as accurate as possible.

Much of the impression that you leave will be outside the scope
of your legal research and writing. You will likely be invited to firm
functions, firm meetings, client functions, or client meetings. These

are the real opportunities to get to know the lawyers at the firm. Do your best to engage as many people as possible in meaningful conversation, showing a genuine interest, yet trying to avoid sounding too eager. When appropriate, submit your opinion on matters of interest. Treat everyone with the utmost respect, and do not be afraid to let some of your real personality shine through.

DO THE WORK YOU WANT TO DO

One of the most common complaints of summer students is that they ended up doing work that did not interest them. The best way to avoid this is to align yourself with partners and associates who work in your area of interest. This could mean dropping a short email to them, indicating your interest in their area of expertise. It could mean knocking on their door to say hi at the beginning of the summer, letting them know who you are and that you have an interest in their area of law. Further, you can let your principal know of your interest and ask them if they could align you with the appropriate people. If you can do these things successfully, you should be able to fill your desk with items of interest to you. The trick is to avoid work that you do not want to do. You can feel free to let an approaching lawyer who wants to hand you some work know what you are currently working on, what your current deadlines are, and whether or not you will be able to readily accommodate the requested deadline for this project. However, do not become known as the summer student who says no to everything that doesn't interest them. Balance things by accepting a reasonable amount of work from other lawyers. Remember that you are there to further develop your legal skills, and a variety of work can lead to new interests, or at a minimum, a working understanding of a new area of law.

Do not bring your work or attitude down to that of your summer workmates. Avoid gossip. Avoid negativity. Remember, you are competing with them. Not everyone gets an articling offer at the end of his or her summer. Be sure that you do.

ACCEPT AN ARTICLE OFFER OR NOT?

At the end of your first summer, if you are at a firm or at an establishment that offers articles, you may have the opportunity to be offered an articling position, even after your first summer! This is a great gift for some people. For others, it can cause a very serious dilemma.

On one hand, accepting an articling position takes a ton of pressure off you. You now can relax for the next two years knowing that you do not have to go through the application or interview process. It seems weird, I know, but these firms seem to place confidence in this early decision. They will have watched you for four months, and are willing to bet on you.

This apparent stress-free scenario can have its downfalls. For one, it can cause you to become complacent in your second and third years of study. However, the truth is that you really do have to learn the law. Some people are scared enough by the idea of showing up on the first day of their article and not being able to answer basic legal questions. Nevertheless, many others that are in this situation do become indolent and end up hurting themselves. Remember, getting the article is only the first step. You still have to impress the firm enough for them to keep you after your article, and you still have to pass the bar exam or the CPLED courses!

The other big drawback to accepting an article early in your law school career is that you are now unable to see what the rest of the market is like. A classmate of mine pined during the application and recruitment period, wishing that he could check out all of the firms that I was visiting, second-guessing the decision that he had made after his first summer. He wondered if he could have gotten a better salary, better benefits, and perhaps even a better fit somewhere else.

Some firms will try to pressure their summer students into giving them an answer right away about whether they would accept an article offer. Do not be pressured. It is a very big decision, and it is still early in your career. Very early. Let them know that you really appreciate the offer and the confidence that they have in you, but you need some time to consider all of your options. Let them know what you think of their firm if it is positive, but don't sell yourself out because of a little pressure. Try to buy time if you can. Do some more research on other firms that interest you and see if you are really getting the article that you want. Chances are that if you have landed an article offer this early, you will be in good stead going into the recruitment period.

If you do accept an article, congratulate yourself, stay humble (in other words, don't brag to all your friends), and put your head down and plod forward into 2L and 3L. You still have a lot to learn about being a lawyer. Use the time wisely. You have nothing to lose now, so go for it!

SCHOLARSHIP APPLICATIONS

Many scholarship and bursary applications are due in May and June of each year. Be sure to keep on top of these deadlines. Do not let your hectic workload at your summer job get in the way of obtaining free money! It's a great idea to gather all of the scholarship information, contact information, and deadlines into a spreadsheet and keep it with you at work and at home. I do not advise working on applications during work hours.

CHAPTER 6: SECOND YEAR (2L)

If law school is so hard to get through...
how come there are so many lawyers?
— Calvin Trillin

SECOND year law school is much different for many people from first year law school. Depending on the location of your law school and what city or town you plan to article in, the second year can be the most important of your three years in law school. This is often the most important year for making an academic impression upon recruiters.

MARKS, MARKS, MARKS?

If there is a time to make sure you are at the upper end of the curve, it is during your second year. It is true that first-year marks were important towards gaining a summer job in your first year, but the truth is that those positions were few. In second year, you are now in the running for a larger pool of articling positions. However, be aware that the number of positions is always less than the number of applicants. You will want to give yourself the very best chance that you can to gain the article that you want. You would much rather be in a position where you are declining article offers than having to scramble for a single offer.

Nobody can predict the future, but providence favours the prepared, so prepare yourself for the battle and build up your arsenal.
The best weapon you will have is your transcript, so take it seriously.

Although marks are very important in your second year, there are
also some other important considerations that can provide you with
a more complete résumé, excellent experience, and a whole lot of
fun. I provide some examples below. Be sure to balance these activities so that you can give yourself enough time to do well on your
papers and exams.

Obiter Dictum

My first year marks were very important to me because I wanted to
make my wife proud of me and to ensure her that we made the right
decision for me to return to school. I did very well in that year, and
so I have continued to put a lot of pressure on myself to keep up my
marks. If one wishes to be involved in their school's law review or is
interested in clerkship, good first year marks are really important.

Second year marks are definitely important in applying for articling
positions. Although not the only thing a law firm will look at, they
can definitely get one an interview.

Third year marks, assuming one has obtained an articling position,
are not that important anymore unless one wishes to pursue graduate
work. I would like to keep my options open and so I still focussed a
lot on getting good grades in my last year.
— *Lorne Randa, Law Graduate, 2005, Associate, Brownlee LLP*

As the saying goes, "In 1L they scare you to death, in 2L they work
you to death, and in 3L they bore you to death." In 1L I was motivated to work hard for good marks because of an intense fear of failing. Unfortunately I got caught up in the drama of law school (what
was the top mark, who got the top mark, etc.) 1L marks are also important if you are planning to summer in 2L. But generally marks are
most important in 2L. You interview for articling positions after 2L
and even if they say marks aren't important, firms do look at your
marks. I was told in an interview, "Everyone in law school has a
pretty amazing résumé. Our only objective indicator is marks." As

for 3L, if you have your article, you typically just want to get it done with. Marks are not as important unless you are still looking for an articling position or if you plan on attending a graduate program.

— *Carissa Browing, Class of 2008*

We go through law school hearing how important marks are. I believe they are not as important as our profs (all top students), the top ten firms (the McCarthys, Gowlings, and Oslers), and our career counsellor would have us to believe. Unless you plan to work for a top-ten Bay Street or Calgary firm, potential employers generally want to see that you are: a) competent, and b) genuinely interested in the work that they do. Anyone in the top two-thirds of the class is probably competent; someone with lower grades might need to fill the gaps with extracurricular activities. I also truly believe that having one or more specific interests is very important. Then you can demonstrate to the firm honestly why you will be good fit for them. My marks were only slightly above average, but I ended up with a job at one of my hometown's largest firms, because my résumé and activities demonstrated that I was truly interested in the work that they do. My grades didn't even come up in conversation.

— *Michael Gunther, Class of 2008*

LAW REVIEW

Not all law schools have a Law Review or similar student run academic journal. If your chosen school does not, please ignore this section.

If your school does have a Law Review or other student run academic journal, you should seriously consider participating on its editorial board or committee.

In the US, Law Reviews are very serious business. Depending on the Canadian law school, Law Reviews can be serious business as well. In most US law schools, only those who are invited get to sit on the Law Review editorial board. Only the cream of the crop ever gets the opportunity. Law Review is considered very highly by employers, and is almost always a requisite for graduate studies in law.

As an example, the Alberta Law Review, a publication that has been in print for fifty years (established in 1955, with its predecessor, the Alberta Law Quarterly, established in 1934), follows the same basic format as the United States Review system. Second-year students apply to the Law Review, and applications are reviewed by the Law Review executive (co-editor-in-chief or treasurer) and faculty advisors (usually four). Each casts a single vote, and from this vote, fourteen to sixteen new members of the editorial board are chosen. It is a great honour to be selected to join the committee. Many applicants are turned down. For the most part, grades are the prime criterion for selection. However, the editorial board is broken down into various committees, so it is possible for a student to gain acceptance even if their grades are not at the top of their class, provided they can offer unique and useful skills that will assist the Law Review in running smoothly. The Alberta Law Review is a business with an operating budget of over Can$100,000. As a result, committee members are given a lot of responsibility, and it is very important to ensure that committee members have the requisite skills to complete their assigned tasks. Doing well on law exams does not necessarily demonstrate this ability.

If you are selected to the editorial board (you apply in the first week of 2L), you will have a two-year commitment, consisting of fifty-two hours of work a year for each of the two years for a total of 104 hours. These 104 hours are broken down into editing and committee work. Each member of the editorial board must complete a minimum of two full edits (usually twenty to eighty hours of work each) over the two-year period. The rest of the time is consists of committee work. As a reward for your hard work over the two years, you are given credit for one three-credit course in the last year of your final semester. As well, as a member of the editorial board, you have the option of registering for the Law Review Research Paper course, which requires you to write a twenty-page case comment and to present it to a group of editorial board members. Both credit opportunities can really take a load of pressure off your shoulders during your last year of law school.

Other benefits of being on the Alberta Law Review include a personalized letter from the Alberta Courts inviting you to apply for clerkships with the Alberta Courts. This is a nice "in." More importantly, recruiters tend to look very highly on experience with the Law

Review. Inclusion indicates that you are most likely the best of the best, that you have gained considerable experience in legal research and writing, that you have developed an eye for detail, and that you are aware of a number of current legal issues. As well, if you are considering going to graduate school in law, inclusion on a Law Review will go a very long way for you, especially if you apply in the United States. It is a well-kept secret that Law Review does not hold quite the same status in Canada as it does in the US.

A further opportunity is available during your third year of law school if you are elected as editor-in-chief (as I was). This is a full-time paid position during the spring/summer of after your second year, and a part-time paid position during your third year. This is an excellent opportunity to beef-up your curriculum vitae, make amazing contacts, and learn leadership skills. I was able to converse often with leading academics, practitioners, and judges during my term. I also had the opportunity of having dinner with the chief justice of Canada, and of having dinner meetings with former members of the Supreme Court of Canada, the Court of Appeal and the Court of Queen's Bench of Alberta. Along with other key things, I attribute this opportunity to landing me so many interviews and subsequent job offers during the articling recruitment period.

Each law school will have somewhat of a different process and organization for their law journal. Be sure to inquire with your law school early and find out how you can become involved. Some schools will offer more or less credit than the Alberta Law Review.

MOOTING PROGRAMS

I include the major competitive moots here, but there may be more that I am not aware of in other provinces. Links to these moots may be accessed from www.CanadianLawSchool.ca.

The Philip C. Jessup International Law Moot
International—the world's largest moot competition—more than fifteen hundred students from more than three hundred law schools

in just less than fifty nations on six continents. National and international division rounds. (From U of A Web site)

Kawaskimhon Aboriginal Moot

Open to all law schools—Aboriginal law. Kawaskimhon means, "speaking with knowledge." The moot is typically based on a current high-profile case in which Aboriginal rights are an issue. Law schools from across Canada represent a party or interested intervener in the case. Each team is required to prepare written factums and give oral presentations on matters arising out of the moot problem. The format of the moot is based on the traditional Aboriginal talking circle consensus building process. The Native Law Students Association of the Faculty of Law, University of Toronto held the first Aboriginal Rights Moot in 1994. You do not have to be Aboriginal to participate. (From Queen's and U of A Web sites)

The Laskin

The only national, bilingual moot. Open to all law schools in Canada. Usually constitutional administrative law. (From U of A Web site)

Gale Cup

Sponsored by the Canadian Bar Association—Ontario—Supreme Court decision—national division and international division—open to all law schools; English and French. (From U of A Web site)

Clinton J. Ford

Department of Justice of Alberta—criminal or constitutional/criminal topic—University of Alberta. (From U of A Web site)

Western Canada Trial Moot

Six teams—one from each Western law school.

Sopinka Cup Trial Moot in Ottawa. (From U of A Web site)

Labour Arbitration Moot

Several law schools—sponsored by Mathews, Dinsdale, and Clark. (From U of A Web site)

Alberta Court of Appeal Moot

Criminal law, civil law (contract, property, or tort law), and constitutional law—between Calgary and Edmonton. (From U of A Web site)

The Canadian Corporate/Securities Law Moot

Sponsored and administered by Toronto law firm Davies, Ward, & Beck. (From U of A Web site)

Niagara Moot

The Niagara Moot is an international law competition that brings together approximately fifteen Canadian and American law schools from the Great Lakes region. At Queen's, International Law (LAW 540) must be taken as a pre- or co-requisite. (From Queen's Web site)

Wilson Moot

The Wilson Moot focuses on equality issues raised by various provisions of the Canadian Charter of Rights and Freedoms, including but not limited to section 15. This national competition is usually held in the Federal Court Building in Toronto. Ideally, students should have some background in Charter jurisprudence beyond Constitutional Law and Public Law in first year. (From Queen's Web site)

Client Counselling Competition

The international Client Counselling Competition provides an opportunity for students from law schools in Canada, the United States, the United Kingdom, and Australia to learn and practice interviewing and counselling skills. The competition simulates a law-office interview in which teams of two students from each school interview a 'client' and are judged according to agreed criteria (e.g., the ability to establish a good working relationship with clients and to develop strategies to help clients resolve their problems). Beginning with a regional competition, the winners at each level proceed to a national and ultimately an international final. (From Queen's Web site)

Arnup Mock Trial
The Arnup Mock Trial is an annual competition involving two-person teams from each of the six Ontario law schools (Osgoode, Ottawa, Toronto, Western, Windsor, and Queen's). This competition requires the examination and cross-examination of witnesses, submissions on motions, and opening and closing addresses to the jury. The competition usually alternates each year between civil and criminal trials. The competition is regularly held at the courthouse in Windsor and the winners go on to compete for the Sopinka Cup in Ottawa. Candidates from Queen's must have taken Evidence (LAW 320). (From Queen's Web site)

British Columbia Law Schools Competitive Moot (U.B.C. / U.Vic. Moot)
The British Columbia Law Schools Competitive Moot is a moot competition between the law faculties of the University of British Columbia and the University of Victoria. The competition is held in early February at the Law Courts Building in Vancouver or Victoria on an alternating basis. The Begbie Trophy, a sculpted trophy donated by the superior court judges of British Columbia, is awarded to the winning school. (From the U.B.C. Web site)

ABA Negotiation Competition
The American Bar Association (ABA) organizes a negotiation competition for law students each fall, which takes place at the regional, national, and international levels. (From U.B.C. Web site)

Online Mediation Competition and Online Negotiation Competition
These competitions run simultaneously. Problems are handed out in January and the moots occur in February. The mediation team, which is comprised of two mediation advocates and one or two mediators, will participate in two online mediations. The two-person

negotiation advocacy team also participates in two negotiations. The first mediation or negotiation is open for one week and discussions can be synchronous or asynchronous; the second mediation or negotiation is scheduled to be twenty-four hours in length and may pose different challenges depending on the time zones of participants. (From U.B.C. Web site)

MacIntyre Cup—Western Canada Trial Competition (Sopinka Cup—Ottawa)

Open to second and third-year students, annual external competition for Western Canada (first and second place teams go to Ottawa for Sopinka Cup Trial Competition). (From U of C Web site)

Moncton-Ottawa Competition (French)

The Moncton-Ottawa Moot is a French-language appeal proceeding on a private law issue. The two-member team is required to prepare a factum and present its argument orally before the Supreme Court of Moncton-Ottawa. The competition is held alternatively in Moncton and Ottawa. (From Ottawa Common Law Web site)

Mathews, Dinsdale & Clarke Labour Arbitration Competition

The Mathews, Dinsdale, & Clarke Labour Arbitration Moot is for students who have an interest in labour law. The team consists of two students who must be in their second year. This moot is held in Toronto in late January. Students prepare oral arguments only, but each team prepares arguments for both union and management sides. (From Ottawa Common Law Web site)

Harrison Shield Moot—UNB

The school's most prestigious in house moot is limited to third-year students. (From UNB Web site)

Trilateral Moot

The Trilateral Moot involves competition with UNB, University of Maine, and Dalhousie University. (From UNB Web site)

There are a number of internal moot competitions for upper-year students at all Canadian law schools. Some of these competitions are qualification rounds for regional, national, or international moot competitions.

RESEARCH FOR ARTICLES—COMPARING FIRMS

One of the biggest challenges that I faced in law school was when it came time to choose firms to send applications to. There really is a large number to choose from. It can be an arduous task to sort through all the information.

Most information about the different firms can be gleaned from a few places. First, your career office should have some files on hand that they have gathered from various firms, which should outline basic information about the firm and their articling program. Second, Quicklaw™ now provides a lot of information on firms and articles. Most importantly, you can gather a large amount of information from individual firm Web sites. I include government articles in this discussion.

When I first started my research, I was faced with well over forty firms that I was considering. They were in two major cities and two smaller centres. I noticed that many of my classmates were starting to pull out their hair because they were frustrated with trying to keep all of these firms straight. Salaries, billable hours, benefits, areas of law, number of lawyers, how many articling students they accept each year, retention rates, key contact persons, and many other pieces of information were swimming around. On top of that, when the rumour mill started working, firm reputations could either become clearer or muddier.

I was determined to give myself the best advantage possible. I saw one solution in creating a database for the above information. I created a Microsoft Excel® spreadsheet containing all of this information, including firm addresses, phone numbers, key contact email addresses, and fax numbers. As well, I used some basic math formulas in the spreadsheet to analyze the numbers—salaries for articling students and first-year associates, billable-hour expectations, vacation length, and other benefits. This analysis told me a lot! By laying this database out in front of me, I was able to see more clearly which firms corresponded to what I was looking for in an article, and in a potential career destination.

The numbers themselves were very revealing. I learned (for the first time—can you imagine that) what these billable-hour quotes really meant. By doing some basic math and making some standard assumptions (e.g., using a 1.6 factor for what a billable-hour equated to in real work hours), I started to get a better idea of what my life might look like working at these particular firms. I came to the conclusion that firms were quoting an actual workweek (using an arbitrary, but good guess using a 1.6 factor) ranging from 32.65 to 58.78 hours. My factor was probably low, but it gave me a good indicator nevertheless. The numbers also showed me that the hourly wage using the factor above ranged from $18.83 to $28.85 an hour.

Now, these numbers may not be accurate reflections of the real workweek hours or the real hourly wage for an associate. However, because I used the same factor for every firm, it was still indicative of the range of expectations and remuneration. 32.65 hours is very different from 58.78 hours! $18.83 an hour is very different from $28.85 an hour! This exercise was a real revelation—firms were paying drastically different remuneration to lawyers who were basically equal in legal experience and potentially, ability. Worse, I had heard many rumours that the higher end firms expected somewhere between 2,000 to 2,400 billable hours each year. I could not imagine a sixty-hour workweek, and am horrified at the thought of an eighty-hour week (or more).

Your needs and expectations for the beginning years of your legal career may differ from mine. The point that I am making here is that a thorough analysis of the numbers and other criteria can go a long ways to making a decision that is good for you, your partner, or your family over the long run. The numbers were not the only criteria that I based my own decision on, but I think that I considered them a lot more closely than many of my classmates did. From my perspective, many of them based their decisions on firm reputation, how fancy the firm offices were, and in some cases, merely on the starting salary, regardless of billable expectations.

Many classmates have argued with me that in the end it all balances out—that once you are four to six years into your career, salaries balance out and billable hours become more reasonable. Although that may happen to some extent (it is my belief that the pressures at higher-end firms never really cease), if you could avoid the high pressure and lower hourly salary in your early years, and still manage to obtain an equally rewarding practical legal education and similar career opportunities, why would you subject yourself to something more arduous?

My approach to the problem was that I wanted to find an article, and hopefully a subsequent associateship, at a firm that valued my time the most in the early years, offered a solid article with a lot of support, and valued community and family over significant profits. Your criteria might be very different from mine. You might be at a time in your life where you would not mind burning the midnight oil for a few years. I was not willing to make this sacrifice. I had come from a career before law school that demanded heavy weekly hours. I knew what it really entailed. I knew that it was not something that I wanted to subject my family to.

A spreadsheet and an analysis can also have other benefits. For one, you may come to the conclusion that you want to strive for the most prestigious, highest paying article with the possible intention of moving somewhere else later on that is more in line with your long-term career goals. I almost made that choice. Another added benefit is that the spreadsheet can make your application process go much quicker and more smoothly as you can use your spreadsheet to do mail merges for applications and for envelopes. I did this, and it saved me hours. The spreadsheet will allow you to collect all contact information and save it in one spot so that you can easily cut and paste or use a merge feature using Microsoft Office® software. Make sure that you check and double-check all contact information in your spreadsheet. It is imperative that you get it right to avoid embarrassment and a lost application opportunity.

If you would like a copy of this spreadsheet so that you can modify it for your own needs, please send me an e-mail at adam @CanadianLawSchool.ca and I will email it to you ASAP. You can fill in the information for firms that you are interested in, along with the corresponding numbers and information. If you are familiar with spreadsheets, you may like to use the *Sort* function (*Data—>Sort*) to filter your information and sort it by billable hours, hourly wages, etc.

I also found it useful to put personal notes beside each firm. This might have included general impressions, rumours about reputation, or whatever personal criteria that might be important to you. I also used the highlight function to highlight those firms that interested me. As I went through the application and interview process, I used the spreadsheet to track progress and results, keeping everything very organized. For example, as interview calls came in, I recorded the date, time, and place of each interview. I could then easily print off the spreadsheet and bring it with me each day during interview week.

CAREER DAY

Career day, if your law school has one, is one of the most important days of your law school career. Absolutely, for no reason whatsoever should you miss this event. Career day is an opportunity to meet with a large number of firms and establishments and their representatives. It is a good chance to collect brochures from each firm, and to get some cool free swag. Most importantly, it is your chance to mingle with potential recruiters. I have only two points of advice for this event.

1. Dress your best and be on your best behaviour—this day, for many, is the first step of the interview process.

2. Talk to as many people as you can from these firms—this is your chance to ask questions without much risk. Although you can use this chance to make a good impression, you are one face among many, and may not even be recognized at future meetings. More importantly, this is a fantastic free opportunity for you to ask as many questions as you would like. It is kind of like being given a *chance* card in Monopoly®—you never know what you are going to find out. You may find that gem among the candidates, or perhaps that you really do not want to work for a particular firm.

THE KILLER RÉSUMÉ

You can find a large number of sample cover letters and résumés on the web or in various books on the subject. I decided to include a sample of my own in this book for a couple of reasons. First, it worked for me. I am a believer that if something works once, it has a good chance of working again. You may use this sample as a template, but be sure to fill the cover letter and résumé with your own information. I include the sample here more as an example of formatting and to show you what kind of content may be included. This sample may also be useful for your summer job or law school applications. Customize as necessary.

You can find other sample résumés at www.CanadianLaw School.ca.

I sent out my cover letter and résumé templates to a large number of classmates and professional colleagues. I also took the time to have them reviewed by our career officer at my law school. I did not take everyone's advice, as it was often conflicting. While there are different schools of thought regarding résumés, here is what I think is really important.

1. Make sure there are absolutely no errors in these documents. A single spelling error can put your application into the reject pile extremely quickly. Law is a field of precision, and an error on your application automatically categorizes you as someone who does not take the proper care required for important documents.

2. Use the name of the person that has been indicated as the key contact person for applications. Make sure that their name is spelled exactly right. Include their position if it is available to you.

3. Make sure that you get the address correct on both the cover letter and the envelope. There are few things worse than having a person from an articling committee open a letter from you addressed to a competing firm.

4. Try to fit your cover letter onto a single page. In retrospect, I believe my cover letter to be rather wordy. If you are able, cut it

down even more. Get the important information out as quickly as possible.

5. Try to fit your résumé onto two pages or less. This may be difficult if you have had extensive experience, both at work and with volunteering. Be choosy about what you include. Leave the best impression possible for yourself.

6. Include a list of references available as an attachment to your package. Unless requested, do not bother with copies of letters of reference. Unfortunately, most recruiters do not take the time to read these. However, if reference letters are requested, ensure that these are available to the recruiter within the timeframe indicated.

7. Create a personal Web site—it will catch a recruiter's attention, will allow them to see your pretty face, and will allow you to tell a lot more about yourself than you can on a few pieces of paper. If it piques a recruiter's interest, it may cause them to spend a lot more time on your application than on your competitor's.

8. Generally, do not use fancy textured or patterned paper. Stick with white.

9. Make sure everything is stapled securely together and that everything is neat and tidy (no coffee stains!).

See Appendix C for copies of the cover letters that I used for my applications, and for the résumé that I used for my applications.

Obiter Dictum

I have known since about week two of law school what my dream-firm to article with was. I came to law school with a very specific interest, and there is one firm in my city that is well known for its proficiency in this area. I made sure that I sat with that firm's representatives at Career Day, and chatted them up at their booth. I even told them at Career Day that they were my ideal firm. From there, I submitted my articling application very early. I interviewed with the firm, played up my undergraduate background (which is beneficial for this firm), and once again told them bluntly that they were my #1 choice. At the second interview, I did more of the same. I knew I was going to get the job after interview #2. They called me to let me know several days later. Firms often seem very insecure about themselves; telling a firm that they are your solid #1 choice definitely helps your cause (but only do this if it's true).

— Michael Gunther, Class of 2008

Personal Web Site?

The best thing that I ever did related to my legal career was to create a personal Web site. I am convinced that this Web site helped me gain acceptance into law school. It also assisted me in obtaining numerous scholarships and bursaries, played a huge role in gaining summer employment, and ultimately helped me land a great article.

I was lucky to have the skills to design and program my own personal Web site. I constructed it about six months before applying to law school. It included the following information.

1. Résumé—an extended version with links to pertinent Web sites, e.g., corporate Web sites

2. Awards

3. Volunteer work

4. Accomplishments

5. Travel information and photographs

6. Volunteer information and photographs

7. Reference listings

8. Adventures and hobbies

9. Contact information

I included photographs throughout the site. I tried to make it very user-friendly and easy to navigate. I made the design with law-firm Web sites in mind, trying to maintain a professional-but-fun atmosphere.

I was amazed by how many interviewers, application assessors, and hiring committee members commented on my Web site. I included my URL address on all correspondence, cover letters, and résumés. I also carried a personal business card with my URL and email address on it. More often than not, interviewers had visited my Web site out of curiosity. Now that all of my readers are advised of the advantages of a personal Web site, and as more of you gain the skills required to build a personal Web site, it may not be such a novelty. However, I still believe that it is worthwhile; a personal Web site offers an opportunity for further exploration of your skills, achievements, interests, and experience. It puts a face with a name and shows real initiative. Not everyone will be interested, but I am convinced that it cannot hurt to include a URL address with your résumé and cover letter.

It did not cost me anything to build except time. It cost me about Can$50 a year for hosting (go to http://www.doteasy.com). If you do not have the requisite skills, I suggest that you approach someone to do it for you. A personal Web site, such as the one that I have described above will cost you between $1,000 and $2,500 to have built with a professional design firm. I have built sites for other law students (I have built over one hundred Web sites altogether in my career) and all of them have said that it paid off for them. If you think that you would benefit from a personal Web site, please email me at adam@CanadianLawSchool.ca and I can either provide an estimate for you or refer you to someone who can assist you. The cost for this service will be somewhere in the range of $500. I believe that the investment in a personal Web site is worth it.

APPLYING FOR COURT CLERKSHIPS

As I did not receive a position with the courts, I asked a colleague of mine to write this section. Her experience and success is convincing.

My name is Kim Yee and as of 2005, I was a second-year student at the Faculty of Law at the University of Alberta. I recently went through the process of applying for a clerkship position with the Court of Queen's Bench in Alberta, the Alberta Court of Appeal, and the Supreme Court of Canada. I ultimately accepted a position with the Alberta Court of Queen's Bench commencing in 2006.

In navigating my way through the application and interview process, I learned some things that I think would be useful to students going through an experience like this. The following are some questions I had, and I think that you may have similar questions when thinking about whether or not to apply for a clerkship position.

I caveat my discussion about clerkships by saying that the answers that I have provided are based on my own personal experiences and observations thus far. As of this writing, I have not yet commenced my clerkship so my opinions are derived from going through the interview experience myself, and talking with judges, professors, people who have completed clerkships, and the career services officer at the law school that I attend.

What is a clerkship?

The term *clerkship* can mean a variety of things. A traditional clerkship would involve working closely with one particular judge, but it can also refer to a position in which the clerk serves a number of judges. The duties of a clerk include researching various points of law, preparing memoranda, writing judgments, discussing cases and case law with the judges, attending trials and hearings, and other various duties. The type of work that is assigned to students may vary according to the court. For example, if you are clerking with a court of appeal, the assignments may differ a lot from those that you would receive in the Court of Queen's Bench in terms of length and the level of analysis required. What I think most clerkship positions share is the fact students have a chance to work very closely with members of the judiciary.

What made you decide to apply for a clerkship position?

When I was in my first year of law school, I attended an information session hosted by the Alberta courts. During the presentation, the speakers outlined what sorts of things the students were able to participate in while clerking, what sorts of skills they wanted to foster, and what former clerks had gone on to do in their legal careers. After hearing the presentation, I knew that this was something that I wanted to do. If your law school offers a presentation such as this, I would highly recommend attending, even if at first blush you don't think that this would be something that you would want to do. When I entered law school, I certainly did not think that this was something I would want to pursue, but once I learned what it was all about, I was convinced that this would be a fantastic opportunity and would be a great fit with my personality and interests.

What are the benefits of a clerkship?

There are so many. The following is a list of the main benefits.

- The opportunity to participate and observe how the justice system works from a very unique perspective
- Establishing working relationships with judges and other staff who you may be appearing in front of or working with later on in your career
- Exposure to a range of different practice areas (this is really beneficial if you are unsure of the type of law you want to practice in the future)
- An opportunity to see what sorts of things judges consider to be important when analyzing the law or the facts of cases
- The chance to hone your research and analytical skills (this will serve you well, especially if you want to go on to do any graduate work in the future)
- The opportunity to see the law in practice
- The chance to see a variety of different written and oral advocacy styles
- Most future employers will see a clerkship as an asset

Are there any drawbacks to doing a clerkship?

I think there are very few drawbacks to choosing the clerkship route, and the benefits heavily outweigh any potential setbacks. In talking with people that had completed clerkships, I heard very few negatives about their time at the courts. One drawback that I have heard about is the fact that doing a clerkship as part of an article may actually extend the length of your article. In Alberta, for example, if you article with the courts, your term there will be ten months, but you must also complete a five-month article with a firm. This is a three-month difference from those who simply article with a firm for twelve months before their call to the bar. For many others, including me, this is not a major drawback at all.

I have also heard from students that a potential downside to clerking with the courts is that when they do finally arrive at the firm they will be articling with, they feel behind when compared to the other articling students, at least initially. One person that I spoke to said that even though he felt this way he said it was very temporary; and on the upside, he had more experience than the other articling students in other areas, especially in procedural matters.

What does the application process involve?

This will vary slightly from province to province and with the level of court to which you apply. However, generally the courts will want the following.

- A cover letter stating why you are seeking a clerkship position
- A current résumé
- Current transcripts of all post-secondary marks
- Letters of reference, including an academic letter of reference from a professor
- Possibly, a short writing sample such as a case comment or an essay.

Each court will have a different application deadline. Be careful not to miss the deadline, as it will often be many months in advance of when your position will commence. For example, for me, the deadline for the Alberta Courts was in December of 2004 but the position will not commence until June of 2006.

Once I applied, I heard back within a couple of weeks. In most instances, I was notified by e-mail that I had gotten an interview.

In determining which courts to apply to, I did some research about what sorts of work the different levels of court did and what sorts of experiences former students had with the different courts. The sorts of cases and the type of work that clerks do will vary widely from court to court.

What is the interview process like and how can students prepare?

I interviewed with the Court of Appeal in both Edmonton and Calgary, the Court of Queen's Bench in Edmonton, and the Supreme Court of Canada. All of my interviews were very different, but the one thing I think they all shared was the fact that at the end of the day, the judges were really just trying to get a sense of the applicant's personality. As a result, the questions were geared towards that end.

For the Alberta courts, the process was very much the same—the courts appointed a justice or two to conduct the interviews for the entire court. In all of my interviews, legal counsel to the court played a large role in the interview and selection process. They were also present during the interview and asked questions of the applicants as well. The interviews lasted for about twenty to thirty minutes.

The Supreme Court of Canada was quite a different experience from the Alberta Courts. I applied to the court as a whole but each justice chooses who he or she would like to interview. Theoretically, one could have nine different interviews. Some justices will want to talk about the law, others will ask questions about the applicants themselves, and some may ask a combination of both sorts of questions. The interviews have a strict time limit of thirty minutes, which goes by very quickly. Unlike with the other courts I interviewed with, legal counsel did not sit in on the interviews.

In general, I found that the appellate courts tended to ask more questions about what my legal interests were and what sorts of research and writing skills I possessed. There was definitely more of an emphasis on these skills and academic ability.

In terms of preparation, I would suggest approaching it the same way you would any other job interview. You want to emphasize the attributes you possess that they are looking for. For the courts, this would be research, writing, communication, interpersonal, and analytical skills. The most important thing is to relax and be you. I know that it sounds trite, but once you have been granted an interview, you are generally in pretty good stead. The justices are now trying to get a sense of who you are and what you would be like to work with on a daily basis. The interview process can be quite intimidating, but I think that there are things that you can do to make it less unnerving, such as being well-prepared in terms of knowing your attributes, what sorts of work the court does, and knowing a bit about the judge interviewing you. Knowing some recent case law from the particular court is an asset as well, especially if you are interviewing with an appellate court.

How important are marks?

I think marks are important, but they are generally less important than applicants think they are. A certain level of academic achievement is required to get you in the door, but not all students that are chosen for clerkships are dean's list students. Additionally, if marks were the be-all and end-all, then the courts would not need to conduct interviews at all. They would just take the top applicants that applied. Research and writing skills are important, so if you are not on the dean's list but you have research and writing experience, perhaps from being on the editorial board of a law review, doing research for faculty or employer's, or involvement with large writing projects in your legal or undergraduate studies, you should definitely emphasize this in your résumé and cover letter as well as in your interview.

Also, if you have anything in your background that is particularly interesting, mention it in your résumé, even if it is not an academic attribute or even remotely related to law. One lawyer that clerked with the Supreme Court shared with me that the majority of applicants have the academic ability to do the job in the judge's opinion. So what determines whether an interview is granted or not is if you stand out from the other applicants in some other way. If you do get an interview, something interesting in your résumé will often be a topic for conversation between you and the judge.

My advice would be to strive to get the best marks possible, especially in your research and writing courses, if you are thinking you may want to do a clerkship. However, do not disregard the idea of applying if you find that you are not at the top of your class. After all, there is nothing to lose by applying. You may be pleasantly surprised and get an interview.

What other things can students do to increase their chances of getting a clerkship position?

- I would recommend getting involved with both law related and non-law related extracurricular activities. The courts (and other potential employers) are looking for well-rounded students.
- Get to know a few of your professors quite well, especially those who will have an opportunity to see your writing. This will make it easier for them to write a good letter of reference, should you need it. They also have their own insights about the clerking experience that they are usually happy to share with students.
- If you are interested in clerking, talk to fellow students in upper years that have gone through the experience of interviewing with the court that you are interested in.
- If your law school hosts an information session, you should attend and try to introduce yourself to the judges, legal counsel, and clerks that are in attendance. These will likely be the people who will be choosing who will get interviews and who will ultimately get clerkships.
- Apply for a position on the Law Review if your school has one. This is a great chance to gain exposure to legal writing and I know that the courts pay a lot of attention to this on a résumé. That being said, this is not the be-all and end-all either, as I know people who were not on the Law Review who got a position with the courts.
- Get as much experience as you can with interviewing. Some schools offer workshops or similar things to help students prepare. I think this is a great idea and will only help you to feel more at ease if you do get an interview with a judge.

Does a clerkship have to be done as part of an article?

This will vary from province to province and from court to court. I know that in Alberta you must be an articling student to apply, as the program that they have in place is actually an articling program. However, the Supreme Court of Canada will take applicants who have completed their articles and who have been called to the bar.

Are costs covered for an interview at the Supreme Court of Canada?

My travel costs, including my, flights, meals, and taxis, were covered when I travelled to Ottawa.

How important is it to speak both English and French for the Supreme Court of Canada?

Being bilingual is definitely an asset when applying for a clerkship position at the Supreme Court of Canada. While I was there, I observed a lot of conversations in French between the clerks, justices, and support staff. However, I did talk to someone who had clerked there and did not speak any French at all. She said that it was not a problem and that there are positions available for those who are not bilingual.

What kind of hours do you work with a clerkship?

From what I hear, the hours are a bit shorter at the courts than they would be at a firm, and weekends are not required. At the information session I attended, the justices said that on occasion, if they need something done right away, a student may have to stay late, but that it is not the norm.

You can find a list of over seven hundred students who have clerked at the Supreme Court at http://www.thecourt.ca/clerks-of-the-supreme-court.

Obiter Dictum

For summer 2L, I interviewed with a small firm that did mainly wills and real estate. Although the interviewer was a nice enough fellow, he seemed very unprofessional and a bit sketchy, in a "Lionel Hutz" sort of way. He wore jeans and an untucked t-shirt. He bragged about how I would be doing sh*t work as a summer student, and getting paid nothing. The second half of the interview he boasted about how financially lucrative his business was, and how if it weren't for the huge real estate boom, he'd retire somewhere warm and quit law. I left a little shell-shocked and wondering if I really wanted to become a lawyer.

— Michael Gunther, Class of 2008

My worst interview experience was with the Federal Court of Canada. I knew very little about what to expect and our career advisor in the faculty provided little help. I had three interviews with judges— two in person and one over the phone. Two out of three went well, despite not expecting substantive law questions in the interview. The worst interview involved a question asking me what three Supreme Court of Canada decisions...[I thought] influenced the law the most. I was not expecting such a question, went completely blank, and could not think of any case names. It was quite embarrassing.

— Lorne Randa, Law Graduate, 2005, Associate, Brownlee LLP

The interview process as a whole is very strange. In 1L, I participated in OCIs (On Campus Interviews) that felt like speed dating. While I was interviewing for an articling position I participated in the Match Program, which crammed all interviews (first and second) with all firms (including dinners/receptions) in one week. Let's just say the thought of running around in heels, nylons, and a perma-smile on a hot day still makes me break out in a cold sweat.

— Carissa Browing, Class of 2008

APPLYING FOR 2L SUMMER JOB

The process for applying for second-year summer jobs is really the same as for first-year summer jobs. Be sure that you are aware of all deadlines, do as much networking as possible, and consider all possibilities that were mentioned earlier in this book.

CHAPTER 7: SECOND SUMMER

English Law prohibits a man from marrying his mother-in-law.
This is our idea of useless legislation.
— Anonymous

WHAT SUMMER JOB IS BEST?

YOU will want to do your research in advance to determine which summer will be best to submit job applications in your chosen city. Some cities have a trend of hiring summer students in their first year of law school. The reasoning behind this trend, from what I can tell, is that these firms are looking for a level of loyalty. They are interested in applicants who show a genuine interest in articling and practicing in their city. Hiring early also helps firms plan for the next two years. Remember, a summer job at a firm is really an extended interview. It allows the firm to consider you carefully for a potential articling position.

Other cities have a trend of only hiring second-year summer students. The reasoning behind this trend is that these firms are more interested in hiring applicants that are more experienced. As a result, these students will often end up with responsibilities that are more substantial.

ARTICLE APPLICATION PROCESS

Timing

For most of you, this will be the preeminent experience of your law school career, and the one that you will want to give the most attention. Regardless of your grades in your first two years or how many extracurricular activities you have been involved in, you can succeed during the recruitment period. However, there are some important (key, in fact) considerations that you must address during the two months surrounding recruitment.

For many students, the timing of the article application process is impractical. You may be busy with a summer job, out of town (surfing, perhaps?), are probably tired or are even burned out from your second year of law school. I hate to be unsympathetic, but too bad. Now is the time to turn on the after-booster and really get to work.

So, clear your schedule as much as possible. Talk to your summer supervisor. Most firms will allow some time to accommodate the recruitment period. Let your boss know well in advance what recruitment will entail for you—when they should expect you to be missing from work and how much time you will be spending on arranging appointments.

Obiter Dictum

To gain an articling position I would advise other students to make as many professional connections as possible. It is not that a connection will lead to a job, but it likely will lead to an interview, which can be the biggest hurdle. Meeting and impressing others already in the profession will allow for your face to be remembered when an application shows up in the future.
— *Jamie Johnson, Law Graduate, 2005, Associate at a major Canadian municipality*

Application Packages

Many of my classmates have indicated that they wished they had prepared their application packages before May came around. In fact, they wished that they had prepared their packages in March, before exam preparation. This is good advice. At the very least, you should have your résumé and most of your reference letters prepared and available. It may be difficult to get reference letters from the professors you have during your second semester of 2L, and these may have to wait until the last minute. You are also well advised to prepare a template cover letter in advance.

It is up to you to submit a full package. Be sure to read very carefully the application instructions for each firm or establishment and follow them to a tee! One simple omission could risk potential rejection at the point of opening your application.

Keep your application materials neat and clean. Do not do your preparation work while drinking coffee or eating breakfast. Everything should look perfect and professional. You should consider using a conservative font, paper, and envelopes.

If possible, prepare a thorough spreadsheet or database of potential articling employers. If you would like a copy of such a template, please email me at adam@CanadianLawSchool.ca and I will send you a free copy for your use. This can keep things organized, but can also save time if you know how to use the mail merge feature on your word processor.

Multiple Cities?

Many people wonder and ask whether they should apply to firms in more than one city. In the US, it is a given that most students apply for jobs post-law school in more than one city, often in more than one state. That is the nature of the legal profession there. In Canada, things tend to be more localized. Although it is definitely possible to gain employment in a city other than the one where your law school is located, the percentage is relatively low. Firms tend to put a lot of emphasis on where you are from and what connections you have to a particular city. They are making a serious investment in you as an articling student, and it is in their best interest to hire people who will be loyal. It is part of the due diligence process to find out where you are from, where your family or friends live, and what your longer-term plans are.

I applied for jobs in three cities and one town. I had not yet decided where I wanted to settle down with my family. There were very attractive firms all over Alberta. I felt that I needed to go see firsthand what the firms in all of these places were like before I could cross them off my list. It ended up creating additional work and travel for me, but I do not regret my decision to apply to multiple places. Had I restricted my applications to the city where I graduated, I would have always asked "What if...?" As it was, I ended up going to the city that was initially last on my list. Why? Because I loved the firm, what they stood for, and I loved the idea of raising my kids in a smaller community. Do not limit your possibilities just because of the potential for some inconvenience over a couple of weeks.

That said, you should be very careful during the recruitment process—especially during interviews—to keep your cards close to your chest, so to speak. If, by chance, you are called on the fact that you have applied to more than one city (the legal community is surprisingly small, and this happens more often than one would imagine), do not be intimidated by the fact that the recruiter has found this out. Be forthright with them. Let them know that you were merely looking into the possibility of another firm, but that you would love to stay in or go to the city that you are currently interviewing in (assuming this is not a lie—don't lie!), and that you are basing your decision more upon the firm rather than the location. If applicable, point out again the connection or nexus that you have with the relevant location of the firm you are interviewing with. In other words, make this a non-issue to the best of your ability. Sometimes, it will be a make-or-break issue for the recruiter, but if that is the way it goes, there is not really much you can do about it. So, do not sweat it.

Hidden Rural Gems

I was unsure if I should include this section in this book, as I believe it is one of the best-kept secrets out there in the Canadian legal world. Please forgive me for my bias. I realize that there are many options available to law students, and it is ultimately up to you to decide what is best for you. Some of you may want to skip past this section—those of you who love the fast pace, the excitement, and the fun of the big city. Those of you who are either repelled by these things, or who seek after a more balanced, relaxed, family-oriented atmosphere, please read on.

There are numerous opportunities to both article and practice in small to mid-sized non-metropolis firms, and at sole practitioner offices. They are not as plentiful as big city firms, and do not advertise for articles very often, but they offer a legitimate opportunity to practice law in a more relaxed rural-based centre.

A firm outside of a major centre may offer many advantages to the up-and-coming lawyer. One of the biggest advantages may be the reduced expectations placed upon both articling students and young associates. While billable hour expectations are stated between 1,500 and 2,400 at big-city firms, at a firm outside a major centre, you are likely to find lower expectations between 1,000 and 1,500, or in many cases, no set billable hour requirements at all. What does this mean? Let me provide an example. If I was comparing a big-city firm who indicated a 1,700 billable-hour goal a year, this would equate to thirty-four billable hours each week, assuming a fifty-week year (two weeks for holiday). The small-city firm who expected 1,000 billable hours annually would equate to twenty billable hours each week, again based on a fifty-week year. Fourteen hours a week sounds like very few hours, doesn't it? But, on average, one billable hour equates to 1.5 to 2.4 hours of actual work, as you will often have administrative, networking, business development, and other distractions. Using an average of 1.6 for a conversion factor, the big-city firm's 34 weekly billable hours would equate to 54.4 actual work hours. Using the same factor of 1.6, the small city firm's 14 weekly billable hours would equate to 32 actual work hours. The difference of 22.4 working hours a week is significant—imagine what you could do with an extra 22.4 hours every week!

A more realistic comparison would be to look at a firm that had an expectation of 2,000 billable hours every week. Although you may be told that there is a billable-hour expectation of 1,500 or 1,700 or 1,800, the actual expectation, due to very high competition between associates and a bonus structure, may be much higher than that. You may have higher expectations than 1,000 billable hours, for example, at a small-city firm, but even so, you will only ever be as high as the very lowest billable-hour expectation at the big-city firm. So, for fun, let's do a comparison between the 2,000 big-city billable hours and 1,200 small-city billable hours. The actual work hours (using a 1.6 factor and assuming a fifty-week year) will be 64 and 38.4 hours respectively. That is a difference of 25.6 hours. That is a lot of extra free time!

My comparisons are not scientific by any means. However, they open your mind to the actual ramifications of high billable-hour expectations that you will inevitably find at big-city firms. The truth is that my numbers are probably pretty low regarding the factor rate, the real-life billable-hour goals, and the competition. This is why you hear of lawyers working eighty to one hundred hours per week. An eighty-hour week is equivalent to 11.43 hours a day, seven days a week! Or, you can take it easy on weekends, and only work five hours each on Saturday and Sunday, or crunch it all in on Saturday and work ten hours. This will leave you with a mere fourteen hours a day during the week. Not bad, eh? It seems preposterous, but this does happen!

I like to look at this problem in terms of hourly pay rates as well. Some people think this is a petty way to look at things. They are career people, and the money is not the important thing. Or, the money will come later, when they make partner. This may ring of truth. Nevertheless, consider this: Let us take a sixty-hour work week (pretty common at top-ten firms in major centres). As of 2005, an average first-year associate position in Calgary, Alberta is paid an estimated $65,000 annual salary. You will work around 3,000 real work-hours during the year. Working sixty hours a week will give you an hourly rate of $21.67. The same salary given for eighty hours a week breaks down to $16.25 an hour. I know quite a few non-professional jobs where you can make this much money an hour, and you have evenings and weekends off (and law school was not required). Just something to consider. Now, if you were at a small-centre firm where you worked 1,200 billable hours annually, you would actually work around 1,920 hours in a year. Assuming a salary of $45,000 (an estimated first-year associate salary). This puts you at an hourly rate of $23.44. It is not a smashing hourly rate, but it certainly beats $16.25, and is better even than the $21.67 an hour quoted above for the big firm. At the big firm, you only get paid $20,000 more a year, but you end up having to work so much more. Another great thing about small centres is that the cost of living is usually much lower. Houses are bought and sold for much less than in big cities! I plan to explore other moneymaking opportunities in my spare time. What do you plan to do with your spare time?

I mentioned that some small-centre firms do not have a billable-hour scheme. These firms will often comment on how they can still thrive with everyone working a nine-to-five-type schedule. Time will have to be put in when an important case or file requires it, but on the whole, partners and associates, and even some articling students, will express that they spend most weekends and evenings at home or with their family.

It boggles my mind that most graduating law students go into their article and their associateship without really thinking about the ramifications of the billable-hour scheme at the firm they have chosen. Classmates and colleagues seem to shrug their shoulders and say that is just the way it is. Although it is my personal opinion, I believe that it is not just the way it is. This scheme is a product of huge mergers and of well-tenured partners who need to keep fuelling the partner profit pool. In order to do that, they must keep bringing in and turning over, if necessary, young and relatively cheap associates. Your work will be billed out at a much higher rate than what you are paid. You are cheap labour. Don't kid yourself. (Ouch! I apologize if this hurts, but it really is the truth).

Don't get me wrong. I realize that you might not get all of the same experiences at a small-centre firm as you would in a big city. You probably will not get as many high profile cases or the fancy corporate files. However, you will probably get a more hands-on experience with more access to clients and the court system. This does not turn everyone on. If you are not excited about meeting clients or going to court, do not worry. It is not requisite for a small-centre lawyer to do these things.

A colleague of mine recently made a very astute comment while we were running together. He mentioned that when considering the whole billable hour thing, it probably makes a big difference if you have a family. I asked him what he meant. He told me that for youthful law graduates who are often relatively inexperienced with the working world, the high expectations are not as daunting as maybe they should be. A person with a spouse or partner, or more significantly, children, or a person who has worked in a high pressure, high hours job before law school will have a great advantage in understanding what high billable hours can really mean. He said that when you have children, you have a better understanding of how difficult it can be to accommodate your children's needs. You can better appreciate any spare time, such as the spare time indicated in my examples above.

A high billable hour scheme can often trap a young person who is planning to have a family some time in the future. Imagine the twenty-four-year-old law graduate. He gets his article at a top-ten firm. He is happily and regularly putting in twelve- to fourteen-hour days. He decides to buy a new house and a new car—he is making good money—why shouldn't he? Then, he finds his dream girl and marries her. The wedding is expensive, but he puts it on credit—he is going to be rolling in money as soon as he hits partner. He starts wishing he could spend more time with his spouse, but both of them appreciate the good money that is coming in. Besides, they decide that they want to start a family, and there are some expenses that come with that. They buy a bigger house, and a minivan to augment their car. The children start coming. Children bring a whole bunch of potential expenses with them.

So, now our young lawyer has children. A couple of years go by. He starts really wishing that he had more time to spend with them. But, now he is totally trapped. He wants to make partner. Once he makes partner, he can really start making good money, and hopefully start working a little less.

The truth is, in my opinion, all of this can be avoided if you seriously consider what you are getting into right at the beginning. You may not like the idea of a smaller centre, or a smaller firm. But, start thinking about the future, about what you want your life outside of the office to look like. Even one hundred less billable hours a year can make a huge difference. At the 1.6 factor, one hundred billable hours is 160 actual work hours a year, which is equivalent to 3.2 hours each week (assuming a fifty-week year). You can be spending those 3.2 hours each week with a spouse, partner, or with your precious children.

I am passionate about this topic because I have four wonderful children who I love to be around. I want as much free time as possible. I also worked very heavy hours in business before entering law school. I had a good understanding of what a sixty, seventy, or eighty-hour work week required of me and my family. I was always wishing I could have more time with my spouse. Because of these things, I chose to article in a small centre. Again, I realize that I have a definite bias, and that these factors do not relate to all of you. You will have to make your own decisions based on your own situation and values.

We had a presentation at my law school on small-centre articles and firms during my second year of law school. At that presentation, some math was discussed that really raised my eyebrows. I will use the Alberta statistics, as the presentation was by Alberta lawyers. I think that the concepts will transfer to almost any province.

According to a presenter at my law school who worked in a small city, the Canadian Bar Association (CBA) conducted a study about six or seven years ago (the CBA could not find a copy for me before publication of this writing). In this study, the CBA tried to come up with the most optimal number of lawyers, compared to a city's population, so that every lawyer could make a good living. The optimal number that they came up with was about one lawyer for approximately 1,200 people (1:1200). The ratio in Edmonton at the time of this presentation was about one lawyer for 550 people (1:550)! In Calgary, the rate was 1:450! I was astounded. This could not be right! Then, the presenters gave the ratios for small cities in Alberta. In Red Deer, the ratio, including the metropolitan area is around 1:2,400. Lethbridge has a similar number.

What do these numbers mean? It means that there are many more lawyers in big cities (per capita), and that it is more difficult for everyone to have a decent piece of the pie. It also means that perhaps there are not enough lawyers in smaller centres. With law school graduation numbers staying the same, or in some cases, increasing from year to year, it seems to me that more graduates should be looking to smaller centres to establish a living.

Consider these ideas, both for smaller centres, and for smaller firms within big centres. Prudent consideration early on can save you literally thousands of hours of work. You will have been in school for a long, long time. You deserve a little free time, don't you?

2nd Edition update: I am now living the dream that I contemplated above and absolutely loving it. I cannot imagine going back to a big city to practice. I make a lot of money, I have a lot of free time, and have unlimited autonomy over my life—it's great. It's not for everyone, I am sure, but I am living proof that it can be done and that it can be enjoyable.

Match Program

Depending on the city where you will be applying for an article, the match program may apply to you. Be sure to ask your career officer for a full explanation of how this system works, as it can be rather complicated. It is a system that is meant to make things fair for the students and the firms, but there can be problems for those who do not follow a simple path. Do not feel that you must only apply to match program firms.

The Alberta Matching Program is described in full at http://www.natmatch.com.

If you are juggling match firm interviews with non-match, be aware that you must get out of the match before you accept any offers from a non-match firm. This is difficult, but one can receive comfort from the fact that you can be open with the firms about your interest and they can tell you if you are in their top ranks. They cannot ask you to tell them how they rank with you, but they can reassure you of your standing with them.

Scheduling Interviews

One of the most prevalent comments made by articling applicants is that they have not left enough time between interviews. This is especially true for students who are applying to more than one city.

What type of interviews and how many will depend on the city that you are applying in, and the firms to which you are applying. You should count on your first interview at a firm to take at least an hour. Some only take twenty minutes, but make sure that you leave a lot of time, just in case. You will find that some firms use the first interview as a quick filtering system to get rid of undesirable applicants promptly. Other firms will try to consolidate their time and efforts and make the first interview the only interview. It is hard to predict what format a firm will follow.

Another prevalent comment made by applicants is that they did not make sufficient time to accommodate second interviews. You should account for a second interview for every firm that you apply to. As such, you should try to reasonably crunch in as many first interviews early on in your recruitment schedule. With second interviews, you should schedule up to two hours at a minimum. Again, some second interviews may last only twenty minutes—it might be a situation of simply getting a second opinion from a second or third interviewer. Others could last a long time, and might even include a lunch, dinner, or drinks. Third interviews are rare, but possible, so be prepared for them.

If you decide to apply to multiple cities, you may find great difficulty in scheduling interviews that fit perfectly into your plans. Some firms will want to bunch their interviews into certain times of the recruiting week, and therefore will not readily accommodate you. If you are able, try to schedule all interviews in your second-choice city on the same date. Also, try to leave one day open at the end of your recruitment week to accommodate any possible second interviews in that same city. This is difficult because you do not know who will actually call you back until they call. It is hard to be logical when you feel uncertain or even desperate. You need to prioritize and even gamble a bit.

I applied to firms in two major cities. I personally found it to be a scheduling nightmare. I ended up having to drive to the second city directly after one interview to attend a dinner interview, and then having to drive back at 11:00 p.m., arriving home around 2:00 a.m. Then, I had to get up for another interview for 8:00 a.m. I was not very fresh at either of those interviews, and wished that I had scheduled things differently. I ended up having to drive back and forth four times. I would not recommend trying to apply to multiple cities, unless the recruitment week is different in each city. You may feel like you are improving your odds, but I think that you may be putting yourself at a disadvantage because of being drowsy and therefore unfocussed in your interviews.

Because of scheduling conflicts, fatigue, or deciding that they have found the firm of their dreams, students will sometimes feel that they should cancel an interview later on in the recruitment week. Do not feel bad about doing this, but do it with tact. Some firms will take it personally and will not treat you nicely for cancelling on them. This may be especially true if you cancel on a second interview. However, you can have an attitude that recruitment week is for you more than it is for the firm. There are plenty of qualified applicants out there who can fill the position. There may only be two or three firms that fit your bill. When you call (do not e-mail to cancel!), ask to speak to the interviewer(s) directly. If they are not available, leave a message with their assistant. Let them know why you are cancelling. In some cases, a firm may call you back to try to reschedule if you are encountering scheduling difficulties—especially if the firm is interested in you. If you have already chosen the firm(s) of your dreams, the recruiters will probably appreciate knowing as soon as possible that you are out of the running for them. I do not advise mentioning why you do not want to work for the particular firm you are cancelling on. It simply does not achieve anything for either you or the firm. Just politely cancel and move on.

Phone Message

It is a very good idea to make sure that your voice mail or answering machine message sounds professional and cheerful, includes information about how you can be contacted (e.g., cell phone number), and perhaps indicates when you will be able to return messages (e.g., by the end of the day, within twenty-four hours, etc.). It should also include your full name.

If you live with roommates, parents, siblings, spouse, or partner, advise them of how you would like the telephone to be answered. Let them clearly know how important it is for them to sound cheerful, professional, and serious. I have heard nightmare stories about mothers talking to recruiters about their sons and daughters, or of a roommate answering the phone with a burp. Promise to take housemates of concern out for drinks or dinner if they will just behave for the next couple of weeks. It is very important. Also, advise them to take good notes when receiving a message. Supply a message pad and multiple pens right beside the telephone. If possible, have them forward messages to your cell phone immediately so that you can reply as quickly as possible.

Cell Phone?

I found a cell phone to be an indispensable device during the recruiting period. It allowed me to receive telephone calls from recruiters immediately, or to return messages as quickly as possible. It can be useful to only include your cell phone number on your résumé if you would like to answer all calls directly and avoid the housemate issue mentioned above.

A cell phone also came in very handy when offers were being made. It meant that I was not pinned to my landline all day. Offers will often come in later in the day, when first- or second-choice candidates decline offers. There is a good chance you will be third or fourth, and you want to be available to take that precious call when it comes.

If you do not use a cell phone very much, like myself, you may want to consider purchasing an inexpensive phone and purchasing a pay-as-you-go card. Top up your phone with enough to last for the recruiting period. If you run out of time, you can simply purchase a bit more time. This way, you are not locked into a contract that you may not need later.

There are some rules about cell phone use. Make sure that it is deactivated or at least silent whenever you are going into an interview. There is almost nothing worse than disrupting an interview with an irritating telephone ring. You will cause embarrassment both for yourself and the recruiter. It is highly unprofessional! Also, do not take calls when you are on a loud train or going under a light rail transit tunnel. It will sound bad on the other end.

Set up your voice mail according to the message rules above. Answer all calls professionally and cheerfully, indicating your full name. Even if it is a secretary calling you, you want to sound as professional and cheerful as possible. They may pass on their impression to a recruiter. It is best to play it safe.

What to Wear

There is only one rule about what to wear to an interview; you cannot overdress. This is one of the most important events of your life, falling somewhere behind your wedding and the birth of a child, or something like that. As such, put in the effort to look your best.

Make an investment in a decent to good suit. You will end up using the suit when you article, so it is probably a good investment. Do not buy a cheap suit. Borrow money if you have to, but do not go to your interviews looking anything but sharp. You will want to choose a conservative colour. However, there is no specific rule about having to wear a grey, black, or blue suit. Wear a colour that is attractive on you, and one that you are comfortable with. Make sure it fits well, and you will be set. Just to be clear, do not wear khakis, sport jackets, or anything that is not a business suit. You will show up to your interview rather embarrassed (or at least you should), and will immediately stick out negatively. This is not an opinion—it is a rule. Also, buy good shoes. People do notice shoes (I have seven interviewers look me up and down—all the way to my shoes). Shine your shoes— do not let them get dirty. Good shoes are also very important as you will put on quite a few miles during interview week, and it will save you a lot of pain. Break shoes in before interview week if you can.

For men, buy a few good dress shirts and have them pressed prior to interview week. You will have to change a number of times, both due to perspiration, and to avoid wearing the same thing to a second interview. There is a debate about whether you should wear a white shirt or jump into colours or patterns. It is my opinion that it does not really matter. Just make sure that your shirt is contemporary, subtle, and attractive. I wore patterned shirts of subtle colours to all of my interviews. Purchase a few attractive ties. Try to match colour to your personality. If you are a fun person, choose a fun pattern and colours, but do not go too crazy. You may want to match patterns and colours with the firm you are interviewing. A tie that is darker than your shirt looks best. If you can, coordinate your tie with your shirt and your suit. If you know that it is a conservative firm, wear a conservative tie. If you know the firm is more forward looking, hip, and young, wear a tie to reflect that. I kept a few ties that were pre-tied in my attaché case and switched if I needed to between interviews. You should probably avoid bow ties, bolo ties, or anything of that sort. Save that for when you are well-established at the firm. You can find out more about choosing ties, tying ties, and more at http://www.tie-a-tie.net.

Men should avoid jewellery other than watches, wedding rings, class rings, engineering rings, or some other subtle ring. Earrings should be avoided, even if you are trying to make a statement about your personal agency. You may have a belief that you would not want to work at a firm that would judge you for wearing an earring. However, remember that you probably will not be working directly with the interviewers once you are hired. In my opinion, such a subject is better addressed once you have started the job. You may want to keep an eye out when you are touring the firm for men that are wearing earrings. If this is important to you, you can get a feel for what others are wearing. Things are a lot more liberal these days, but why eliminate yourself from the running for a great article to make a jewellery statement? A good dress watch can really set off your suit Cuff links are even a possibility, if it suits your personal style. Again, you cannot overdress.

You may want to invest in a good attaché case. It looks professional, provides a space to put your résumé, cover letters, map, cell phone, snacks, and other items. However, be prepared to be teased by fellow classmates that you meet on the street. It is very easy to spot articling applicants by their fancy suits, shiny shoes, and shiny attaché cases. Do not be affected. You want to look polished, professional, and on top of your game.

Get a good haircut about a week in advance of articling week. Do not gamble on a hairstyle that is far off from your regular look. Depending on the type of firm you are applying to, you may want to choose a more conservative look. However, I am aware of students that have been hired with long hair, spiky hair, and other styles that are considered out of the ordinary. I am in no position to suggest personal style to you. However, the general rule is that you do not want to give an interviewer any reason not to hire you. On the flip side, an interviewer may appreciate that you have contemporary style, including your haircut, especially if the interviewer is relatively young.

You might want to avoid facial hair unless it is your regular style. A subtle beard, goatee, or moustache may be acceptable, but I would recommend going to an interview properly shaven. You may want to avoid contemporary styles such as soul patches, razor blade, side burns, and things like that. Any one of these things could set you apart as not taking the interview seriously.

There is a lot of controversy about what women should wear to an interview. I am not a fashion consultant, but I do have some strong opinions about this controversy. Wear what you want to wear. If you want to wear a skirt with your suit, wear one. If you do not, do not. In this case, unlike the earring issue above, you do not want to work for a firm that will judge you based on the bottom half of your suit. The earring issue is more of a professional standard issue. The skirt issue is discrimination. Again, this is only my opinion. A number of my classmates have expressed that they chose to wear a skirt to avoid elimination from any potential firms. Again, it is up to you.

Women should follow the same general advice written above for the men. Avoid perfume, or keep it to a very bare minimum as a courtesy to your interviewers who have to stay all day in one room. That is, unless you have found perfume to be to your advantage in the past.

Women should also have a few blouses available to change into. You may be able to mix and match your suits as well to achieve a different look for multiple interviews at a single firm. Again, perspiration can be a problem solved by having multiple shirts. Jewellery should also be kept to a minimum and rather conservative. Avoid multiple earrings in each ear, and avoid facial piercings. Again, do not provide any reason for rejection.

Do not take any of this advice personally. It is for your benefit. It is not a rejection of your personal style, or an attempt to bolster the already too-stuffy and too-conservative atmosphere of the legal community. It is advice given to provide you with the best possible chances to obtain that coveted articling position. You might want to prove me wrong. Go ahead if you want to. However, you will be fighting the odds, and I do not see why you would want to make an already challenging experience tougher on yourself. Law is a professional career. Conservative attire comes with the territory. There is more relaxation today compared to even five or ten years ago, but interviews are the time to look your very best. Wouldn't you rather be in a position of turning down offers than scrambling to get even one offer? This is the truth of the situation, and I recommend that you give yourself the very best chances.

These rules and this advice apply equally to formal and informal interview situations. Even if a partner invites you to lunch or out for coffee, you should not consider removing your tie or dressing down in any way. Even if it is casual Friday at the particular firm, do not give in to the temptation to follow suit and dress down—not even for after-hours receptions or drinks. You are always being scrutinized. The interview never stops until you are in your car, on the train or bus, or going to your next interview or home. Again, you can never overdress for an interview.

If you have experiences contradicting or supporting my advice, please share them at the http://www.CanadianLawSchool.ca website.

Interviewing

Interviewing is an art. There is no right or wrong way to conduct yourself. However, a few tips are worth mentioning. First, you should attempt to be as professional and as courteous as possible. This includes basic manners such as saying please and thank you, holding the door for others, and waiting for the person(s) on the other side of the boardroom table to seat themselves first. It also includes avoiding gum chewing, distracting mannerisms, putting your legs up on the table, and other potentially offensive behaviours. Most of these are common sense, or at least they should be.

Law interviews tend to be very laid back (except for government interviewers, from my experience). They will often take on a conversational tone. Welcome this tone. However, do not become so relaxed that you appear unprofessional. Avoid vulgar language and off-colour jokes. Steer clear of putting others down, even if the other side goes this way. Maintain integrity and composure at all times.

It is a great idea to shift the focus towards the firm and the interviewers if you have the opportunity. Once you see a gap in the conversation, feel free to ask questions about the firm and about the interviewers. People love to talk about themselves. However, do not forget to tell about you and your experience. Take the conversation as it comes, and remain confident.

It is a good idea to avoid interrupting an interviewer. Let them have their time to share with you. You will often be able to pick up on key points, such as what the firm is looking for, what areas of law are important to the firm, and so on. However, if you feel that the interview is being monopolized by the interviewer(s) (this is a common problem), feel free to interject at an appropriate time and either ask a question, or offer some useful information about yourself.

The interview will often extend beyond the boardroom. You may have the opportunity to tour the firm with a current articling student. You may be introduced to associates, partners, and support staff. Use this time wisely. Do not let your guard down. But remember that you are interviewing the firm at the same time and use these opportunities to get a sense of the culture and tone of the firm. Current articling students may give you a sense of the reality of the firm better than the wining and dining partners.

You are being assessed during this time just as much as you were in the interview room. Lawyers, apparently, will often ask articling students and support staff, as well as other associates and partners, about what their thoughts on you are. This also applies to dinners, luncheons, and wine and cheese events that you are invited to.

The bottom line is: be on your best behaviour, come across as relaxed, and let your true self (at least your better self) shine through.

If you face a difficult or compromising question, do not lose it. Take a few moments, take a breath, and think about how you should respond. If it was an inappropriate question, feel free to let the interviewer know that you feel it was unsuitable and why. If the matter is pushed, let them know that you will not answer that type of question. If you are wondering what types of questions I am talking about, imagine being asked if you are married or have kids, if you are gay, if you drink, if you are part of a political organization, etc. These have no bearing on your ability to fill the role you are interviewing for, and should not be tolerated. If the interviewer insists, you might just want to shut the interview down. You do not want to work at that type of firm anyway.

From the "Inappropriate Questions" section of the 2007 University of Alberta Articling Handbook:

"Many female lawyers gain weight. How are you planning on avoiding this?" (actual question!!!)

If you think that you have bombed an interview, do not fret. I thought that I bombed a particular interview and ended up landing an offer from that establishment. I never would have thought that would happen. But, it turns out that the interviewers appreciated my honesty and forthrightness. Never say die!

Obiter Dictum

My first interview [for a summer position] was by far the worst but only because I was very nervous and I thought it went really badly. That said, two years later, when I was interviewing for an articling position at that same firm they said they remembered me from that first interview, were impressed, and that was why they wanted to see me again. Even the worst interviews might not actually be so bad.
— *Robin Penker, Law Graduate 2005, Risk Manager and Legal Counsel, Maple Trade Finance*

At one particular firm, I was about half-way through an interview and it seemed we were really just having a hard time making conversation. At that point the interviewee stated that "sometimes you have to sacrifice your family for your career." I immediately determined that this wasn't the firm for me. To finish off the interview I was asked if I had any questions for the firm. My mind went completely

blank on anything that I had read about the firm and I couldn't come
up with a single question.

— *Jaime Johnson, Law Graduate, 2005, Associate, major Canadian munici-*
pality

Even though the firm I ended up with is generally viewed as a conservative firm, there is always room for humour in the interview. We
ended up discussing Will Ferrell and his cowbell skit from *Saturday*
Night Live. I was amazed how informal the interview process actually
is. I think they already have ideas on who they want to hire based on
your résumé. They interview to make sure that you are a decent guy
(or girl), and your personality meshes with theirs. And any firm that
thinks highly of Will Ferrell will undoubtedly be a terrific place to
work!

— *Michael Gunter, Class of 2008*

Be "Yourself"

For me, this was the most frustrating and confusing mantra reported by fellow students, former students, career advisors, and networking contacts. What does it really mean to "be you," and does
this advice really carry any weight?

Does "be you" mean that you should recite a poem if you are a
poet? Does it mean that you should talk about hockey if you are a
die-hard hockey fan? Does it mean that you should be exuberant if
you are a born extrovert? Does it mean that you should tell jokes, or
show your wit if you are a person of humour?

This mantra made a lot more sense to me post-articling week.
Law interviews are a very funny thing. With only a few exceptions,
my interviews were extremely casual affairs. There was very little to
no discussion of the law. Discussions included current affairs, sports,
my children, travels, ancestral background, networking contacts, personal business experience, and even a mountain biking accident I had
had a few years earlier (I included photographs on my personal Web
site). There were references and questions about law school experiences. In my case, there were no discussions about particular professors, particular classes and their usefulness, the Law Review, extracurricular activities related to law school, etc. The exceptions to this

rule were with government-related articles, where substantive legal questions were asked. These were not difficult questions, and were easily prepared for.

As the articling week progressed, I realized increasingly that interviewers already knew a whole lot about me before I even entered the interview room. They had read my résumé rather carefully, had perused my Web site (sometimes to a greater extent than I thought they should), and in some cases had spoken to other people about me. As well, some of them had already contacted references that I had provided. Wherever possible, I had also asked networking contacts to put in a good word for me. So there was really no reason to try to impress by pretence.

The interview is really an opportunity to get a feel for each other. You will hear quite often that interviewers are looking for a good fit. This rings very true in my experience. You are also best served by trying to look for a good fit. What is a good fit? This is where things become very subjective. For me, a good fit was a firm with a family focus, and one with a large range of potential legal practice areas. I was also looking for relatively low billable hours and many hands-on solicitation and litigation opportunities. I wanted a smaller firm size with few articling student positions, so that I could get the attention that I deserved as a student-at-law. I was also looking for genuine sincerity in my interviewers. For you, criteria might include good humour, a mature atmosphere, a young and energetic atmosphere, a quick partnership track, lots of social events, etc.

I would like to provide a caveat for the idea of finding a good fit. For the most part, law firms are identical. Most of them run on the same billable-hour scheme, have more male partners and associates than females, are profit-focussed, have annual ski trips, family picnics, associate retreats, benefits, article rotations, etc. It is hard to find firms that have a unique way of doing things. You will find more distinctiveness in smaller firms, as they tend not to be quite as profit-focussed and are willing to look outside of the big-firm box. My caveat is the fact that most law firms are identical in many ways, and also that interviewers are not always a true reflection of the firm at which you are interviewing. As a result, you are best served to meet as many people as possible at the firm that you are interviewing at. If you are offered the opportunity to meet with current articling students, jump at the opportunity. These students are as close as you will get to the truth within the walls of the firm. They are not far removed from where you are, and will often be quite candid about certain things, such as what their real work schedules are like. They will also provide some of the ins and outs regarding certain associates or partners that are great or not-so-great to work with. If you have the opportunity to meet with partners or associates, also jump at the opportunity. Time spent doing this can pay off immensely down the road. If you can, sit down with these people face-to-face in a closed office. People tend to be more truthful behind closed doors.

So, what does "be you" mean? It means all kinds of things. I have told you some things to expect at your interview. The rest is really up to you. Be relaxed. Be confident that the interviewer is genuinely interested in you. You will have already made it through a huge cut. Often firms will receive upwards of 100-150 or more applications. Most of them only make time to interview thirty or less applicants. This means that you are high up on their radar screen. My theory is that once you have made it through their doors, you are on equal ground with the rest of the interviewees. Now is your time to shine. Now is your time to impress upon everyone you meet that you will be a fantastic person to work with, to play with, and to show off at firm meetings and most importantly to clients. However, do not feel that you need to come across as something that you are not. Put in the time to get a good number of interviews, and then just relax.

Obiter Dictum

Once you get an interview, I think the most important thing in gaining an article is to at least appear self-confident. Even if you feel like you are in way over your head or are under-qualified, walk into the interview as though you belong there: smile, shake hands, [and] speak clearly... in a conversational tone. If the interviewers see that you feel confident about your abilities, they will be more likely to think that you actually do have the abilities they are looking for.
— *Robin Penker, Law Graduate 2005, Risk Manager and Legal Counsel, Maple Trade Finance*

Be the kind of person the interviewers would want to have dinner with. Be pleasant, appropriately humorous, and give the appearance of being driven … be relaxed. The idea is that everybody should be comfortable in their own skin.

— *Rob Nelson, Law Graduate 2005, Associate in Dubai, United Arab Emirates*

This means being comfortable and acting as you would around friends and family. This also means being proud of who you are and what you have accomplished—but don't brag or be cocky. However, one must ensure they are still being professional.

— *Lorne Randa, Law Graduate, 2005, Associate, Brownlee LLP*

You don't want to come off as "affected." However, you have to go into interviews with a sense of confidence in yourself. As well, you want to present yourself as someone that your interviewer could see working side by side with.

— *Mike Kariya, Law Graduate, 2005*

I think that [being you] means to just let … your personality come through in the interview so the interviewer(s) can get a sense of who you are in a short period of time. The firms will be interviewing a large number of very good students and I think that personality is what sets people apart.

— *Kim Yee, Law Graduate, 2006, Associate, Brownlee LLP*

I know it sounds trite but be yourself. If you are trying to be someone you're not, you might end up in a firm you hate to work at. Make eye contact, smile, and come prepared with extra copies of your résumé, transcripts, and references. If you are interested in the firm it is very important to LET THEM KNOW. They see hundreds of résumés and if it comes down to two people with virtually the same marks and personality fit they will choose the person that showed the most interest in working at the firm.

— *Carissa Browing, Class of 2008*

Don't talk about scholastic achievements. You are smart enough to work at the firm otherwise you would not have gotten the interview. Talk about extracurricular interests, travels, and know a little about the city/school of the interviewer(s). Don't be a boring schmuck who the interviewer would dread meeting in the copy room of the firm late on a Thursday night.

> — *Shawn Davis, LLB/MBA Graduate, 2005, Associate, Shearman &*
> *Sterling LLP, Abu Dhabi, United Arab Emirates*
>
> Be relaxed and don't be someone you're not. Law interviews are re-
> markably informal—they're like a conversation. But don't forget they
> are interviews. You have two goals: 1) sell yourself and 2) find out
> who the firm actually is.
>
> — *Ari Singer, Class of 2008*

Prepare

Practice, practice, practice. I wish I had practiced more. I had a
willing audience in my wife and some fellow classmates, but I was
too proud to take them up on their offers. I think that it would have
helped me greatly, especially in my early interviews. I ended up using
my first two to three interviews as practice, and only then did I finally start to relax. Had I practiced beforehand, I might have put
myself in a better position for my earlier interviews.

Know your résumé and cover letter inside and out. Know the
dates, know the names of all referees, employers, professors, etc.
Generally, do not include something in your application that you are
not intimately familiar with. There is nothing worse than being asked
a question about your résumé that you cannot remember details
about. It is embarrassing, and really tarnishes your trustworthiness. If
you have an opportunity, review your cover letter the night before,
or at the very least, right before the interview. If you have dropped a
name in your application, make sure you remember their name, position, and their connection to you.

Know where you are going. Double and triple check your addresses before articling week. Write them down in multiple locations
on your person (e.g., in your attaché case, your suit, and perhaps on
your Palm Pilot or planner). I used MapQuest™ (http://www.
mapquest.ca) to create and print out maps for any firms where I was
unsure of the location. This helped immensely to save time while
travelling from one interview to the other.

Call to confirm times, addresses, and names of interviewers if you
are at all unsure. Be very polite when you are doing this, and let the

person who you are talking to know that you simply want to ensure that you do not miss this very important meeting.

It is imperative to review the Web sites of firms you are interested in very well. Read the interviewer biographies if you know who the interviewers will be. Read about the areas of law that the firm practices and the articling student section. Read up on firm history, their clients, the managing partners, and anything else you can find to give you an edge.

Ask the Right Questions

After reviewing the firm Web site carefully, prepare a set of questions that are specific to the firm. Add these to your general questions that you will have prepared before interview week begins.

What are the right kinds of questions? This is definitely subjective, and I cannot tell you exactly what types of questions to ask, as your needs and desires will be individual. However, you should consider the following types of questions.

- *Can you give me an example of a case that you are working on?* Ask this question of partners, associates, and especially current articling students.

- *What did you do last weekend?* This will reveal how much the person works on weekends, and what kind of outside interests the person has, which might provide an opportunity to find a common interest.

- *What kind of feedback do you provide to articling students?*

- *How often do your students-at-law go to court?*

There are many other great questions that you can ask. Be creative.

Reveal Your Intentions

One of the most common mistakes made by articling applicants is being afraid to reveal their intentions. There is a general feeling that things should be kept quiet, and that they should reveal as little as possible, thus giving them the upper hand. In my experience, the exact opposite is true. When you do not make it blatantly obvious that you are very interested in articling at a given firm, you make the decision much more difficult for the interviewer. If it is between you and another person, they will usually go with the person who shows the most interest.

This is a tricky area, because you may want to avoid any kind of dishonesty. If you think that you would rather work at two or three other firms better than you would like to work at this particular firm, then you will have to frame your comments carefully. You may want to say something like "If I were to receive an offer from you, I would be very excited about the upcoming articling year." You would be telling the truth, assuming that you only received an offer from this firm, as any offer is better than no offer. If you think that the firm is in your top three, tell them that they are in your top three. Tell them that you would be thrilled if you were given an offer. It is better to turn someone down once they have given you an offer than to take yourself out of the running by not properly communicating your desire for a position with a firm.

In my case, I received an offer from every firm where I expressed something like what I have written above. In two other cases, I knew that I was in the top three or four positions, but because I didn't come across as being absolutely excited about a potential offer, I did not receive an official offer. In my case, that was all right, because I was sure that I would receive offers from some other firms that I liked better. However, if you are feeling like your chances are not as good as you would like, you will want to be sure to extend an impression, as honestly as possible, that you would be delighted to work at that particular firm.

You could also help yourself by blatantly telling the interviewers that you intend to make your home or keep your home in the city where the firm is located. Provide as many connections and reasons for living there as can think of. This cannot hurt you, and will probably help immensely. Of course, nothing is written in stone, but you want to show a real intention. If you are honest with yourself, you *will* have a real intention to live and practice where you are applying.

If you will be clerking with a court, be sure that you express this, and let the firm know what you intend to do—that you plan to complete your clerkship as quickly as possible and return as an associate at the given firm.

Obiter Dictum

I picked a firm that would be a good springboard in case things did not work out. At the same time, I chose a firm that I thought would provide me with fantastic articling experience.
— *Rob Nelson, Law Graduate 2005, Associate in Dubai, United Arab Emirates*

Try to be Honest

The section above expresses that you should frame comments as honestly as possible. I cannot emphasize enough the importance of honesty. On a personal basis, I really believe in honesty and integrity, but that is not why I advise you to frame your comments truthfully. The reason that I implore you to remain as honest as possible is because the legal world is incredibly small. It is common to have articling committee members from distinct firms that are friends or colleagues outside the office. Remember—they were potentially classmates not so long ago. I have heard of committee members from different firms getting together to talk about candidates, or even talking on the phone about potential candidates. You absolutely do not want any discrepancies coming across. This will immediately take you out of the running at both firms. This may sound paranoid, but it has happened. You do not want it to happen to you.

In addition to this reasoning, it is better to be honest and end up at a firm that suits your needs, concerns, and desires than to try to pretend to be someone that you are not. If you put enough effort into your preparation, you should be able to rest on your qualifications, interview skills, and your personality to get that job of your dreams.

Bow Out When Appropriate

If you find that you would not fit in at a particular firm, or if you feel confident that you will be able to get a better offer at a firm that is better for you, you should contact that firm as soon as possible. You are in a great position, and should not feel the need to block up a spot at that firm. Remember your poor classmates who are not as qualified as you and are still desperately trying to get a job. This is also the classy thing to do in terms of the firm. They will appreciate your polite decline to a second interview or offer. It will make their job easier. Be sure to let them know why if you can. Do not tell them that you think their firm would be miserable to work for. Let them know that you have found a firm where you believe there is a good fit, or that you are interested in practicing in an area that is not offered by their firm, or that you have decided to move to another city.

The Thank-You Letter

This is essential. It is difficult to fit this in to your already busy schedule, especially if you have a very hectic interview week. However, this step is very important. Many applicants overlook this practice, and I think that it hurts many of them. A thank-you note is a great opportunity to get your name in front of the interviewers again, especially after a day of mind-numbing interviews. It is also an opportunity to express how well you thought the interview went, how there is a great fit between the firm and you, why you think you are the perfect person for the job, and why you would be thrilled to accept an offer from the given firm. Again, use honesty when framing your note.

The note itself can take a few forms, depending on your personal style, the time that you have available, and what you think the interviewer(s) would be most comfortable with. I have sent e-mail messages directly to the interviewers. It is important that you send your note to the interviewer as soon as possible, preferably the same day of the interview. You may want to send another quick e-mail message at the end of recruiting week. Another method is to send a letter or card through the mail, but this can be slow. My favourite technique is to keep a stack of small, subtle, and professional looking thank-you cards with me at all times. If I was able, I would sit in the foyer for a couple of minutes and give the card to the receptionist, or if I was jumping from interview to interview, I would take a few minutes writing the cards, and then quickly swing by the firms where I had interviewed to drop off the card. You may think that this is overdoing it—I do not. You will make a great impression, and the interviewer will probably appreciate the personal touch. As well, a handwritten card will likely grab the interviewer's attention more than e-mail. Lawyers receive hundreds of e-mail messages every day, and it is difficult for them to pay close attention to all of them during interview week. A nice personal card delivered to their desk or mailbox will definitely stand out more than e-mail. Another technique is to leave a voicemail message. This can be as effective as a handwritten card. However, be sure to rehearse what you will say, or use the rerecord function if you are not happy with your first try. Come across as professional as possible, and as sincere as possible, but don't overdo it.

I reemphasize the importance of the second thank-you message at the end of the interview week. This is a great time to remind the interviewer of your keen interest. This will immediately put you ahead of other candidates.

Callback Interviews

The majority of firms will conduct a second interview for those candidates who interest them. If you get a callback, congratulations. You are now in the top tier of applicants, and your odds have increased dramatically. Now is the time to really turn on the charm and convince the firm that you are the person for the job. These interviews can differ in style from firm to firm. In some cases, a second, third, or fourth interviewer will interview you—and perhaps other members of the hiring committee. It may be a more formal interview or a more casual interview, depending on the firm and on the interviewers. A single partner or multiple partners who have the final say may conduct the interview. You may be taken on a tour of sorts, briefly meeting a number of associates and partners. Some will even have you sit down individually with associates or partners. I understand that this is less common in Canada, as compared to the US. You may be invited to a lunch, a dinner, or out for coffee or drinks. Some invitations end up in group situations where several candidates are invited to dinner or cocktails together. Remember, in any of these situations, you are being interviewed. Unless you are expressly told to take down your guard (i.e., specifically told to take off your tie or remove your shoes) you should always be conscious about your conduct. Be sure to schedule plenty of time for these second, or in some cases, third interviews.

The Witching Hour

The witching hour is that hour between 8:00 a.m. and 9:00 a.m. on a previously determined day when firms can begin making offers. This is the time when applicants are anxious, perched by their phones, praying for that elusive offer. It is a very nerve-racking and important time. Because it is such a critical time, it is very unwise to schedule anything during this time. Stay close to your telephone or cell phone. You do not want to miss an important call and risk losing an opportunity.

It is very important to be realistically considering options ahead of time and prepare to have a choice. Choose a wise friend to talk to during this stressful time for advice, perspective, and stress-relief.

Accepting an Offer

So, you received an offer. Congratulations! You are now in a position of great power. If you have received more than one, you have even more power. However, you must treat that power appropriately and ensure that you get off on the right foot with your future employer.

Some students get excited when they receive their first offer. They often accept right away. I would advise against this. As I said, you are in a position of power. It is a good idea to let this idea settle for a while. It is also a good idea to see what other offers come your way. You may be pleasantly surprised. Even if you were not on the top of the list at other firms, as offers go out and other students reject those offers because they want to go somewhere else, the firms move down their list of candidates until they find a successful match. Therefore, do not be too anxious to accept an offer on the spot.

The appropriate way to buy additional time is to express that you are very flattered and excited about being offered articles at the firm. Let the recruiter know that you are very seriously considering their offer, but would like to think about it and discuss it with your family, etc. Let them know, clearly, when you will get back to them (they will usually want to hear back within twenty-four hours). You may want to ask further questions of them, or ask for another tour of the firm and an opportunity to meet more members of the firm to help you make your decision.

Once you have done this, you can now sit back and revel in the fact that you now have an article. Do the same with other incoming offers. Take time to consider all of your options. Sit down and figure out what is important to you. Is it money? Is it more free time? Consider carefully the salary and billable-hour expectations. Consider the amount of holiday time offered, benefits offered, what kind of office you will have, etc. If you have offers from more than one city or town, sit down and do a pro and con assessment of living in each centre. Use these twenty-four hours wisely and you will end up in a situation that is best for you.

Once you have decided which offer you will accept, you may want to phone the firm and ask some more questions about the offer. You can ask whether the salary is negotiable, or whether any other point is negotiable. Some firms will not budge. However, some firms are open to negotiation. Do not worry about offending the recruiter or the firm. It is your right to ask these questions. Remember, they expressed that they want you to work for them. Now they need to convince you that they are the best firm for you, and that they will meet your interests. Going through this process can have great financial benefits, and can provide you with a sense of control going into your article and your career.

Do not *demand* more money or benefits. Remember, it is a negotiation. Also, do not tell the firm that you are balancing their offer with another firm, and that the highest bidder wins. Use tact and be courteous. Maintain a professional relationship through this period and it will pay dividends once your article begins.

Now, some of you will be very happy to accept an offer right away from your number-one choice. That is your prerogative. However, you may want to adopt the strategies above before you do this to increase your satisfaction with your choice. If you are afraid of stepping on toes, don't be. It is your right to ask questions, to negotiate, and to make an informed decision.

SCHOLARSHIP APPLICATIONS

In the midst of all of this excitement during your 2L summer, it is important not to miss important scholarship and bursary application deadlines. Along with this, you should obtain letters of reference well in advance, hopefully near the beginning of your break from school. Once you have received your grades, you can approach professors and instructors that you did well with, or with whom you have established a good relationship. I have seen quite a few students slap their forehead during June, July, and August because they were too caught up with work and articling applications and neglected to submit a scholarship or bursary application. This is literally too costly a mistake to make!

CHAPTER 8: THIRD YEAR (3L)

*If Moses had gone to Harvard Law School and spent three years
working on the Hill, he would have written the
Ten Commandments with three exceptions and a saving clause.*
— Charles Morgan

WHAT CLASSES?

CHOOSING classes in your last year of law school can be somewhat tricky, or it can be as easy as you want to make it. There are two ways to go about it.

The first is to contact the firm that you will be articling with and ask them if they would recommend any courses for you, based on what area they think you are best suited for. Be careful with this approach, because you may be pigeonholing yourself too soon. However, some firms may want you to take particular courses such as trusts, sale of goods, or taxation, for example, just to get a good rounded familiarity with particular areas of law. You may be able to figure this out on your own based on the information you already know about what areas of law the firm practices in.

The other approach, and the one that I think is most beneficial, is to take courses that you find interesting or that you think you might like to practice some day (even if it is far off in the future). I believe that you should not try to kill yourself in your last year. In my case, I was beat by my last 2L semester. I wanted courses that would catch my attention on a daily basis. I was attracted by more practical courses, as they interested me more than theoretical ones. You might be the opposite. Although it was recommended by some "experts" that I should take certain courses to prepare me for the bar exam or CPLED courses, I did not take that advice. I figured I would learn that material when the time came. The truth is, most law students will have some major gaps going into their articling year. It is simply not possible to cover everything.

Thus, I recommend having as much fun as possible in your last year. Consider the professor teaching the course. By now, you will have picked some favourites. Consider the class size. It might be more or less fun to be in a smaller class, depending on your preference.

Some people really sweat over this topic. I say let them sweat. You will have more fun, will be less burned out going into your article, and will enjoy better long-term health.

Obiter Dictum

I chose upper-year courses based mainly on two things. First, I looked for ones that interested me but would still add possible value to my future career. Second, I listened to suggestions from articling interviews and upper-year students.
— *Jamie Johnson, Law Graduate, 2005, Associate at a major Canadian municipality*

I took classes that I wanted to take (along with the required ones). I view that most of the work in law school is really about learning how to learn, along with some pivotal basics. But a lot of the practical information will be from researching in actual practice, so I decided to take classes that I was interested in and those that would give me a good foundation for my goals for my career.
— *Ari Singer, Class of 2008*

I took classes that I was interested in, regardless if I would practice law in that area or not. If you take classes that you enjoy, you will learn more and do better. But I would also recommend taking at least a couple courses that are typical areas a lawyer may face such as wills or estates, land titles or real estate transactions, judgment enforcement or personal property security, trusts, and bankruptcy. These classes will help one become well rounded in the various areas of law.

— Lorne Randa, Law Graduate, 2005, Associate, Brownlee LLP

MOOTS?

Moots are a fantastic opportunity to gain some practical advocacy, research, and litigation experience. If you are leaning even slightly towards litigation, negotiation, or other alternative dispute resolution mechanisms (e.g., mediation, arbitration, etc.,), a moot in your last year can do wonders for increasing your knowledge and confidence. It is also a fantastic way to boost your GPA, as moot coaches or instructors tend to give pretty high marks, as the rules about grading curves do not usually apply to registered moots.

Moots are hard and require intensive work. However, you can learn more in a moot than in most classes. Further, most moots do not take a whole semester to complete, including research, writing, and oral practices, thus freeing up time and energy for your other courses.

PASS OR FAIL COURSES

Pass or fail courses are a great option in your third year. They are also great in your second year. However, I think they are best done in the last year. By this time, most of you should not be too worried about your GPA, unless you do not yet have an article, or if you are considering legal graduate work. If you are in these situations, a pass or fail course is still a great option, as it will not affect your GPA. Your average will be based on your remaining courses.

Pass or fail courses tend to be a little more laid back. The pressure of the grading curve is gone, and you can use your energy to actually learn the practical aspects of the given course. Be warned, however: pass or fail courses often involve role-playing exercises of some kind.

RESEARCH PAPERS?

Research papers, for some students, are the best thing since sliced bread. Many law schools offer the option of conducting independent research and writing a major paper on the subject. There is usually no corresponding scheduled lecture. As such, you are free to manage your own time, to pursue an area of law that has struck a chord with you, and to practice your legal research and writing abilities. You will have to obtain a faculty supervisor for your research and paper. This person will provide a certain level of guidance, including suggestions for topics, analysis of your paper outline, and will ultimately assign a grade to your paper. Most professors take on four to six independent research papers each year. Grades tend to be on the higher side for these papers. This may correspond with a relatively better quality of research and writing. In turn, it may correspond with the low number of people on the grading curve. In any case, it can be to your advantage.

The important thing with independent research papers is to begin your research as soon as possible. It is easy to become lazy and to procrastinate. Many students hammer out their research and writing at the beginning of a semester. This can be a great advantage to you both for reducing stress during your semester, and when exam time comes along.

Many lecture-based courses include a major paper as the main or only method of evaluation. These can be wonderful experiences, especially if the course subject interests you. Some professors will assign a participation mark, but some will not. In any case, it is not difficult to skip classes if you so desire, without much chance of repercussion. If you are getting burned out, either in second or third year, a paper-based course can be a real relief.

It may surprise you, once you enter a paper-based seminar, how many of your classmates will be diligently taking notes. It is my personal opinion, shared by a select few, that this is a complete waste of time. I personally hated taking notes all throughout school, as I found it to be a real distraction to actually learning the material discussed in class. I also found it very tiresome to concentrate on transcribing a lecture for fifty to seventy-five minutes straight, sometimes for two or three classes in a row. Unless you are aiming to create a personal library of notes to refer to when you are bored during your article year, it is not necessary to take notes during paper-based lectures. The exception is when your paper topic is being discussed, or when a particular item comes up that you think might relate to your paper topic in some way. Otherwise, I believe that you should sit back, listen intently, and relax. This is a great opportunity to engage in discussion, practice your oral advocacy skills, actively analyze a particular area of the law, and to formulate personal opinions about the law.

I know some students who chose to skip most of the lectures and to work on their paper during that scheduled time. Be careful about this plan, as most people have difficulty adhering to a self-imposed schedule like this. For some people, I suppose, feeling obligated to go to a lecture can be motivating. I tend to tune out more often than not in this style of lecture. It is not my fault. I am a visual, tactile learner, and lectures have never worked for me. I would much rather read a book, or formulate a fancy spreadsheet with all of the legal concepts involved all right in front of me. I like to draw diagrams that help me to connect the dots as well.

Be careful not to take too many paper-based courses. It may seem like a dream to have fewer lectures and fewer exams, but papers can be very demanding in their own right. As well, avoid these classes if you have any sort of motivational challenges, as nobody will be putting a gun to your head to prepare on a daily basis, or to work on your paper regularly.

Obiter Dictum

I much prefer papers. Papers give you the ability to learn an area of the law that you are interested in and provide a depth of study that exam-based courses do not. Also, paper-based courses give you greater control over your grade. An exam, on an off day, can kill your grade but a grade on a paper is more directly related to the work you put into the paper.
— *Robin Penker, Law Graduate 2005, Risk Manager and Legal Counsel, Maple Trade Finance*

I prefer papers because there is less chance that you will miss a key issue after having conducted considerable research.
— *Shawn Davis, LLB/MBA Graduate, 2005, Associate, Shearman & Sterling LLP, Abu Dhabi, United Arab Emirates*

I preferred courses with exams over courses with papers because I found that paper-based courses had twice the workload for the same amount of credit. This is because with paper-based classes the student is assigned readings each class, plus they often have to prepare for a presentation on top of research for their paper. For an exam-based course, the workload is focused just on the curriculum and does not require any additional research and work. However, if one is required to write a paper during their degree, like at the U of A, I would recommend taking an independent research course (especially if they are dedicated and can self-motivate).
— *Lorne Randa, Law Graduate, 2005, Associate, Brownlee LLP*

WHAT TO DO IF YOU DIDN'T GET AN ARTICLE (YET)

Learn the art of patience. Apply discipline to your thoughts when they become anxious over the outcome of a goal. Impatience breeds anxiety, fear, discouragement and failure. Patience creates confidence, decisiveness and a rational outlook, which eventually leads to success.
— Brian Adams (not the singer)

Depending on the year that you graduate law school, and depending on what city you originally apply to article in, you may find yourself in a group of students who enter third year without obtaining an article position. This realization should not be accompanied with any sense of shame. This does happen. There are limited spots available in mainstay law firms and organizations. The truth is that law schools churn out more graduates than the system can currently handle. So, where does this leave you? There is no best answer to this problem. However, I do have some words of advice that may help you.

First, it is time to regroup. Go back to your 2L assessment. Do you need to seek some help from a mentor or from a book or two, in order to improve your GPA? If so, get right on that. Second, if you think that your GPA is within a respectable range, you should begin applying to unconventional places. Two of the offers that I received were at firms that did not post an articling position. I sought them out first. You may have to do this. Small communities are often excellent possibilities. Sole practitioners in larger centres and non-profit organizations may also be options. The key is to approach these individuals, firms, and organizations with a real plan. Most of them will need to be guided through the process and made to understand what having an articling student would entail. You may find yourself in a situation where you will need to obtain the funding, perhaps along with the organization, for your articling year.

You may want to take a year away from law. You can enjoy one more year of freedom, take a temporary job that you will enjoy, and try again the following summer to find an article. By then, hopefully your GPA and résumé will be stronger.

Another option is to look to more remote communities. Firms in the NWT, Yukon, and Nunavut often have a difficult time filling articling positions. Sometimes the situation is similar in more northern provincial centres as well.

Have your résumé reassessed by a career officer and by colleagues. You might even consider asking for feedback from lawyers that have interviewed you. Approach them with tact, and let them know your situation. Let them know that feedback from them will be greatly appreciated and will help you to obtain that important articling position. Most, if not all, lawyers will agree to help you. Ask them for constructive criticism. Take it with some humility and try your best to incorporate their comments. You may also want to ask colleagues to do a few mock interviews with you to polish up your interviewing skills.

The key is to not give up. Apply for all open positions that are within reason for you and your family, if you have one. Open your mind to all possibilities. I believe that the person who has tenacity and a true desire to succeed will eventually do so.

ARE GRADES STILL IMPORTANT?

This may come as a shock to those who have not been initiated into law school. Except for the select few who don't have an article, or who are in the running for gold, silver, or bronze medals, or who plan to do legal graduate school, grades are unimportant in your third year of law school. In fact, there are many jokes that go around among articling students and associates regarding that fact. In many, if not most cases, hiring firms do not look at third year marks when they have hired you the previous year. Why should they? You have already proven to them that you are a capable learner, and that you have the ability to analyze and apply the law. You have shown your competitiveness, and most importantly, you have shown your loyalty to the firm by accepting an article with them.

Some of you may be thinking that this is a crazy notion—"What's the use of third year then?" You are not alone in thinking like this. Many third-year students are frustrated by this fact. It makes it difficult to remain motivated. You may begin resenting second-year students in your class who are diligently taking notes in class, and spending umpteen hours in the law library each day. You may be daydreaming about your upcoming holiday, or be focussed on a new hobby, now that you have some breathing room. Do not feel too bad about this.

For those of you who decide that you want to go on to graduate school, grades will remain very important. It may be even harder for you to remain motivated. However, the fact that many of your classmates in third year will become lackadaisical will be to your advantage when it comes to the bell curve grading. In addition, there will be a small number of people vying for the dean's list, a very honourable bragging right that you can carry with you for the rest of your career.

Don't forget about learning for intrinsic reasons and not just for someone else. Grades and the evaluation methods used trick us into forgetting that law school is about learning the law!

For those of you who decide to stop caring, consider this: In less than a year's time, you will be entering the practice of law. A student-at-law is not expected to know everything that they need to know (in fact, far from it). However, you will be expected to have a minimal level of competency. Further, you will enter preparation for your call to the bar. The more preparation you do in third year, theoretically, the less strenuous your bar admission or CPLED course preparation will be. Some students claim that their classes do not help them to prepare for bar exam. Others claim that certain classes are imperative, and that doing well in those classes lends itself to success on the bar exam or CPLED courses. The best thing is to ask colleagues who are currently articling and studying for the bar exam what their experience has been. It will likely depend on your particular law school and its curriculum, and will depend on your particular provincial bar admission course curriculum.

CHECK CREDIT AND COURSE REQUIREMENTS

It may seem ludicrous, but students have arrived at their last semester of law school, or even graduation, suddenly realizing that they are short on their credit hours. You may think that this advice does not apply to you, but I suggest that you check and double check and triple check that you are on schedule to meet your credit requirements, and that you perform this check well in advance. In fact, be sure before you even begin third year. If you end up having to juggle your schedule at any point, be sure to check again that you have all your credits to graduate. Can you imagine facing your articling principal and asking them to defer your article for another semester so that you can take that one last lousy course to graduate?

This same principle applies to required courses. Many law schools have particular course requirements for upper-year students. Be sure that you have scheduled these in, because you cannot graduate without meeting these requirements.

HELP THOSE BELOW YOU

The reason that I wrote this book was because I was constantly hoping and wishing for upper-year wisdom to flow down to me. On a few rare occasions, I was the recipient of kindness from an upper-year student. A little hint regarding law school administration, mooting strategies, what courses are most useful, what professors are most enjoyable, what firms are hiring, what firms to avoid, upcoming networking events, exam strategies, and legal discussions are all examples of extremely useful information that can really help your up-and-coming legal colleagues. You might think of those behind you as competitors that don't require help. However, the more respect that you show during law school, the more potential opportunity there is to work in harmony post-law school. The world of law is a small one, and a good referral or legal source can be extremely valuable to your personal legal career. It is much better to make friends than enemies.

The best thing that you can do for a classmate or a lower-year student is to refer them to this book. It will contain most of what they need to know. If the book is missing anything that pertains to your law school or experience, let that person know, and let me know as soon as possible (adam@CanadianLawSchool.ca), so that I can amend the book or Web site and pass on that valuable information.

OPPORTUNITIES FOR NON-FACULTY CLASSES

Some faculties will accommodate one course outside of the law faculty in your upper year(s). Consider this option. It can be a great way to take a course that you always wanted to take in your undergraduate studies. Many people choose to take language courses if they think they might face a bilingual situation in their law career. Others take the opportunity to take introductory or brush-up courses in business, especially if they are embarking on a corporate law career.

Most faculties ask you to provide a brief application, including reasons for taking the out-of-faculty course, how it will apply to your legal career, and that sort of thing.

REGISTER FOR BAR EXAM COURSES / CPLED

Make sure that you do not miss any application deadlines. You do not want to delay your articling start date. Determine the application dates far in advance and be sure to mail the applications on time.

ARRANGE STARTING DATE FOR YOUR ARTICLE

You might have arranged a starting date when you accepted your article. If you did not, now is the time to ensure that you have a start date written in stone. See if there is any flexibility on the part of the firm. You might not want to rush into your article. You have just been through three of the hardest years of your life. Many students choose to go on a vacation to Europe, Australia, or some other dream destination. It may be your last chance to do something like this for a while. In any case, allow for at least one month to wind down, take care of your living arrangements, and make time for those neglected family members and friends. Or, you may want to begin earlier because you are desperate for an income.

3L EVALUATION

To look backward for a while is to refresh the eye,
to restore it, and to render it the more fit for its
prime function of looking forward.
— Margaret Fairless Barber

You have done it! You have graduated from law school. Way to go! So, now what?

You will usually have a month or two (or sometimes more) to sit back and ponder your three years of law school. Many students take the opportunity to travel, to get away and to regroup before embarking on their articling year. This is a fantastic idea. It is a good idea to get plenty of rest, as the articling year usually proves to be very challenging; mentally, physically, and emotionally. Many people say that it is akin to your first year in law school, and by now you will have some very vivid memories of that time.

You will want to take stock of what you have learned. Now is a good time to organize all of the notes that you took during the last three years. Organize any important textbooks. If you can, gather CANS or outlines from courses that you did not have the opportunity to take, as these may help you during your article. If you feel that you need to brush up on some areas that you know you will be involved in, take some time to casually read that material.

You have succeeded through a rite of passage. You have taken one huge step forward towards becoming a lawyer. Congratulate yourself. Revel in the feeling that you have made it this far. Not many people make it into law school. Even fewer graduate from law school.

Not everything is roses in law school. I think you will have come to that conclusion on your own after reading this book. There are many hurdles to overcome, and many routes you can take. There is no right or correct way to become a lawyer in Canada. The adventure is yours to pursue. I hope that you enjoy yourself as much as I did and still do. So, you want to be a lawyer, eh? I wish you the very best of luck!

NEW! CHAPTER 9: THE ARTICLING YEAR

I had some idea of what the articling year would be like, but for the most part, I went into it cold and unprepared. I imagine most of my classmates felt the same way, unless they had previously spent a summer at their chosen firm. I am sure that everyone's articling year will be slightly different; as such, it is impossible to completely prepare you. However, I include some commentary and a few tips to help you through this last part of your journey.

Most of you will start your article between two weeks and two months after your graduation from law school. Don't be too overanxious to get going. I began my article about a month after graduation. I worked for the Centre for Constitutional Studies during that month.——big mistake. I realize now that I should have taken the month off to relax and get ready. If you have the chance, take a break, travel, and enjoy your family and friends. You won't see them much for a while once you start working.

Each articling student is assigned a principal lawyer. This principal can vary greatly from one situation to another. Some principals are extremely helpful—almost acting as a coach. Some are extremely hands-off, and simply view their role as signatories to your law society paperwork. Still others see their role as facilitator, helping you to kick things off with other lawyers. My principal was fairly hard-nosed. He was, in my opinion, a workaholic. (Sorry, Sir). But that didn't matter to me. I made my own choice about how much and how hard to work. My tendency is to work harder than I should, and that proved useful for my article.

At first, my principal was very difficult to communicate with. I found that I had to almost barge into his office in order to get some face-time. Once I learned this, things became much easier for me. My principal was also very reticent to give me work. I couldn't tell if he was just overprotective of his files, he couldn't find time to organize himself enough to pass along a file, he was not accustomed to delegating, or whether he was simply distrustful. I had to be quite persistent. After a while, I found that it was much more useful to seek work from a variety of lawyers at our firm. Within a few months, I found two or three lawyers that I really enjoyed working with and sought out work from them most often.

Students-at-law, the designation of an articling student, must follow strict rules regarding their work with clients. They must designate themselves as students-at-law on all correspondence. They cannot pass themselves off as lawyers—in other words, they must let the client know that they are a student-at-law. They are able to go to court, but are somewhat limited when it comes to appeals, indictable offences, and trials.

Some principals and law firms are more lenient about these rules, and some are very strict. My firm was more lenient, and I ended up working directly with many clients. I enjoyed this very much. I have many classmates who did not get to work directly with clients during their articling year. I have other classmates that simply did legal research and writing their entire article. This is definitely something to consider when choosing your firm—ask how much contact you will have with clients.

Some firms will expect you to meet billable goals. They are not really supposed to do this—it is supposed to be a year for learning. However, especially in some of the bigger firms that hire a large number of articling students, you can literally be fighting for an associateship, and the numbers are definitely used as a gauge.

Firms have different rotation systems. The Law Society expects articling students to receive a well-rounded article, with exposure to a number of areas of law. Most firms will try to accommodate this. However, this can be difficult if you article at a boutique-type firm, where they only practice in one or two areas. If this is the case, see if there is a way that you can be seconded to another firm for a while, or make some other arrangement. For example, my firm did not practice criminal law. As such, they set up a two-week rotation with the Crown Prosecutor's office at the courthouse. This was a very useful and enlightening experience, and helped me to gain some valuable exposure to court procedure. It was well worth my time, even though I will likely never practice criminal law.

Some firms will split your year into a solicitor-type rotation and a litigation-focused rotation. This is a great opportunity to help you begin to focus your practice. Many classmates have expressed that they ended up going to a practice group in litigation upon being called to the bar when they swore that they would never do litigation. Vice versa, other classmates have ended up working in municipal or construction law, even when they were very determined they would be a litigator in law school. The articling year is there for this purpose—to expose you to as many files and areas of law as possible, in a safe environment.

Here is a list of important tips to help you get through your articling year.

1.   Get as much information as possible from your principal before you start your article. Find out your salary, how your benefits will work, what your expected hours and goals will be, how you will be paid, where you will work, and what your rotation(s) will look like.

2.   Meet with your principal as early as possible. A short visit before your article begins can be useful for breaking the ice and making the transition smoother.

3.   Find out how much time will be allotted, if any, by the firm for you to complete bar admission requirements. If they do not have a current policy, work with them to set up a concrete policy that everyone is comfortable with. Try to arrange for at least one afternoon a week to work on bar admission courses or studying.

4.   Have conversations with any lawyers that you think you may be dealing with in the articling year. Introduce yourself; let lawyers know what your interests are, if you know them yourself. Discuss potential policies on accepting new work.

5.   Set up in your own mind a policy for accepting new work. Practice saying no in front of a mirror. Come up with statements that are politically correct, such as "That file sounds really interesting. I would really like to try my hand in that area of law. However, if I say yes to that assignment right now, I will have to make arrangements with (partners) to extend my deadlines for their assignments," or "I expect to have a more reasonable schedule within X days. Would it be possible to begin work on your matter at that time?" Don't be afraid to say no if it is appropriate. However, don't become known as the articling student who will not take on any work.

6.   If possible, find out early who you do not like working with. Do work for lawyers that you enjoy working with.

7.   Make friends with the most important people—your legal assistant, the law librarian, the courthouse clerks, and the receptionists.

8.   Learn to use dictation quickly—it can save hours and hours of time if used correctly.

9.   Put aside time-intensive hobbies for at least a year.

10.   Have discussions with your spouse, girlfriend, boyfriend, family, and other friends—let them know that you are going to have a very heavy year. Let them know that it is a really important time for you. Set particular times to meet with these important people. When you are with them, give them your full attention.

11.   Learn to use online databases and other library resources if you don't already know how to use them.

12.   Don't rush your work. Double, triple, and quadruple check everything that leaves your desk. This applies even when you

perceive that you are under strict deadlines. The lawyer you are working with should hopefully appreciate accurate work over quick work.

13. Don't be afraid to ask for help, more help, and yet more help. Don't let pride get in the way of your learning experience. You are there to prove that you are a hard worker, not that you are already an expert lawyer.

14. Give yourself appropriate rest periods. Get to bed early, try to take as many weekend days off as possible.

15. If you are having trouble keeping up with the bar admission requirements, let your firm know that you need more time for that purpose, or that you require some help.

16. Follow all bar admission requirements very strictly. Do not try to cut corners—it will only make your articling year more stressful, and can cause unnecessary delays towards passing the bar.

17. If possible, try to strike up relationships with the local judges—this is a fantastic learning opportunity.

18. Track down as many precedents as you can during this year. Precedents are the lifeblood of a lawyer. However, ask permission to use such precedents—many lawyers are very possessive about their templates. Start organizing and backing up these precedents so that you can take them with you wherever you may go in the future.

THE BAR ADMISSION COURSE

I completed the Canadian Centre for Professional Legal Education (CPLED) program, which is the bar admission program in my jurisdiction. This program covers Alberta, Saskatchewan, and Manitoba. I cannot directly comment on the program in other jurisdictions, but I think that my general comments and tips can be useful to you, whatever program you are under. It is my understanding that there is a good chance that the CPLED program will be instituted in other jurisdictions soon.

There is a lot of debate about the difference between the new CPLED program and the standard bar admission courses. However, no matter who is telling the stories, the storyteller is always adamant that their experience was much worse than your experience. No matter what program you fall under, you will find the experience challenging. For some, it may even be crushing.

The CPLED program consists of a series of learning modules instead of tests. They are really tests in and of themselves, but more like take-home tests. The modules are completed online, and you may communicate with a facilitator on a daily basis (a volunteer lawyer). You are expected to complete some practice questions and then answer a series of problems or questions. There are strict submission guidelines and deadlines which must be met. Under this program, you are assessed by the facilitator, and it is a pass or fail grading system. You are not allowed to fail any modules. You can appeal an assessment, or you can redo modules up to three times. Failing a module can cause great delays in your bar call. I do know some classmates who failed the CPLED program altogether, but not unlike the first year moot in law school, everybody gets through it.

Tips for Your Bar Admission Course

1. Read all of the rules, policies, and prodecures very, very carefully. Follow them. There is no reason not to give yourself this advantage.

2. Get help wherever you can—within the rules. Ask your principal and other lawyers for general help, for a step in the right direction, while being sure to stay within the policies of the program. You don't want to fail a module or test unecessarily. Also, don't be afraid to look to other resources at the law libraries or online.

3. Do not plagerize!!! This has killed the dreams of a few people— don't let it be you. This is a black stigma that you will not be able to shake. You might think that the program people are not as

smart as you. That might be true, but it really isn't worth taking any chances.

4. Double, triple, and quadruple check all of your work. Or, if you are studying for a test, be sure to memorize the necessary facts. Test yourself numerous times.

5. Answer the question in front of you. This is a pass or fail situation. You don't have to knock the facilitator's socks off. You just need to pass. You know that scene in "The Firm" with Tom Cruise where they are comparing his bar score to the rest of the firm for the state bar. Maybe that's what it is like in the US, or in the movies. But in Canada, nobody will ever ask you what score you got on your bar exam. They may ask you how many times you had to take it over or whether you had to appeal any results, although they shouldn't. Just make sure you pass. Don't go off on tangents.

6. Pretend you are a real lawyer. Start thinking like a lawyer. Think of contingencies. Think of how the client might perceive your work. Think of how a judge might perceive your work.

7. Stay away from the theoretical. This is the time to be practical. For many of us, it's exactly what law school did not teach us. That's all right—it's time to be a lawyer now anyway. Get to it.

8. Hand things in on time. This means allowing for plenty of time to work on bar admissions stuff. Don't miss an assignment or a test unless it is an absolute emergency! If it is necessary to miss, or you are late, be sure that you have an excellent excuse, and then confidently appeal to the head honchos.

9. Don't let this stuff overtake your practice or your life. If you are doing things right, you should still have a bit of time to go to a movie once a week, to exercise, and to have a conversation or two with your significant other. However, the time it will take will vary greatly between individuals and their articling circumstances.

10. Work really, really hard. This is the last step in your long journey. It's time to initiate your final kick. Come into the finish line with your arms held high.

11. When you are done (i.e., when you pass), be sure to give yourself a proper break. Take a couple of sick days (you might really be sick, after all). Try to get out a bit and speak to your friends again. Then, get back to work. You still have some things to prove to the hiring committee.

NEW! CHAPTER 10: WHAT IS IT LIKE TO BE A LAWYER?

Lawyers, I suppose, were children once.
— Charles Lamb

W HAT is it like to be a lawyer, anyway? I wanted to include this section in the first edition, but did not have a good line on a lawyer to provide insight. Now that I am a lawyer, I feel that I can provide some useful comments on this subject.

I must admit that before I considered going to law school, my exposure to lawyers or anyone in the legal profession was extremely limited. I had read a number of John Grisham books, and had seen some John Grisham movies. Obviously, I was exposed to a number of legal scenarios through other movies and television. I had been to court a few times, both as a witness and as an applicant. I had dealt with lawyers on occasion in my various business ventures, but that was about it.

I would venture to say that most of us would have similar experiences as what I have described above. There are some of us who have had increased exposure to lawyers through various experiences. Many people have purchased or sold homes, have hired a lawyer's to have their wills drafted, or have been involved in the defence or prosecution of a matter that needed to be heard by the courts. However, I would venture to say that those individuals who have had such experiences would not be able to tell you what the day-to-day life of a lawyer would look like. In this section, I will provide you with a brief description of my day-to-day life as a lawyer. Please realize that these descriptions are not a full exploration of this particular topic, but rather it is one form of a cross-section of the life of a lawyer. It is my hope that this section will help you in your decisions to become a lawyer.

In my opinion, my work-day as a lawyer is quite exciting. I own and manage a law firm in a city of about 100,000 people. I also run a law office in the small town of 3,500 where I live. My firm employs an associate lawyer and three staff. In the past fifteen months, I have opened approximately 280 files for a variety of clients. I practice mainly in the areas of real estate, wills and estates, civil litigation, Aboriginal law, dependent adult law, and corporate law.

I get to choose my own clients. Because I live in a rather small community, I get a number of calls to my office, both in person and by telephone. People call me throughout each day (and sometimes at night) in regards to a variety of topics. I try to stay as focused as possible in my practice, referring legal issues that I am not familiar with or not comfortable with to other lawyers in my geographic area. However, sometimes I enjoy extending a telephone call or interview if I am intrigued by a new topic.

One of the great challenges of being a lawyer is the absolute necessity of keeping secrets. As a lawyer, we are under oath to keep all client information completely confidential. This is sometimes challenging when I come home to my wife or am visiting friends. I often feel the desire to tell stories. Some of these could be truly entertaining. Some are dumbfounding and some are downright offensive. I love to tell stories, and really have to keep myself in check.

For the most part, I really enjoy meeting with and speaking with clients on the telephone. Every new potential client and every new file opened poses interesting, and often challenging problems to be solved. Although these problems are sometimes very stressful, I enjoy using the training that I received and using my intellect and common sense to assist clients in achieving various goals, whether those goals are obtaining a new home, planning an estate, collecting on a debt, or defending a vexatious litigation claim.

I personally spend the majority of my day in my office. However, I attend court from time to time and sometimes pay personal visits to clients at their homes and offices. I also try to go to lunch as often as possible with lawyer colleagues, business associates, or clients that I am interested in.

One of my favourite parts of running a law firm is business development. As such, I like to spend a lot of time in developing relationships with people, whether as friends or as potential clients. Many lawyers enjoy this part of the job. Whether a seasoned partner, or a new associate, it is important to feed relationships in order to grow your personal law practice.

Sometimes it can be very stressful to deal with clients who are faced with stressful situations of their own. Every once in a while, I am abused by a client and need to deal with them so as to avoid further abuse. This requires some genuine patience and tact, as I try to alleviate various concerns, show the client that I am competent and that I care, all while solving the problem at hand. Sometimes, I must fire a client, as I do not see eye to eye with them, or I do not wish to adopt their principles. This can be difficult, but is very important towards maintaining a sense of dignity and control over your personal practice. Luckily, I have yet to be fired by a client; however, I do see this happen from time to time to other lawyers. Sometimes it is due to incompetence, but more often it is because the lawyer does not want to follow unreasonable or even silly instructions from the client.

In the areas that I practice, some of my favourite activities are dictating or formulating letters to clients, drafting contracts and other various agreements, drafting statements of claim and statements of defence for civil litigation, and drafting wills and other estate documents. To balance these activities, I also enjoy preparing for and attending court. This experience can bring new challenges and forces you to stay on your toes as you engage with judges and other lawyers, along with witnesses. I also enjoy interviewing clients and educating them. I have found that in my personal practice, I enjoy helping people to avoid problems much more than solving existing problems.

I also enjoy the practice of real estate law. It is very gratifying to assist people to obtain their first home, an investment property, or a home for their children. People are always excited, sometimes nervous, and usually overwhelmed. It is fun to guide people through the process, to educate them on the pitfalls of buying a property, and to make sure they fully understand what they have gotten themselves into. I also enjoy solving various problems that arise in various real estate transactions. Sometimes, a deal goes sideways, and I am required to put it back on track, to litigate the matter, or to negotiate on behalf of my clients.

One of the greatest challenges of being a lawyer is the difficulty of leaving your work at work. Often, I find myself thinking about particular files as I am eating dinner, showering, or even while having a conversation with my spouse. (She wouldn't like to hear that, I am sure). Lawyers are problem solvers, and it is difficult to turn off your legal analysis tendencies, even when you want to. It takes practice to switch gears and to be a "normal" person outside of the office. Many of my lawyer friends say that they suffer from the same condition. Sometimes it is also difficult to turn off adversarial mannerisms. As lawyers are often in an argumentative mode, especially when dealing with other lawyers, this mode can sometimes creep into your personal life. I have found that it is important to take a few moments before I enter the front door of my house to cool down.

Another one of the challenges of being a lawyer is the constant requirement of accuracy. Although I have an English degree, and have been a professional editor for years, I still catch myself sending out correspondence or sending out documents that have small errors in them. I get angry with myself when I flip through a file and find such errors on documents that have already been sent out. I find numerous errors in other lawyers' documents, and this sometimes reflects on their legal abilities. I have also had other lawyers call me on such errors.

My principal during my articling year would often tell me, "The devil is in the details, Adam." This is often true. Small errors or omissions can often bite you back later on. Sometimes, it can seem tedious to go over a document repeatedly, when what you really want to do is be done with it and send it out. However, I remind myself that this is what I am being paid for—to ensure that all the i's are dotted and all the *t*'s crossed, and to ensure that my client is being represented in the best way possible. In litigation, attention to detail can be the difference between winning and losing an application or a case. Forgetting to ask a particular question in examinations for discovery, or on cross-examination can result negatively on the outcome for your client. Maintaining organized and detailed notes, and organized trial binders is imperative. I have come across a variety of lawyers unprepared for court. Without fail, this does not impress the judge, and I cannot help to think that judges have a bias against dishevelled lawyers with files falling out of their briefcases. Judges are much more willing to listen to a well-dressed, organized lawyer. This takes a particular kind of personality and for some it can be hard to maintain.

Another major challenge for many lawyers is the financial end of things. Regardless of where you practice, you will be forced to record your time and fees. Accounts receivable (the money still owing from your clients) can make or break a practice. Partners will not be impressed if you have not actually collected fees owing, even if you have broken billable-hour records. As a sole practitioner, accounts receivable are essential to meet overhead costs. This takes organization, and a good legal assistant is invaluable! Finances require attention, and you must remain diligent in keeping track of everything.

One of the biggest challenges in being a lawyer is to focus on particular types of law. Too many lawyers stretch themselves too thin by trying to cover too many areas of law. I started out wanting to try everything, but am now starting to narrow it down, and will probably narrow my focus even more in the future.

In law school, we are constantly challenged to learn as much as possible about as many areas of law as possible. However, it is important to start focusing fairly early on in your law practice. This is why you see so many lawyers who advertise themselves as practicing in particular areas of law. In Canada, lawyers are not able to claim that they specialize in an area of law, except in some rare circumstances, such as intellectual property law, but we can declare certain focuses.

Telling clients that you don't practice in a certain area of law can be discouraging, both for the client and for yourself as you refer the client away to someone else. I have personally referred away very lucrative files because I did not feel comfortable in the given area of law. However, I have come to realize that in the end, being honest with my clients allows me to avoid unnecessary stress and to serve the client much better.

Working at a large firm can be advantageous in many ways. There is usually a never-ending supply of work. It is nice to be able to consult with more senior lawyers, or younger associates when required. Most mid to large firms have well stocked legal libraries and ready access to other resources. Most of the larger firms have law librarians that are excellent at helping the lawyers in their legal research. Working as a sole practitioner or at a small firm can also have its advantages. You can have more ready access to clients, more flexibility in your time, and less billable pressures and time spent at the office.

One of the biggest complaints for most lawyers is the number of hours worked. At many of the larger firms, you are expected to work extremely long hours. On the other hand, many sole practitioners claim that they end up working many more hours than they would like. In my experience, this can be curbed through effective and assertive communication with your clients or with more senior lawyers, and through effective time management. However, even with assertiveness and proper time management, the clients really never go away. Many lawyers feel guilty when they are taking some down-time for themselves and convince themselves that they are letting their clients or firms down.

Many lawyers have a tendency towards anxiety, depression, and self-destructive behaviours. There is a lot of research about this, but most of it is inconclusive about the reasons for these tendencies. Most sources cite long work hours, high pressures, and unreasonable expectations from other lawyers, as well as a tendency towards type-A personalities as the reasons for these ill effects.

Some lawyers thrive on deadlines and others can't seem to get out from under them. No doubt, lawyer-work is often very time sensitive. You are usually up against a closing date, a trial date, a deadline for discoveries, a limitation period, or a billing period deadline. Sometimes, you will be working against false deadlines created by more senior lawyers, clients, and you. Many lawyers justify their long hours based on these false deadlines. Again, time management is an essential skill for a lawyer. You will find that a strong and competent legal assistant and a paralegal, or both, is the real lifeline of a good lawyer. Some deadlines are extremely important. A missed real estate or corporate transaction can have dire circumstances. However, everything in a law practice must be kept in balance, and unreasonable expectations must be kept in check.

One of the great advantages of being a lawyer is the relatively high income. New associates in most major Canadian centres can expect to receive annual gross salaries from $60,000 to $100,000. The pay scale rises dramatically in your first five years. There are firms that cannot match these kinds of salaries, but on the whole, most young lawyers are receiving better-than-average salaries.

Partners at major firms can expect salaries upwards of $250,000, and sometimes even into the millions. These days, in Alberta, there are some partners who are lured from one firm to another with exorbitant signing bonuses.

There are many sole practitioners or owners of small firms, or lawyers at small firms who make very decent money. I know one lawyer who runs a firm in Northern Alberta who consistently takes home half a million each year. I know another lawyer in another small community in Alberta who takes home $300,000 a year. My own practice has proved fairly lucrative and I am probably taking home more than my classmates who decided to work at big law firms.

The increase in income can be enjoyable; especially if you can keep the number of hours that you work in check. However, some lawyers are not able to do this, and seem to be unable to enjoy the fruits of their labour. Some lawyers seem to be unable to find the time to spend their money or enjoy it. Many lawyers put off taking holidays for years, and end up suffering extreme burnout. But, for the most part, most lawyers that I know try to enjoy their new-found wealth.

With the increased costs of attending law school, you may find the first few years full of debt payments. If you are single, or if you are able to keep your cost of living reasonable, I highly recommend paying off as much debt as possible early on, opening up flexibility and options as you move on in your career.

Is it scary to be a lawyer? Sometimes it is, but most of the time, I find it to be an exhilarating job. There is always a small fear at the back of your mind that you will make a mistake, or act negligently, or even be disbarred. However, as long as you are honest, upfront, and as diligent as possible, there is little need to harbour this fear.

One of the greatest advantages of a legal career is the plethora of areas of practice. There seems to be no end of specialties and sub-specialties of law. Below is a list of potential areas for you to practice in.

General Corporate Law
Commercial Lending
General Commercial Transactions
Residential Real Estate
Commercial Real Estate
Family Law
Elder Law
Criminal Defence
Criminal Prosecution
Civil Litigation
Municipal Law
Aboriginal Law
Poverty Law
Estate Law
Dependant Adult Law
Small Business Law
Corporate Securities
Mergers and Acquisitions

Privacy Law
Personal Injury
Insurance Defence
Competition / Antitrust
Energy Law
Employment Law
Labour Law
Entertainment Law
Sports Law
International Trade
Tax Law
Intellectual Property
Administrative Law
Oil and Gas Law
Class Actions
Constitutional Law
Environmental Law
Immigration Law
Regulatory Law

NEW! CHAPTER 11: IF I KNEW THEN WHAT I KNOW NOW

In retrospect there were failures enough to go around.
There were failures before the storm and failures after the storm.
— Jeff Sessions

A great advantage of reading this book is the benefit that you have of learning from my mistakes. Retrospect is always much more clear than the present vision. For this second edition, I thought that I might add a rundown of pitfalls that I could have avoided had a mentor apprised me. There is no way to avoid the challenges of law school, but maybe I can make it a bit easier on you. Some of these thoughts are sprinkled throughout this book, but here it all is in one spot.

1. Decide as early on in your post-secondary career whether you want to attend law school.

2. Write your LSAT as early as possible, giving you time to take it again if necessary.

3. Apply to as many law schools as possible, given your geographic limitations.

4. Talk to as many lawyers as possible before applying to law school. Spend a few days with lawyers to get a feel for what their life is really like.

5. Live as meagrely as possible during law school; debt after law school is a big ball-and-chain.

6. Make friends with top students; learn their secrets.

7. Keep extracurricular activities in law school to a minimum; get involved in some things, but take it easy—grades are MUCH more important than anything else.

8. Don't sweat it if you bomb a course—almost all recruiters give you at least a couple of "mulligans".

9. Make friends with the law librarian—they can save your life, especially for your Research and Writing course.

10. Don't fret if you don't get a law summer job at a firm in your first year—almost everybody does eventually get an articling job—spend your energy on improving your grades rather than worrying about your future employment.

11. Don't work part-time during law school—spend your time on studying instead—the dividends are much higher.

12. Don't ever be afraid to approach your professors or instructors when you are feeling challenged—you are not the only one.

13. Get a laptop and use it from day one.

14. Don't get bogged down in your textbook reading or class notes—synthesize, synthesize, synthesize—and do it early.

15. Procrastination will kill you in law school.

16. Study for every exam like it is your last one—your career really does depend on your results.

17. Find out whether you are more comfortable with exam writing or paper writing early on and stick to your strengths.

18. Choose your courses based on what you are interested in (and on what will help your GPA) rather than on what an employer or bar admission course might dictate.

19. Attend the law school where you will be happiest—getting good grades at any law school will get you to the top.

20. Make your intentions known early to any employer—you can't be too blatant on this subject.

21. If you are able, choose the article that will bring you the most HAPPINESS—money, prestige, and name dropping do not bring you happiness.

22. Choose the article that will allow you as much free time as possible—so many lawyers get burned out in their first five years—don't become a statistic.

23. Remember that there is more to life than the law—a lot more. Remember your family, your friends, your hobbies, and your passions.

24. If you end up in a law job that you hate, change it up—try a new firm, a new type of law, go to public practice, try an alternative legal career, try being a sole practitioner for a while. You have put too much into this career to give up so early on.

CHAPTER 12: CONCLUSION & FINAL THOUGHTS

A GAIN, thank you for buying and reading this book. Please feel free to tell your friends, colleagues, and associates about its contents and about how it has helped you sort through the complex task of becoming a lawyer in Canada. Please respect the copyright existing on the contents of this book and do not pass along the book for free. You may be tempted to do this, especially if you have purchased the electronic copy. Who will ever know, right?

This book is how I am paying off my student loans, so please be honest. I have put hours and hours of time into researching and writing this book. I know that we are all facing a financial crunch because of high tuition and the high cost of living, but as someone studying and practicing the law, I think you can appreciate the importance of maintaining copyrights, and of paying the author for the work contained in this book. Thank you, sincerely, for your consideration.

Become a lawyer. If it truly interests you, don't let any of the negative stuff included in this book stop you from achieving your dream. It is a great career if you choose your steps wisely. Prove it to yourself that you can do what it takes.

APPENDICES

APPENDIX A. ALTERNATIVE CAREERS FOR LAWYERS

The following is a small list of individuals who have law degrees who never went on to focus on lawyering

Fidel Castro—Dictator
John Cleese—Actor
Colonel Sanders—KFC Founder
Howard Cosell—Sports Writer and Commentator
John Grisham—Author
Julio Iglesias—Singer
David E. Kelley—Screenwriter and Producer
Tony LaRussa—Baseball Player and Manager
Geraldo Rivera—Reporter and Talk Show Host
Portia di Rossi—Actor[13]

There are many career options out there for persons with backgrounds in law. Here is a small sampling:

- Politician (fourteen of Canada's twenty-two prime ministers were, or continue to be, lawyers. Included among the prime ministers who were not lawyers was a doctor, a diplomat, a labour expert, and a printer)
- Legal researcher
- Business Executive (here is a compelling case for lawyer-CEOs)
- Consultant
- Member of various board of directors (I have heard of some people who actually make a living doing this!)
- Lawyer for Contract (have a say in your hours and types of work!)

[13] From http://www.law.arizona.edu/Career/Handbooks/alternativehb.pdf —The Alternative Careers Handbook 2007/2008—**The University of Arizona Rogers College of Law.**

- Legal Publishing (what lawyers refer to as "where lawyers go to die" or "where law students get overpaid whilst studying")
- Policy work (in government)
- Real Estate Agent
- Law Professor (you need an LLM in Canada to do this)
- Author (Any future John Grishams out there?)
- Sports Agent (almost every one I have ever known was a lawyer or had a law degree)
- Mediator
- Judge
- Real Estate Agent or Broker
- Mortgage Broker
- Negotiation Consultant
- Career Headhunter
- Law Librarian
- Paralegal
- Career Services Officer
- Legal Media Consultant
- Alternative Dispute Resolution Specialist
- Arbitrator
- Corporate Arbitrator
- Mediation Coordinator
- Crime Analyst
- JAG Lawyer (army)
- Patent Administrator
- Patent Examiner
- Trademark Administrator
- Privacy Officer
- Immigration Officer

There is a funny list of alternative legal careers at http://www.indissent.com/altlegal.htm.

APPENDIX B. LAW SCHOOL ADMISSION INFORMATION

School	Avg LSAT	Avg GPA	LSAT/ GPA Weight	# of Applicants	# Admitted	Total Student Body	Yrs Under Grad Req'd	App. Deadline	Combined Programs	Tuition
UBC	163	82%	50/50	1679	200	620	3	1-Feb	MBA, MAPPS	$9,363.60
U Vic	85-92%	3.7-3.87	30/70	N/A	105	315	3	Feb 1(rolling)	MBA, MPA, MAIG	$9,100.00
U of Alberta	161	3.6	70/30	1143	175	510	3	1-Nov	MBA	$9,437.00
U of Calg	158	3.52	N/A	843	72	N/A	2	1-Feb	MBA, MEDes	$11,000.00
U of Sask	159	3.54	50/50	965	116	300	2	1-Feb	B.Comm., B.A., B.Sc.	$7,293.00
U of Manitoba	158	3.75	50/50	900-1000	101	N/A	2	1-Feb	MES MBA	$10,000.00
Osgoode Hall	82%	3.57	N/A	2500	295	N/A	2	1-Nov	MBA(MPA), MES	$15,116.00
U of Toronto	95%	85%	N/A	1900	170	525	3	1-Nov	Cert. Enviro Stud., Coll M.A. (Int'l Rel.), M.A. (Crim, Econ, Russ. & East Euro Stud.), M.B.A., M.I.St., M.S.W., Ph.D. (Econ, Phil, Poli-Sci)	$17,280.00
Queen's	161	81%	50/50	N/A	160	N/A	2	1-Nov	MIR, MPA, Civil, MBA	$10,452.00
Western	160	3.7	50/50	2400	160-165	N/A	3	1-Nov	MBA, HBA, MIT	$12,300.00
Windsor	N/A	N/A	N/A	1600	N/A	N/A	N/A	1-Nov	JD, MBA,	$9,263.00
U of Ottawa	156	83%	N/A	3156	200	850	2	1 Nov	LLL, MBA, JD, MA (Int'l Affrs),	$8,912.00
McGill	160	3.7/83%	N/A	1509	170	797	2	15-Jan	BCL, MBA, MSW	$3,036-$5,951
U of New Brunswick	158	3.7	40/60	845	80	230	3	1-Mar	MBA	$8,646.00
Dalhousie	81%	3.3	60/40	N/A	155	N/A	3	28-Feb	MBA, MPA, MLIS, MHSA	$10,577.00
U of Moncton	Not Req'd	3.3	N/A	N/A	55	N/A	3	30-Apr	MBA, MAA, MES	N/A

*Table Current as of August 2007

APPENDIX C. SAMPLE COVER LETTERS AND SAMPLE RÉSUMÉ

Please note that I included my own personal information within these samples. I did so not to make myself look good, or because I thought they were the ultimate samples. They are simply what I have available to me, and I did not want to make one up. It was a lot easier to just leave them as they were and allow you to customize them for your own needs. Further, they worked very well for me.

Sample Cover Letter #1:

55555 55 Avenue Edmonton, AB T63 4B3
(780) 555-5555 adaml@ualberta.ca
www.AdamLetourneau.com

May 3, 2004

Fraser Milner Casgrain LLP
30th Floor, Fifth Avenue Place
237 - 4th Avenue S.W.
Calgary, Alberta T2P 4X7

Dear Mr. X,

Mr. Y of ABC and Mr. W and Mr. M of Fraser Milner Casgrain LLP, all of whom I met last summer during my time at ABC Legal Services suggested that I contact you to discuss the possibility of an articling position with your firm. I am currently enrolled in the Faculty of Law at the University of Alberta and will graduate in May 2005. I am applying for an articling position at Fraser Milner Casgrain LLP for the 2005-2006 term. I am particularly interested in Corporate/ Commercial Law as well as Intellectual Property & Technology, although I have other interests as well.

I am extremely disciplined, have excellent time management skills, and am accustomed to setting goals and working hard to achieve them. As my résumé indicates, I have experience in successfully managing and developing companies, along with advanced expertise in publishing, computer programming, and Internet technology. Recently, I helped launch an electronic publishing company. I have also assisted in the start up of a publishing house, a youth magazine, a web design and editing company, an online liquidation company and an online shopping Web site. I am a published editor and writer, and have first-class research and writing skills.

My summer employment at ABC Legal Services has provided me with valuable legal insight and my experience as Co-Editor-in-Chief of the Alberta Law Review will undoubtedly familiarize me with interesting and diverse legal issues. Further, my participation in the Kawaskimhon National Aboriginal Moot has honed my oral and written advocacy skills.

I hold B.Sc. and B.A. degrees, speak and read French at an intermediate level, and have a Métis background. I have been very involved in volunteer activities, most recently with the Alberta Law Review (Co-Editor-in-Chief), Aboriginal Law Students Association (President), Club Tout Droit (President), and the Oratory Association. The Web site I have designed (www.AdamLetourneau.com) elaborates on my skills, experience, and extracurricular interests.

I would be very pleased to meet with you to discuss the possibility of articling with your firm. I can be reached at (780) 555-5555 or adaml@ualberta.ca.

Yours faithfully,

Adam Letourneau
Enclosures: résumé, references, transcripts

Sample Cover Letter #2

55555 55 Avenue Edmonton, AB T63 4B3
(780) 555-5555 adaml@ualberta.ca
www.AdamLetourneau.com

May 4, 2004

Ms. X
Justice Canada
211 - 10199 - 101 Street
Edmonton, AB T5J 3Y4

Dear Ms. X,

I am applying for an articling position with Justice Canada for the 2005-2006 term. I am Métis and I attend the Faculty of Law at the University of Alberta. I will graduate in June 2005. I am particularly interested in Litigation, Intellectual Property & Technology, International Law, and Aboriginal Law, although I also have other interests.

I am extremely disciplined, have excellent time management skills, and am accustomed to setting goals and working hard to achieve them. As my résumé indicates, I have experience in successfully managing and developing companies, along with advanced expertise in publishing, computer programming, and Internet technology. Recently, I helped launch an electronic publishing company. I have also assisted in the start up of a publishing house, a youth magazine, a web design and editing company, an online liquidation company, and an online shopping Web site. I am a published editor and writer, and have first-class research and writing skills.

My summer employment at ABC Legal Services has provided me with valuable legal insight, and my experience as Co-Editor-in-Chief of the Alberta Law Review this year will undoubtedly familiarize me with interesting and diverse legal issues. Further, my participation in the Kawaskimhon National Aboriginal Moot has honed my oral and written advocacy skills.

I hold B.Sc. and B.A. degrees, speak and read French at an intermediate level, and Edmonton is where my family and extended family call home. I have been very involved in volunteer activities, most recently with the Alberta Law Review (Co-Editor-in-Chief), Aboriginal Law Students Association (President), and Club Tout Droit (President). The Web site I have designed (www.AdamLetourneau.com) elaborates on my skills, experience, and extracurricular interests.

I would be very pleased to meet with you to discuss the possibility of articling with Justice Canada. I can be reached at (780) 555-5555 or adaml@ualberta.ca.

Yours faithfully,

Adam Letourneau
Enclosures: résumé, references, transcripts; further reference letters to follow directly from referees

Sample Résumé #1:

Note that this entire résumé fits on two 8.5" x 11" inch sheets. It is compressed and somewhat modified here due to page size limitations. You should aim to have your résumé fit on two pages as well.

Adam O. Letourneau
55555 55 Avenue, Edmonton, AB, Canada T63 4BY
Phone: (780) 555-5555 Email: adaml@ualberta.ca

EDUCATION

2005 **Bachelor of Laws,** University of Alberta

2002 **Bachelor of Arts, English,** Athabasca University

1997 **Bachelor of Science, Psychology,** University of Calgary

1992~1995 Advanced French
     - Université du Québec à Trois-Rivières, Summer 1995
     - Collège de Bois de Boulogne, Summer 1992

WORK EXPERIENCE

2004 **Co-Editor-in-Chief,** Alberta Law Review
   * Coordinate quarterly publication of legal academic journal, including management of 30 editors and various committees; Perform chief edits on all articles.

2003 **Summer Student,** Petro-Canada Legal Services Department
   * Assisted 16 in-house lawyers with various legal issues, including contract, commercial, environmental, insurance, employment, Aboriginal and other areas of law.

2000 **Vice President, Operations,** PublicationsUnbound, Inc.
~2002 * Supervised up to 9 staff and 20 contractors. Managed ~150 strategic partners. Directed all Web site development

and maintenance (50+ Web sites). Created strategic plans for e-commerce and distribution of 3,000 e-books via the Internet through a proprietary syndicated network. Coordinated exclusive launch with Amazon.com.

2000   **President / Founder,** OlenInc.
~2003   * Web development and editing firm. Designed created small- to mid-sized Web sites, edited three Masters theses (one LLM, one MBA, one MSc), various editing services.

1999   **Vice President, Editing Operations,** American Book
~2000   Publishing Group
        * Large publishing house. Managed group of 67 editors.

1999   **Vice President / Principal,** aShoppingGuide.com
~2000   * Managed 10 employees and 22 contractors, directed all web marketing and site promotion, community development, site co-branding, strategic partnerships, merchant and affiliate management. Supervised all Web site design and layout.

1999   **Director of Communications,** LiquidationShop.com
        * Directed and designed communication and business initiatives for start-up company.

1998   **Associate Editor / Event Programmer,** The Canadian
~1999   Parking Association
        * Trade Magazine. Programmed annual national conferences & bi-annual world symposium.

ACHIEVEMENTS

- Member of the Kawaskihmon National Aboriginal moot team (2004)
- Elected Editor-in-Chief of the Alberta Law Review (2004)

AWARDS

- Encana Corporation Scholarship (2003 and 2004)
- Faculty of Law Aboriginal Law Bursary (2004)

- TransAlta Education Award (2003 and 2004)
- Roger Carter Scholarship (2004)
- Belcourt Brosseau Métis Award (2003 and 2004)
- Peter Freeman QC Bursary for Indigenous Students in Law (2003)
- Justice Canada Legal Studies for Aboriginal People Program Bursary (2002, 2003, 2004)
- Honours Academic Scholarship; Leadership Scholarship; Outstanding Achievement Scholarship (1992-1993)
- Crescent Heights High School—Ruthorford Scholarship; Citizen of the Year Award; First Class Honours Award; Physical Education Award (1992)

ASSOCIATIONS

- Canadian Bar Association
- Indigenous Bar Association
- U of A Native Student Association

VOLUNTEER

- 2003~2005   Alberta Law Review Editorial Board
- 2003~2004   Club Tout Droit—President
- 2004~2005   University of Alberta Graduation Pow Wow Steering Committee
- 2002~2005   Aboriginal Law Students' Association— Treasurer then President
- 2002~2004   Faculty of Law Oratory Association— Technical Director
- 2003~2004   Advisory Committee Member Indigenous Law Program
- 2002~2004   Cannons of Construction (Law School Newspaper)—Editor, Writer
- 2002~2003   Student Legal Services—Criminal Project; Civil Law Project
- 2003   Philip C. Jessup International Law Moot Court Competition Volunteer
- 2002   Calgary Mountain Bike Alliance—

	Trail Maintenance Leader
• 2001	U of C Native Centre—Resident Tech Head
• 2001~2002	Venturer Group—NW Calgary— Scoutmaster
• 1999~2000	goMagazine Inc.—Contributing Editor
• 1998~1999	Fast Company Magazine - Cell Coordinator

COMPUTER COMPETENCY

Expert skill with many computer applications, web design, programming, desktop publishing, and electronic publishing. Exceptional on-line research skills, including QuickLaw and eCarswell.

LEISURE & INTERESTS

Triathlon, golf, hiking, yoga, Canadian and children's literature, my three children.

APPENDIX D. SAMPLE STATEMENTS OF INTEREST

Both of these sample interest statement letters resulted in acceptance to three or more Canadian law schools. Use them as a reference, but do not copy them. Make your Statement of Interest your own. Make it interesting.

In preparing my Statement of Interest letter, I relied upon the information provided at http://www.accepted.com/mba/dodonts.aspx.

It is aimed towards MBA students, but is equally applicable to prospective law students.

Statement of Interest—Adam Letourneau

I'm not supposed to be writing a Statement of Interest for an application to the University of Alberta Faculty of Law. I'm supposed to be *maintaining* the status quo. I'm supposed to be negotiating a higher salary and more stock options at my next quarterly review. I'm supposed to be thinking of ways to make the company more efficient, more effective.

However, here I am writing it nonetheless. I am writing it because it is important to me. It is important because it will pass the rocking chair test.

Some friends and I belong to a little group that we call "The Rocking Chair Test Club." It's simple—it goes like this: "When I am sitting on the front porch of my house, rocking in my favourite chair, my trusty dog by my side, will I remember what I am doing today and smile?"

One of my favourite test subjects was a weeklong trip to California and Mexico. In a whirling week, I experienced ocean, surf, sand, cities, desert, and adventure! On an absolute shoe-string budget, I lived life to its fullest. No regrets and no self-imposed limitations.
I think that law school *will* be like this for me. When I am old and grey, I will consider the challenge, the diversity, and the opportunity

to do something great! I have friends in law school and they are "living it." They are creating memories with their fellow classmates and professors. They are exploring the complex subtleties of the law and are preparing themselves for a long series of voyages. I want to be there too.

I am applying to participate in the joint LLB/MBA Programme. Although my diverse work experience, along with my educational, cultural, and volunteer background have provided me with a plethora of learning opportunities, I am ready for a new challenge—a big challenge. One that will influence who I become and what direction my life will take, and I believe that the University of Alberta can offer this. I attended the U of C for two years, completing my B.Sc. and enjoyed it immensely. There is nothing that I would rather do than stay in Alberta, a true province of adventure.

I have had the opportunity to be involved in a number of start-up businesses over the last six years. In various roles, with most of them at an executive level, I learned what it takes to rise to a challenge. Bringing to fruition an idea or concept is arduous, risky work. Many times have I experienced defeat when trying to "make it happen", but so far I have not lost the battle, and I do not intend to. I have assisted fine colleagues in creating an online auction house, a full-fledged publishing house, a magazine, and an electronic publishing distribution company, not to mention the many small projects that I have been involved in. I have also been able to establish a number of mentoring relationships, being both mentor and mentoree. These relationships have been invaluable in shaping my business aspirations and my career goals and objectives. As well, I have been able to help a number of young people find direction in their lives. This is extremely rewarding!

I have supported myself since high school and have fully funded both of my undergraduate degrees. I have also supported my wife and two children in recent years. I have always had to work full-time or close to full-time while attending school. I am in decent financial shape currently, but will require financial assistance in order to attend law school this September. I have faith that the funds will be there when required.
Subsequently, I have so much to offer the University of Alberta Faculty of Law. I bring leadership, astute research skills, a keen interest

in thoughtful discussion and dialogue, and a passionate yearning to learn. I have an interesting background, with Cree, French, and Swedish traditions to draw from. I thrive on sport competition and have immersed myself in the world of writing and publishing. I am a self-taught 'techie' and a well-mentored business diplomat. I am also an avid member of the community at large, and an active member of the First Nations community. I look forward to honing these skills within the walls of the University of Alberta.

I have a keen interest in learning about all areas of law, but particular curiosity about the areas of Corporate Law, Environmental Law, and Aboriginal Law. There is so much to learn, and so many opportunities to apply that knowledge in practical ways.

If I am selected from your excellent pool of applicants, I can assure you with confidence that I will bring a level of merit and achievement unsurpassed. I am writing this statement for one reason only—for the opportunity to pass the rocking chair test of all rocking chair tests.

I strongly urge the Admissions Committee to consider my application.

Adam Letourneau

Statement of Interest—Mark Anthony (Names and Places Changed)

I will not be satisfied until I hear the words "Congratulations on being called to the Bar of Saskatchewan 2004!" If it were possible for the Faculty of Law to represent on indices an applicant's sheer desire to undertake LL.B. studies, it is a certainty that you would find the name Mark Anthony in the upper-echelon of all applicants. I have completed a B.A., a B.Sc., and I will complete an M.Sc. next year. I have worked for the Congolese government as a civil servant since September 1996, garnering knowledge of Congolese language, culture, customs, education, and business. Recently, I was offered an English teaching position at a top-tier US university for the April 2000 session. I deliberated whether to accept this position vis-à-vis attending law school. I declined the job offer because I am most compelled to undertake LL.B. studies.

I have great concerns about the environment, as well as the welfare of people with disabilities and aged persons. I am passionately involved in volunteer activities related to these causes. Completing an LL.B. degree would provide me with the tools necessary to lobby for societal change and make positive contributions to the field of law. Law school also interests me because undertaking LL.B. studies would place me in a veritably challenging environment. I need to be challenged.

As an undergraduate B.A. student at the University of Saskatchewan, I often pondered how rewarding LLB studies would be. I am drawn to attend law school at the University of Saskatchewan due to the low student-professor ratio and the increasingly positive reputation of the program. In addition, I will return to Saskatoon (from the Congo) in August of 2000, after having been away from my family and friends for more than three years. Acceptance into the University of Saskatchewan's Faculty of Law would make my homecoming even more special.

The thought of attending law school has long pervaded my thoughts. As I approach twenty-six years of age, having completed two undergraduate degrees, and working toward completion of an M.Sc., I know I now have the personal and academic maturity necessary to excel in my studies. If I am selected to attend law school at the University of Saskatchewan, I will undertake a leadership role in the Faculty of Law and I will be an active contributor to the community.

I strongly urge the Admissions Committee not to overlook my application.

Sincerely,

Mark Anthony

APPENDIX E. LAW LINKS

a. **http://www.CanadianLawSchool.ca**—where you can buy this book, and where you can get updated Canadian law student information beyond what this book has to offer. Includes links to law schools and CANS.

b. **Law, Eh? Blog**—http://canadalawstudent.blogspot.ca—where I post miscellaneous law and law school posts. Lots of stuff that goes beyond the contents of this book.

c. **http://www.LawStudents.ca**—a great law school student forum, with many interesting and useful threads, broken down into specific topics and law schools.

d. **Canadian Law Schools**—
   http://www.geocities.com/canadianlawschools/—brief information for the interested law student. Also includes a discussion board.

e. **Canadian Law Schools Forum**—
   http://p210.ezboard.com/bcanadianlawschools. (Now merged with http://lawstudents.ca)

f. **First year Student Bookshelf** (WestlaweCarswell)—
   http://www.westlawecarswell.com/lawschool/firstyear.htm.

g. **Canadian Law Schools**—http://www.canadalawschools.ca/—A resource for prospective law students, created by the Council of Canadian Law Deans (CCLD). (No longer exists—now just a blank filler page)

h. **Law Buzz**—http://www.lawbuzz.ca—a fun forum for law students and lawyers, broken down into a variety of topic threads and discussion groups. Can get kind of nasty sometimes—be wary of the opinions posted by some of the more notorious characters.

i. **Getting into Canadian law schools—Campusaccess**—
   http://www.campusaccess.com/campus_web/educ/e4gr ad_lacan.htm.

j. Firm Salaries & Other Statistics Charts
   http://www.infirmation.com/shared/insider/payscale.tcl? state=international.

k. **National Magazine**—
   http://www.cba.org/CBA/National/students/

l. Find more links at **http://www.CanadianLawSchool.ca.**

APPENDIX F. LAW SCHOOLS IN CANADA

BRITISH COLUMBIA

University of British Columbia - Faculty of Law, 1822 East Mall, Vancouver, British Columbia, V6T 1Z1,Tel: (604) 822-2818, Fax: (604) 822-4781, http://www.law.ubc.ca/, LLB / Combined Program Admissions Inquiries: borthwick@law.ubc.ca, Graduate Student Admissions Inquiries: graduates@law.ubc.ca

University of Victoria - Faculty of Law, P.O. Box 2400, Victoria, British Columbia, V8W 3H7, Tel: (250) 721-8147, Fax: (250) 472-4299 or (250) 721-6390, http://www.law.uvic.ca/, Admissions Office: lawadmss@uvic.ca

ALBERTA

University of Alberta - Faculty of Law, 485 Law Centre, University of Alberta, Edmonton, Alberta, T6G 2H5, Tel: (780) 492-5590, Fax: (780) 492-4924, http://www.law.ualberta.ca/, Admissions: kjwilson@law.ualberta.ca

The University of Calgary - Faculty of Law, 2500 University Drive, N.W. Calgary, Alberta, T2N 1N4, Tel: (403) 220-7116, Fax: (403) 282-8325, http://www.law.ucalgary.ca/, law@ucalgary.ca

SASKATCHEWAN

University of Saskatchewan - College of Law, 15 Campus Drive, Saskatoon, Saskatchewan, S7N 5A6, Tel: (306) 966-5910, Fax: (306) 966-5900, http://www.usask.ca/law/, law_admissions@usask.ca

MANITOBA

University of Manitoba - Faculty of Law, Room 301, Robson Hall, Winnipeg, Manitoba, R3T 2N2, Tel: (204) 474-9282, Fax: (204) 474-7580 http://www.umanitoba.ca/faculties/law/newsite/index.php, UM-LAW@cc.umanitoba.ca

ONTARIO

York University - Osgoode Hall Law School, 4700 Keele Street, North York, Ontario, M3J 1P3, Tel: (416) 736-5199, Fax: (416) 736-5251, http://www.osgoode.yorku.ca/

Queen's University - Faculty of Law, Macdonald Hall, Kingston, Ontario, K7L 3N6, Tel: (613) 533-6000, ext. 74285, Fax: (613) 533-6509, http://law.queensu.ca/

University of Ottawa - Faculty of Law, Common Law Section, 57 Louis Pasteur, Ottawa, Ontario, K1N 6N5, Tel: (613) 562-5927, Fax: (613) 562-5124, http://www.commonlaw.uottawa.ca/

Université d'Ottawa- Faculté de droit, Section de droit civil, 57 Louis Pasteur, Ottawa, Ontario, K1N 6N5, Tel: (613) 562 5902, Fax: (613) 562-512, http://www.droitcivil.uottawa.ca

University of Toronto - Faculty of Law, 84 Queen's Park, Toronto, Ontario, M5S 2C5, Tel: (416) 978-3718, Fax: (416) 971-3026, http://www.law.utoronto.ca/, law.admissions@utoronto.ca

University of Western Ontario - Faculty of Law, London, Ontario, N6A 3K7, Tel: (519) 661-3346, Fax: (519) 850-2412, http://www.law.uwo.ca/mainSite/

University of Windsor - Faculty of Law, 401 Sunset Avenue, Windsor, Ontario, N9B 3P4, Tel: (519) 253-4232, Ext. 2930, Fax: (519) 973-7064, http://athena.uwindsor.ca/law

QUÉBEC

Université Laval- Faculté de droit, Pavillon CharlesDeKoninck, Québec, Québec, G1K 7P4, Tel: (418) 656-3511, Fax: (418) 656-7714, http://www.fd.ulaval.ca/

McGill University - Faculty of Law, 3644 Peel Street, Montréal, Québec, H3A 1W9, Tel: (514) 398-6604, Fax: (514) 398-4659, http://www.law.mcgill.ca/, info.law@mcgill.ca

Université de Montréal - Faculté de droit, C. P. 6128, succursale Centre-Ville, Montréal, Québec, H3C 3J7, Tel: (514) 343-2356, Fax: (514) 343-2199, http://www2.droit.umontreal.ca

Université du Québec à Montréal - Département des sciences juridiques, C.P. 8888, succursale Centreville, Montréal, Québec, H3C 3P8, Tel: (514) 987-3000, ext. 7047, Fax: (514) 987-4784, http://www.juris.uqam.ca/

Université de Sherbrooke - Faculté de droit, 2500 boul. Université, Sherbrooke, Québec, J1K 2R1, Tel: (819) 821-7511, Fax: (819) 821-7578, http://www.usherbrooke.ca/droit/

NEW BRUNSWICK

University of New Brunswick - Faculty of Law, Ludlow Hall, Box 4400, Fredericton, New Brunswick, E3B 5A3, Tel: (506) 453-4702, Fax: (506) 453-4604, http://law.unb.ca/, lawadmit@unb.ca

Université de Moncton - École de droit, Université de Moncton, New Brunswick, E1A 3E9, Tel: (506) 858-3705, Fax: (506) 858-4534, http://www3.umoncton.ca/UdeM_menu1.cfm?www=http://www3.umoncton.ca/cdem/droit/

NOVA SCOTIA

Dalhousie University - Dalhousie Law School, 6061 University Avenue, Halifax, Nova Scotia, B3H 4H9, Tel: (902) 494-2114, Fax: (902) 494-1316, http://law.dal.ca, Law.admissions@dal.ca

ABOUT THE AUTHOR

Adam O. Letourneau earned a Bachelor of Science in Psychology from the University of Calgary in 1997. He then undertook a career in business, technology, and publishing, gaining valuable experience in business start-ups and executive management. In addition to working on other ventures, Letourneau acted as Vice President of Operations of a high tech publishing company in Calgary, and before  that as Vice President of Editing Operations for a publishing house in the United States. While working in business, Letourneau earned a Bachelor of Arts in English from Athabasca University in 2002. Letourneau earned a Bachelor of Laws from the University of Alberta in 2005. While at the University of Alberta, he was Editor-in-Chief of the *Alberta Law Review*, President of the Aboriginal Law Students' Association and President of the Law Faculty French Club. He also worked for the Centre for Constitutional Studies. Letourneau completed his law articles at North & Company LLP. He then opened up his own law firm, Letourneau Law (http://www. lelaw.ca). He is presently Chairperson of the Board of Directors of Apeetogosan (Métis) Development Inc. In his spare time, Letourneau enjoys running, cycling, photography, and gardening. Letourneau and his wife, Carmen, have two daughters, Zoë Skye and Soleil Rhiannon and two sons, Zane Olen and Samuel Golden.

Writing on Stone Press is currently accepting manuscripts and query letters for non-fiction books. We are especially seeking authors for our Canadian Career Series in the professions of Accounting, Dentistry, Chiropractic Therapy, Education, Architecture, Engineering, Veterinary Medicine, and Pharmacology.

Please forward your inquiries to:
Writing on Stone Press
Box 259
Raymond, Alberta
T0K 2S0
or fax us at 403-752-4815

At Writing on Stone Press, we strive to produce quality books for our audience. If you have noticed any errors in this publication, please let us know so that we can make any necessary corrections for future printings. Thank you.

Got a question on the following?

1. Applying for law school
2. Succeeding in law school
3. Applying for summer jobs
4. Applying for your article
5. Getting through bar admissions courses
6. Getting ready for a law exam
7. Obtaining a great law job
8. Anything else law school or lawyer related

Give me an email – adam@CanadianLawSchool.ca

I am always glad to hear from you and will do my best to answer your question. No question is dumb, and if you want, you can ask on an anonymous basis.

I look forward to hearing from you.

Adam

LaVergne, TN USA
30 August 2010
195179LV00006B/162/A